THE ESSENCE OF GANDHIAN PHILOSOPHY

THE ESSENCE OF GANDHIAN PHILOSOPHY

Its Impact on Our Literature

Dr. Binod

KALPAZ

ISBN : 978-93-5128-053-8
Price : ₹ 850

First Published, 2016

Published by

Kalpaz Publications
C-30, Satyawati Nagar,
Delhi-110052
Ph. : 9212142040
E-mail: kalpaz@hotmail.com

Laser Typesetting : Rudra Computer Graphics, Delhi
Printed at : Chawla Offset

Cataloging in Publication Data—DK
Courtesy: D.K. Agencies (P) Ltd. <docinfo@dkagencies.com>

Binod, author.
The essence of Gandhian philosophy : its impact on our literature / Binod.
pages cm
Includes bibliographical references (pages) and index.
ISBN 9789351280538

1. Gandhi, Mahatma, 1869-1948—Philosophy. 2. Gandhi, Mahatma, 1869-1948—Influence. 3. Gandhi, Mahatma, 1869-1948—In literature. 4. Indic literature—History and criticism. 5. Indic literature (English)—History and criticism. I. Title.

DDC 954.035 23

Dedication

To
my Mother, who left this world for her heavenly abode before the publication of this book and
To
my Father, whose constant talk on Ramayana and Bhagvad Geeta and its impact on the Mahatma kept me inspired to write this book.

Contents

Gratitude

Ishavasam idam sarvam, yatkinchit jagatyamajagat. The whole world is the manifestation of the Supreme Lord. I salute Him as I think that this work is the translation of His wishes into reality.

Gurur bramha, gurur vishnu, gurur devo maheshwarah. I offer my *pranam* to all my *gurus* whom I love beginning from Swami Vivekananda to Shri Shri Ravi Shankar ji Maharaj; whose writings and the lectures keep me inspiring to reach the heights in my life. H.H. Morari Bapu ji while his *Ram-katha* Session at Bodhgaya viewed and discussed my book and expressed happiness to see quotes from *Ramcharitmanas.* My *pranam* goes to him for his blessings to me.

Char padarath kartal jake, priye pitu matu praan sam jake. The four human ends lie in the palm of those to whom his parents are dearer than even his life. I fall upon the feet of my parents whose frequent talks on the *Ramayana* and *Bhagvad Gita* and its impacts on Mahatma Gandhi created in me a curiosity to study Gandhian Philosophy.

I express my deep gratefulness to Dr Karan Singh ji, the former Maharaja of Jammu and Kashmir, the former chancellor of Banaras Hindu University and President of ICCR for writing the foreword of the book. I have no words to express my gratitude to Shri Atal Bihari Vajpayee, Hon'ble former Prime Minister who, kindly consented to listen his poems from me especially his tribute to Mahatma, that I have quoted in this book. I am grateful to Shri Lal Krishna Advani ji who received me at his bungalow 30, Prithviraj Road, and gave me valuable suggestions. I have quoted him from his bock at more than once. Dr A.P.J. Abdul Kalam, Hon'ble former President of India has my warm regards for his kindness to view my book. It was gracious of Dr Ved Pratap Vaidik, Chairman, Council for Indian

Foreign Policy, for giving his impression on my book. I am obliged to Dr Subhash C. Kashyap, former Secretary General of Lok Sabha and the scholar of Constitutional Law and Parliamentary Affairs, for giving his impression on my book. Dr Gauri Shankar Rajhans, former Ambassdor of India in Cambodia and Laos deserve my obligation for writing beautiful remarks on my book. I must thank Shri Inder Singh Namdhari ji, then officiating chairperson, Lok Sabha, who briefed me on Kuka movement as referred in the book. I pay homage to Shri Khushwant Singh ji, the celebrated writer, who recently passed away. He was kind enough to meet me at his house Soujan Singh Park and wrote in the appreciation of the book.

To get the criticism on my book I visited the vice-chancellors and university professors of dozens of leading universities. I express my gratefulness to Prof (Dr) Uday Narayan Singh, Former Vice-Chancellor, Visva-Bharti, Santinikethan, Prof (Dr) R. N. Rai, D.Litt. Head, Dept. of English, Banaras Hindu University, Prof (Dr) Tirtho Prasad Mukhopadhaya, Head, Dept. of English, University of Calcutta, Prof (Dr) Ashok Vohra, Dean, Faculty of Arts, University of Delhi, for writing their impressions on my book. Prof (Dr) Dorlando Khating, Vice-Chancellor, Central University of Jharkhand, Ranchi, Prof (Dr) Saugat Bhaduri, Chairperson Centre for English Studies, Jawaharlal Nehru University, Prof (Dr) Vishwanath Roy, Convener, Comparative Indian Language and Literature, University of Calcutta, Prof (Dr) Sabujkoli Sen Mitra, Dept. of Philosophy and Comparative Religion, Visva-Bharti, Santiniketan deserve my thankfulness for their impression on my book. I can't forget to express my gratitude to Prof (Dr) Chakradhar Prasad Singh, former Vice- Chancellor and Dean, Faculty of Arts, Magadha University, Bodhgaya, Prof (Dr) Radar Mohan Singh, Head, Dept. of English, Patna University for their criticism on my book. I cannot forget to salute my beloved sir Prof (Dr) S.M.P.N. Singh Shahi, Head, Dept. of English, Ranchi University for all the affection and the guidelines that I received from him. Shri Abhay Dubey, Director of Indian Language Program, CSDS, New Delhi and Shri Balbir Dutt, Editor, Ranchi Express, deserve my thanks for giving their opinion on my book.

Dr Bindeshwar Pathak, Ph.D., D.Litt, Sulabh International Social Service Organisation in a meet expressed his happiness and advised me to get the book translated into Hindi so that the Hindi speaking people can get the benefit of it. Dr Buddhinath Mishra, the renowned columnist in Hindi from Dehradun gave me the likewise suggestion. I thank both these scholars for taking interest in the book and I assure them, this will be my immediate project and I myself will work upon this mission and very soon the book will be available in Hindi.

On the auspicious occasion of the publication of the book, I am in receipt of the good wishes from my well-wishers from abroad namely, Dr Susan Gould Fogerite, New Jersey, USA. Dr Naima Gwen Lewis, Atlanta, Georgia, USA, Dr Sat Bir Singh Khalsa, Boston, USA, Prof Ingunn Hagen, Trondheim, Norway, Dr Jose Rogue, Ribeiro, Sao Paulo, Brazil, Prof Predrag Nikic, Belagrad, Serbia, Dr Paulin Jensen, New South Wales, Australia, Dr Miguel Farias, University of Oxford, England, Dr Luciano Bevnardi, University of Pavia, Italy, Dr Christine La Monica Inniss, California University, USA, Dr Carolina Baptista Menezes, Porto Alegre, Brazil, Dr Bishal Sitaula, Norweigian University, Norway, Dr Basu Dev Bajgai, Yonsei University, Korea, Dr Balmukund Bhala, ILFROD, London, Dr Leigh Blashki, University of Sydney, Australia, Gyaneshwar Singh Guddoye, Mauritius, Prof Leung Ping Chung, The University of China and Prof Christopher Garner from Germany. From the very core of my heart, I express my gratefulness to them. I happened meet these scholars in an International Conference on Yoga for Health and Social Transformation hosted by Patanjali Yogpeeth Haridwar, India.

I extend my gratefulness to the Librarian and the Staff Members of National Library Kolkata, University of Calcutta, Rabindra Bharati University, Kolkata, Central Library Santiniketan, Central Library J.N.U, New Delhi, Central Library, Delhi University, Central Library, Utkal University, Bhubaneshwar, Gyan Bharati University, Bangalore, Gandhi Shanti Pratishthan, New Delhi, Gandhi Smriti, New Delhi, North-Eastern. Hill University, Shillong, Tripura University, Agartala and Seminar Library, Ranchi University, for their unstinted co-operation during my academic consultation in these Libraries.

I express my gratefulness to all the authors and the publishers whose works I have studied and quoted to substantiate my ideas. References have been duly given at the appropriate place. I express regret if any references would have been left unknowingly or for mistakes of either type that I'll try to correct in the later editions. With all my humbleness, I invite the suggestions of scholars and the critics.

I am very much obliged to Kalpaz Publication who, on my maiden visit happily agreed to publish this book.

In the final preparation of the manuscript *Advaita Vedanta*, my son helped me very much in many ways. I am very much thankful to him and I have all my best wishes for him.

Finally, I express my deep gratefulness to my beloved wife, Alpana Rani, who has collaborated with me on the research work as well as writing this book from the beginning to the last page.

At last I express my thanks to all my friends in India and abroad who have sent their warm wishes for the publication of the book.

Dr Binod
New Delhi
Ganga Dusshera
June 8th, 2014

Preface

Natwaham Kamaye rajyam, na swargam na punarbhawam,
*Kamaye dukhataptanam, praninamarti nashanam.**

The *sloka* appears in one of our scriptures and is said to have been uttered by Maharaja Rantideva; one of the *Chakravarti* monarch of ancient India. Mahatma Gandhi was so deeply impressed with the vision of the verse that he identified himself with the seer of the *sloka*. This is why he usually sang it in his morning prayers, or to begin the congress session. The verse rendering of the *sloka* follows hereunder:

Neither do I desire,
The perishable kingdom of this Earth,
Nor heavenly amenities
I would like to avail,
What do I desire
Is the redemption of the grief
*of the grief-striken humanity.***

What is the impact of Mahatma Gandhi on the India's mind? Pt Jawaharlal Nehru in his book "Discovery of India" writes:

*Gandhi's influence on India's mind has been profound in the present age; how long and in what form it will endure, only the future can say. This influence is not limited only to those who agree with him or accept him as a national leader; it extends to those also who disagree with him and criticise him.****

---

*Favorite *sloka* of Mahatma Gandhi from our scriptures.

**Verse rendering in English by the author.

***Discovery of India, Nehru, Jawaharlal, Oxford University Press, 1946

The book in your hand is the study of this impact that Mahatma Gandhi, his personality and his ideas i.e., Gandhian Philosophy left on the writers of all the literature of India especially the Indian writing in English Literature. Being a student and a research scholar of English Literature my imperative was to make a study of Indian Writing in English and to find the image of Mahatma Gandhi in it.

So the book is basically a work of Indian Writing in English. The students pursuing M.A. in English and even Honours can immensely benefit themselves from it. Here we have a good criticism of all the works of Mulk Raj Anand, Raja Rao, R.K. Narayan, K.A. Abbas, Khushwant Singh, Chaman Nahal, Manohar Malgaonkar, Nayan Tara Sehgal, Bhabani Bhattacharya, etc. Here it deserves to be mentioned that the works of all of these authors are prescribed in the curriculum of all the universities of India and abroad.

With all my humbleness I would like to say that though there are a number of books available on the subject but most of them are verbose and wordy in nature, and are hardly useful for the students. Contrary to this, this book is very organised and precise one. I would like to assure my young friends that this book is exclusively designed for their requirement. I am very happy that many of the learned University Professors from the leading universities of India have warmly appreciated the thematic and the stylistic pattern of the book.

But the very first chapter titled *Gandhi: the mentor* gives a new dimension to the book. After the award of Ph.D., my interest widened and I decided to make a thorough study of the spirit of our nationalism especially the Gandhian ideas as reflected in all our literature from Kashmir to Kanyakumari. This chapter is the culmination of my effort on the same. Here we have a panorama of the expression of nationalism especially the Gandhian spirit in all the literature e.g., Hindi, Bengali, Gujarati, Assamese, Kannada, Tamil, Marathi, Odiya, Punjabi, Sindhi, etc. A comparative study of all these literatures has made this book a unique work of comparative Indian language and literature. It is a pleasure for me that the convener of CILL of many universities have approved the very content of the book.

Mahatma Gandhi and his philosophy bears the perennial significance. The book as the very title suggests/presents the very essence of Gandhian Philosophy. Here I have tried to study the very basic questions as to what this Gandhism is and what is its relevance for our age and the ages to come? It is a pleasing experience to witness the journey of Gandhi's life: how a man of common caliber reached the towering heights. The allusions of Henry David Thoreau, and Ralph Waldo Emerson from America, Count Leo Tolstoy from Russia, John Ruskin and Edwin Arnold from England, Annie Besant from Ireland, Romain Rolland from France, Prof Fredrich Maxmuller and Albert Einstein from Germany, and Swami Vivekananda, Lokmanya Tilak, Rabindranath Tagore, Dr S. Radhakrishnan and Jawaharlal Nehru, Jay Prakash Narayan etc. from India have given the book a global perspective.

I am very happy many of the eminent Gandhian scholars of our time have warmly acknowledged this book.

To the research scholars pursuing Gandhian studies in the universities, I assure them that this is the book with a difference. This is why it has become a rich possession in each library. Gandhi is the father of the modern Indian Nation. He is the greatest personality of the last two millennium. It is very much relevant and useful work to the people working in the political realm. Gandhi is for all. So this book is worthwhile to be kept and read by all.

Gandhian Philosophy is as broad as the Indian Ocean. There is towering height in his personality and unfathomable depth in his philosophy. How an author can claim that he has grasped the whole in his book. With all my humbleness, I would like to conclude with the words of Ramdhari Singh Dinkar:

Tera virat yeh roop kalpana pat par nahi samata hai,
Jitna kuch kahoon magar kehne ko shesh bahut reh jata hai.

June 17th, 2014 **Dr Binod**
New Delhi

Impressions

A New Horizon to View Gandhian Philosophy

"Gandhian Philosophy is like a deep ocean full of many a gems. Dr Binod, the author has successfully plunged into this unfathomable ocean and has picked up some of the valuable gems, weaved them into a cohesive whole, and presented it as *The Essence of Gandhian Philosophy (Its Impact on our Literature)*".

Dr Karan Singh
Hon'ble MP, President, ICCR, New Delhi

"Dr Binod, the celebrated author of *The Essence of Gandhian Philosophy (Its Impact on our Literature)* has masterly described the impact of Gandhian values on all Indian literature especially the Indian Writing in English. The profound knowledge of the subject and its beautiful delineation has assigned him a lofty place among the contemporary authorities of Gandhian Philosophy."

Dr Gouri Shankar Rajhans
Hon'ble MP(1984-89), Ambassador(former) in Cambodia and Laos

"*The Essence of Gandhian Philosophy (Its Impact on our Literature)* is a spectacular work of our contemporary literature. The author, Dr Binod has done a singular service to the nation by aesthetically presenting our national philosophy as depicted in our literature."

Dr Ved Pratap Vaidik,
Chairman, Council for Indian Foreign Policy, New Delhi
Renowned Scholar and the Columnist on International Affairs

"I am very happy to go through the book *The Essence of Gandhian Philosophy (Its Impact on our Literature)* authored by Dr Binod. The book as the title suggests/shows the very essence of Gandhian Philosophy. There are hundreds of books available on different aspects of Gandhian Philosophy but this book is an exemplary one as it opens a new horizon to view the same. The book will be a valuable possession to the scholars pursuing contemporary Indian philosophy."

Prof (Dr) Sabujkoli Sen Mitra
Dept. of Philosophy and Comparative Religion
Visva-Bharti, Santiniketan, Kolkata

"*The Essence of Gandhian Philosophy (Its Impact on our Literature)* is the result of extensive study and deep research.The author Dr Binod has done a distinct work by writing this book. It has the potential of making an excellent reading.The effort of the author is highly commendable."

Dr Subhash C Kashyap
Secretary-General, Lok Sabha (1984-90)
Well known scholar of Constitutional Law and Parliamentary Affairs

"It is a subject of pleasure that now we have a new book on Gandhi titled *The Essence of Gandhian Philosophy (Its Impact on our Literature)*. The author Dr Binod has beautifully depicted the impact of Gandhian ideas on our literature. The book opens a new horizon to view Gandhian philosophy. Let this book be a rich possession of each library."

Gandhi Peace Foundation, New Delhi,
(Quote from the message)

A distinct work on Indian writing in English

"*The Essence of Gandhian Philosophy (Its Impact on our Literature)* is a panorama of contemporary Indian Writing in English. There are dozens of books available as a criticism on Mulk Raj Anand, Raja Rao, R. K. Narayan and other novelists but Dr Binod, the author here has precisely presented the same in the light of the Gandhian image and the values as projected there. The Book is recommended to the scholars working on either of these authors."

Prof (Dr) Saugat Bhaduri
Chairperson, Centre for English Studies
Jawaharlal Nehru University, New Delhi

"I am impressed to see wide range of references and the scholarship of Dr Binod in his book *The Essence of Gandhian Philosophy (Its Impact on our Literature)*.The book should be recommended as a reliable reference of Gandhian Philosophy and Indian English Literature".

Prof (Dr) Tirtho Prasad Mukhopadhyay
Head, Dept. of English,
University of Calcutta, Kolkata

"Dr Binod's book *The Essence of Gandhian Philosophy (Its Impact on our Literature)* is a sincere effort made in the direction of the explication of Gandhian Philosophy and its impact on Mulk Raj Anand, Raja Rao, RK. Narayan, and other Indian English fiction writers of contemporary era."

Prof (Dr) R N Rai, D. Litt
Head, Dept. of English,
Banaras Hindu University, Varanasi

"The book *The Essence of Gandhian Philosophy (Its Impact on our Literature)* by Dr Binod is a commendable work of literature. It elaborately discusses Gandhian Philosophy and its impact on our literature.The Honors' and the P.G students and those pursuing their research of Indian Writing in English may immensely benefit themselves by close study of this book. I wish a grand success to the author as well as the book."

Prof (Dr) Chakradhar Pd. Singh
Dean, Faculty of Arts
Magadh University, Bodhgaya

"The book captioned *The Essence of Gandhian Philosophy (Its Impact on our Literature)* offers an insightful study of Gandhian thought impacting the writings of Mulk Raj Anand, Raja Rao, R K Narayan, K A Abbas, Khushwant Singh, Manohar Malgaonkar, Chaman Nahal, Nayantara Sehgal, Bhabhani Bhattacharya etc. Each chapter is a delectable read for clarity and seraphic style. The book is a precious acquisition to the Indo-Anglian writings. The book has become unputdownable. Congrats gallore to the writer Dr Binod for this superb success."

Prof (Dr) Radhamohan Singh
Head, Dept. of English,
Patna University, Patna

"That Mahatma Gandhi has left profound impact on the thematic and stylistic pattern of the contemporary writers is the prime concern that author Dr Binod shows in his work *The Essence of Gandhian Philosophy*

(Its Impact on our Literature). The book has become a comprehensive criticism of our Indian Writing in English."

Prof (Dr) Ashok Vohra
Dean, Faculty of Arts
University of Delhi, Delhi

A panorama of comparative literature

"I am very pleased to see the book *The Essence of Gandhian Philosophy (Its Impact on our Literature)*. Dr Binod, the author has beautifully discussed the circumstances that turned a barrister M K Gandhi to Mahatma Gandhi. The allusions to Thoreau, Emerson, Leo Tolstoy, John Ruskin, Edwin Arnold, Dr Annie Besant, Romain Rolland, Swami Vivekananda, Lokmanya Tilak, Albert Einstein, Dr S. Radhakrishnan, Jawahar Lal Nehru etc. have given the book an international perspective."

Prof (Dr) Uday Narayan Singh
(Former) Pro-Vice Chancellor
Visva-Bharti, Santiniketan, Kolkata

"In the prologue of the book *The Essence of Gandhian Philosophy (Its Impact on our Literature)* Dr Binod, the author shows the impact of Gandhian ideas on our Indian Literature, e.g. Hindi, Gujarati, Bengali, Kannada, Marathi, Telugu, Tamil, Malayalam, Punjabi, Oriya, Assamese, Sindhi etc. A good criticism of our Literature has made this book a commendable work of Comparative Indian Language and Literature."

Prof (Dr) Bishwanath Roy
Convener, Comparative Indian Language and Literature
University of Calcutta, Kolkata

"I am happy to view the book *The Essence of Gandhian Philosophy (Its Impact on our Literature)* by Dr Binod. Each chapter in the book covers different aspects which are very informative and educative.I wish that the book will be well received and will encourage further study in the life and works of the Mahatma."

Prof (Dr) Darlando Khating
Vice-Chancellor
Central University of Jharkhand, Ranchi

"Mahatma Gandhi; one of the greatest personality of the millennium, had the tremendous appeal to the masses and his philosophy has left the deep impression on the writers of our time. The book *The Essence of Gandhian Philosophy (Its Impact on our Literature)* gives a comprehensive view of Gandhian impact on our Indian literature."

Balbir Dutt

Editor-in-chief, Ranchi Express, Ranchi

The Essence of Gandhian Philosophy (Its Impact on our Literature) is a work of comparative literature fore-grounding the impact of Gandhian thought on the literary geniuses of century. Dr Binod has sumptuously treated the initiated reader of literary discourse. I am sure this book will be prelude of many other works of high quality by the author.

Abhay Kumar Dubey

Director, Indian Language Programme

CSDS. New Delhi,

Foreword

This is the man who has stirred three hundred million people to revolt, who has shaken the foundation of the British empire and who has introduced into human politics the strongest religious impetus of the last two thousand years.

Romain Rolland

The impression gained by one of the greatest European thinkers of our age strongly shows why Gandhi is regarded as one of the greatest personalities of the last two millennia. The author Dr Binod has done a wonderful work by writing *'The Essence of Gandhian Philosophy' (Its Impact on our Literature)*. The book, as the title suggests, seeks to present the essence of Gandhian philosophy. The author has tried to study basic questions such as to what is Gandhism? what does it stand for? what are its components? what is its relevance for our age and the ages to come? why do its values need to be inculcated in the minds of the younger generations ?

The author discusses the circumstances that turned barrister M.K. Gandhi into Mahatma Gandhi. Here we have allusions to Thoureau, Emerson, Leo Tolstoy, John Ruskin, Edwin Arnold, Annie Besant, Romain Rolland, Swami Vivekananda, Lokmanya Tilak, Rabindranath Tagore, Albert Einstein, Dr S. Radhakrishan and Jawaharlal Nehru.

In chapter one *Gandhi: The Literary Mentor* we find the impact of Gandhian personality on the masses. To the masses, Gandhi became a legend, a tradition and an oracle. They regarded him as an *avatar*, an incarnation who descended upon the earth to destroy the monster of foreign domination and to set *Bharatmata* free from *ferungi sarkar*. The author shows this magical impact of Mahatma Gandhi on the Indian mind that captured the imagination of writers of all the languages of India - especially Hindi, Gujarati, Bengali, Assamese, Marathi, Tamil, Telugu, Kannada, Odiya, Malayalam and Punjabi, in addition to Indo-Anglian fiction, Indian writing in English. The author here presents a panorama of modern Indian literature as well.

In *Gandhian Impact on the Thematic and the Stylistic Pattern*, the second chapter, the author presents subtle literary theories in the light of the Gandhian principles. Literature, says Gandhi, is the means that can speak to the millions. This was the time when the young writers were being drawn towards Marx and Freud. Gandhi counters these foreign influences by arousing in them the feeling of national pride. The author here provides a new perspective to see Gandhi such as Gandhi; the writer, Gandhi; the journalist, Gandhi; the speaker, etc.

Keeping Gandhi as the pivot, the author presents the literary pursuits of eminent personalities around him like C.Rajgopalachari, Sri Aurobindo, Sarojini Naidu, Jawaharlal Nehru, Jaiprakash Narayan and others. Away from the flamboyant language of the time, Gandhi pioneered clarity and brevity in the language. In the *Gandhian values in the Novels of Mulk Raj Anand*, the fourth chapter, the author gives a panorama of Anand's novels and the Gandhian values depicted in it. There are dozens of books available on Anand's novels, but Dr Binod precisely presents them in the light of Gandhian image and principles as projected in them.

The author has dedicated the fifth chapter titled *Kanthapura and the Mahatma to Raja Rao*. He says that the novel captures the true spirit of Gandhian Age. It is saturated with Gandhian thought and imagery and its theme is closely linked to Gandhi's life and philosophy. Here Gandhi is eulogised, romanticised, and mythologised. In the collective unconscious of the village *Kanthapura*, the myth, the legend, the religion, the poetry and the politics all get mixed up, and the village of *Kanthapura* becomes a throbbing heart of India responding to the call of Mahatma.

Into the world of Narayan and Abbas, the sixth chapter presents a criticism of the novels of two great authors of our time, R.K.Narayan and Khwaja Ahmed Abbas. In the last two chapters of the book titled, *Unfavorable treatment of Gandhian ideals* and *Gandhian Philosophy needs Revalidation in the changed contexts,* the author presents the criticism of the post-independence novelists of our time, especially Khushwant Singh, Chaman Nahal, Manohar Malgaonkar, Nayantara Sahgal and Bhabani Bhattacharya.

Gandhian Philosophy is like a deep ocean that bears full of many a gems. The author has successfully plunged into this unfathomable ocean and has picked up some of the valuable gems, weaved them into a cohesive whole, and presented it as *The Essence of Gandhian Philosophy. (Its Impact on our Literature).*

KARAN SINGH
New Delhi
Nov. 12, 2012

1

Mahatma Gandhi: A Literary and Spiritual Mentor

Gandhi: The Literary Mentor

The period-1920-1947-is generally designated as 'The Era of Gandhian Revolution' in Indian literature. Mahatma Gandhi, during these fateful years of India's struggle for independence, dominated the Indian national scene, and Gandhian strategies and approaches shaped the course of India's destiny. Gandhi's image, his personality and his philosophy, influenced millions of people in India, including a large number of poets, novelists, and other men of sensibility. They regarded him as their literary and spiritual mentor. Mulk Raj Anand, a renowned Indo-Anglian novelist himself, writes with regard to Gandhi:

This strange man seemed to have the genius that could, by a single dramatic act, rally multi-coloured, multi-tongued India to himself.[1]

To the masses, Gandhi became a legend, a tradition, an oracle. They regarded him as an *avatar*, who descended upon the earth to destroy the monster of foreign domination and to set *Bharat-Mata* (Mother-India) free from the *'Ferungi Sarkar'* (the British Government). It was this magical impact of Mahatma and his image on India's mind that captured the imagination of many Indo-Anglian novelists and inspired them to express, to reflect, or to probe into his ideas, ideals and ideologies either directly or metaphorically in their works.

This impact has been two-fold; *first*, there are his (Gandhi's) writings. Like other pioneers of Indian Renaissance, Mahatma Gandhi has written in his mother tongue, Gujarati, as well as in English. The major part of his writings, however, had to be in English, for through English alone could Gandhi reach all corners of subcontinent across the linguistic frontiers. This aspect of his contribution has been discussed at length elsewhere in this book.

Secondly, he has been what we may call a writers' writer: while he produced no fictional work of his own, he inspired creativity in a number of fiction-writers. In some of the best writings in all Indian languages we have his counter-signature. Mahatma Gandhi played the role of a catalyst. He brought about catalysis in Indian literature. Dr K.R. Srinivasa Iyengar seems quite justified in considering Gandhi as a "formative influence on writers of the time":

> *The personality of Mahatma Gandhi affected the people of India as powerfully as his pen. It exercises a potent influence on our language and literature, both directly through his own writings in English and Gujarati, and indirectly through his movements generated by his revoluntionary thoughts and practice. The several Indian regional languages acquired a new versatility and power... No apology is needed for considering Gandhiji as a writer and as a formative influence on writers of the time.*[2]

The Image of Gandhi in Hindi Literature

It is interesting to make a survey of the Gandhian impact on our regional literature. Let us have a look into Hindi literature. Sri Ramdhari Singh Dinkar, a great laureate of Hindi poetry, pays rich tribute to Mahatma Gandhi:

Tu kalodadhi ka mahastambh,
Atma ke nabh ka tung ketu,
Bapu, tu martya, amartya, swarg,
Prithvi, bhoo, nabh ka mahasetu.
Tera virat yah rup, kalpana
Pat par nahin samata hai,
Jitna kuch kahun magar kahne ko,
Shesh bahut rah jata hai.
Lajjit mere angaar tilak,
Mala bhi yadi le aaun main,
Kis bhanti uthun itna upar,
Mastak kaise chhu paun main.
Griwa tak hath na ja sakte,

Unglian na chhu sakti lalat,
Vaman ki puja kis prakar,
Panhuche tujh tak manav virat.[3]

Maithili Sharan Gupta, another celebrated poet of Hindi, who has dedicated most of his poems to Indian culture and nationalism, eulogises the Mahatma thus:

You are blessed! Your renunciation
is the basis for the comfort of all.
From this body which has consumed all desire
The world will build a new life
And satisfy all desires.[4]

Sohan Lal Dwivedi, another great poet and a devotee of Gandhi, writes in dedication to Bapu:

Chal pare jidhar do dag mag men,
Chal pare koti pag usi ore,
Gar gai jidhar bhi ek drishti,
Gar gaye koti drig usi ore.
Jiske sir par nij dhara hath,
Uske sir rakshak koti hath,
Jis par nij mastak jhuka diya,
Jhuk gaye usi par koti math.
Hei koti charan, hei koti bahu,
Hei koti rup, hei koti naam,
Tum ek murti, pratimurti koti,
Hei koti murti, tumko pranam.
Tum bol uthe, yuga bol utha,
Tum moun bane, yuga moun bana,
Kuch karma tumhare sanchit kar,
Yuga karma bana, yuga dharma bana.
Yuga parivartak, yuga samsthapak,
Yuga sanchalak, hei yugadhar,
Yuga nirmata, yuga murti tumhe,
Yuga-yuga tak yuga ka namaskar.
Hei yugdrashta, hei yugsrashta,
Parhte kaisa yeh moksha mantra,
Is rajtantra ke khandahar mein,
Ugta abhinava Bharat-Swatantra.[5]

Atal Bihari Bajpayee, the former Prime Minister of India, the legendary politician and a laureate of Hindi poetry pays a rich tribute to Mahatma Gandhi:

Varsh huye hi kitne, path par rahi ek chala tha,
Andhakar ka vaksha chir kar, dipak ek jala tha.
Dainya dasya ka pank dabakar, sat-dal kamal khila tha,
Kaalratri ko bhed jyoti ka prawar punj nikla tha.
Pathar par chalte-chalte hi wah rah ban gaya,
Til-til jalte-jalte hi wah dah ban gaya.
Kaisa tha wah bhakta swayam bhagwan ban gaya,
Kumbhakar ki kirti swayam nirman ban gaya.
Aaj nahi wah kintu panth par charan chinha ankit hai,
Manu ka vanshaj pralay kal se kyun sankit hai.
Aawo yuga ke sapno ko sakar karein hum,
Mritkon mein navjivan ki hunkar bharen hum.[6]

It is thus evident that Gandhi, Gandhian ideals, and the freedom movement he led, have been *upjibya,* i.e. source of composition, for Hindi poetry. The overtone is patriotism, the desire for national independence. Almost all the celebrities of Hindi poetry such as Mahavir Prasad Dwivedi, Makhan Lal Chaturvedi, Subhadra Kumari Chauhan, Balkrishna Sharma Navin and others actively participated in the freedom movement led by Gandhi. Naturally Gandhi is always present in their works, directly or metaphorically.

Let us have a look into the Hindi novel. In its early phase Premchand was in the vanguard. He was thoroughly imbued with Gandhian ideas. In his novels we have depiction of common man with no romanticism, no 'literary' trappings. The words he used were as simple as the lives he portrayed. His humanism was of Gandhian complexion. His novels have *Young-India* type of patriotic fire. His collection of short stories, e.g., *Soze Watan* and *Samar Yatra*, were banned and bon-fired by the British government as they dealt with vital social problems bearing on the lives of the rural masses.

Jainendra Kumar is the next to use the Gandhian philosophy for his creative works. To quote Vatsyayan:

He (Jainendra Kumar) gave creative expression to the Gandhian philosophy of passive resistance, boldly carrying it to the logical extreme of non-resistance to evil and acceptence of suffering.[7]

We also have Nagarjuna and Fanishwar Nath Renu who have depicted the peasantry with much intimacy. Renu's *Maila Anchal* is an outstanding Hindi novel of our time. The portrait of Vaman Deva in *Maila Anchal* is the fine quintessence of Gandhian thought in the form of a living character.

The Impact of Gandhi on Gujarati

Gujarati was the mother tongue of Mahatma. Naturally his impact on it was stronger than any other regional literature of India. He gave a new direction to the works of his fellow writers. Bhabani Bhattacharya, a well-known Indian novelist of English, writes in this context:

> *Inspired by him they turned towards the depiction of the life of the common man, the poor and the illiterate, particularly in the villages. Their prose- style became less ornamental, less designed for the highbrow scholar. Simple, direct, natural, the literature of Gandhian era aimed at appealing not to the classes alone, but to the masses as well.*[8]

As for the poets, they ceased to confine themselves as before to love, nature and God. In the words of a critic: "They chanted songs of universal love and universal brotherhood and misery and human sympathy."[9]

According to Padam Singh Sharma Kamlesh:

> *There are two groups of these writers; there were those who imbibed the Gandhian philosophy and made it the main content of their literature, and there were those who were influenced by Gandhi but adopted an independent line.*[10]

Kaka Kalelkar, Ramnarayan Pathak, Kishorelal Mashruwala and Mahadev Desai are in the first group. Kaka Kalelkar's mother tongue was Marathi but he wrote in Gujarati with great command over the language. Dilip Thakore calls him "the most outstanding representative of Gandhian era." To quote Giridhari Prasad Sharma, "He shared the view with Gandhi that creative literature should help to bring about moral and social upliftment." His *Otarati Diwalo* is based on his experiences in jail. His novels, essays and travelogues are written in a style marked with vividness and charm. These works have been ranked high in Gujarati literature.

Ram Narayan Pathak is described as a link between the 'Pandit Yuga' of erudition and the simplicity of the Gandhian style. Kishorelal Mashruwala has presented Gandhian thought in a scientific manner in *Gandhi Vichar Darshan* and *Gandhi aur Samyavad*. Mahadev Desai was associated with Gandhi as his private secretary for nearly twenty-five years and the 'Diaries' he wrote give vivid glimpses into his master's personality. Gandhi's impact on Gujarati poetry has been profound. Dilip Thakore remarks:

> *Out of numerous forms of Gujarati literature, poetry was more influenced than any other form by Gandhian spirit of freedom.*

Meghani, Umashankar, Sundaram, Khabardar and Sneharashmi truly represent the Gandhian age of Gujarati literature.[11]

Meghani opens up the gateway of a new era. He was the first to present the innermost thoughts of Gandhi in Gujarati poetry. Meghani's poems written in 1930 and onwards were inspired by Gandhi's *satyagrah* movement and attained great popularity. His *Yugvandana* poems show the complete influence of the new era. The Mahatma himself gave Meghani the title of a '*Rastra Shayer*' (The national bard).

Umashankar Joshi was a participant in the *satyagrah* movement. His *Gangotri* and *Nishitha* made him popular. His ideal of universal brotherhood of man and universal peace has been powerfully expressed in his poem titled *Vishvashanti*. This beautiful poem clearly mirrors the Gandhian ideals.

Kanhaiyalal Maniklal Munshi was predominantly a novelist. Gandhian ideals are evident in his works. *Swapnadrasta*, a socio-political novel by him, is concerned with the Gandhian movement. There are numerous other writers in Gujarati whose creativity was roused under the influence of Gandhi.

Gandhi Era in Kannada Literature

If we make a survey of the Kannada literature, we find that the thirties marked the new Gandhian era in it. Dattatreya Ramchandra Bendre has nationalism as the dominant theme of his works, e.g., *Vision in a Dream, Song of Thirty-three Crores* and *The Young Ascetic*. In his collection of poems, *Suryapana* (Vintage of the Sun), we have a poem on Gandhi. The lines are very inspiring. We have another notable poem by him on Gandhi titled *Amara Marana*, i.e. 'Deathless Death'. Several other verses of Bendre are gems of Kannada poetry.

Masti Venkatesa Iyenger is a noted writer in modern Kannada literature. His *The vision of Gandhi* is an inspiring poem. We have a number of Gandhian writers in modern Kannada literature. The names of K.V. Puttappa, D.V. Gundappa, G.K. Hegde, B.H. Sridhara and P.T. Narasimhachar deserve special mention. A fine play on Gandhi is G.P. Rajratnam's *Sambhavami Yuge Yuge*.

R.R. Diwakar, the Chairman of the 'Gandhi Peace Foundation', has been a celebrated name in Kannada literature. His works in English have frequently enriched the pages of the outstanding periodical, *Gandhi Marg*. In one of his earliest works in Kannada, *Halligara Kaipidi* ('The Villager's Handbook'), published in 1938, he has dealt with Gandhi's constructive programmes. *Sereya Mereyally* (Behind Prison Bars) is an account of his experiences in jail as a *satyagrahi*. Diwakar recalls that one day a Congress leader asked Gandhi: "Is there a single instance in the history of a country which got freedom by non-violence?" Gandhi was silent awhile, thoughtful. Then his answer flashed: "We are writing a new history."[12]

K.V. Sitaramayya's poem on the great uprising of Quit India is notable:

These people!
Who can hinder now their onward march?
Who can set the limit to their illimitable hopes?
Towering temples will rise.
And lift their spires to the blue of the skies.[13]

The works on Gandhi's life and teaching in Kannada literature are too numerous to be mentioned. *Udghosha,* the collection of lyrics of different poets, is charged with nationalistic ideas of freedom movements. Adha's *Shoka Chakra,* a notable play, describes Gandhi's assassination. Among the novelists swayed by the Gandhian influence are V.K. Gokak, Basavaraj Kattimani, Inamder, T.R. Subh Rau, Gorur Ramaswami Aiyangar and Kota Shivaram Kanath. M. Yamunacharya, a noted exponent of Gandhism, has said:

> *The prominent note in Kannada literature today is human sympathy towards the poor, the unfortunate, the underprivileged, the neglected and the condemned. This veering round of interest from aristocratic and plutocratic society to the society of the poor and the humble may be directly or indirectly traced to the impact of Gandhian ideas.*[14]

Gandhian Impact on Assamese Writers

There has been an abundance of patriotic verse in modern Assamese literature. Lakshminath Bezbarua wrote remarkable poems such as *Amar Janambhumi*, *Mor Desa*, *Assam Sangit*, and *Bin Baragi.* Kamlakanta Bhattacharya has two notable collections of poems, *Chinta* and *Chintaranga*. The verses of Prasannalal Chowdhury are fierier.

It was 1921 when Gandhi went to Assam for the first time. It became a milestone in the history of Assamese literature. His message of freedom stirred waves of a new impulse throughout the province. The literary awareness was an inherent part of mass awakening. The new human values associated with it found expression in creative activity.

Under the Gandhian impact the Assamese writers also began the portrayal of simple life. The poets began to sing the songs of universal brotherhood. Caste system and social inequality were denounced.

Ambikagiri Rai Chaudhury wrote *Songs of the Cell* describing his jail life in 1942. Nilmani Phukan was inspired to write his collection of poems, *Jinjiri* (The Shackles). Kanak Chandra Sharma wrote a life of Gandhi in verse which was banned by the government in 1931. Hem Barua, who actively participated in the 1942 struggle, and Birendra Kumar Bhattacharya were two active writers writing under the Gandhian influence.

Like poetry Gandhi's life and thought was interpreted in prose also. Notable writers of Assamese prose are Bijay Chandra Bhagvati, who wrote *Gandhivad* (Gandhism), and Mafida Begum, who wrote *Visvadip Bapuji* (Bapu, the Light of the Universe). The dramatists and the novelists also got inspiration from the freedom movement led by Gandhi. The notable names are Jyoti Prasad Agarwala, Satya Prasad Barua, Pravin Phukan, Atul Hazarika, Birinchi Kumar Barua and Dinanath Sharma. Omeo Kumar Das, a noted critic, concludes:

> *The sense of direction which Gandhism brought about is being felt today even more than during Mahatma's life time ... the writer of today is no longer groping in the dark.... Gandhian ideology has consciously or unconsciously awakened the people.*[15]

Nationalistic Fervour in Bengal

Bengal has been the land of national renaissance. Long before the advent of Gandhi on the national stage patriotic writings came into existence in Bengali literature in the middle of the 19th century. Bankim Chandra Chattopadhyaya gave a strong stimulus to it. He was the first renowned novelist of India. In his *Ananda Math*, which is the story of an armed revolt against the foreign rule, we have the song, *Vande Mataram*, which became our national anthem. Here we have strong patriotic fervour at its highest. The song is dedicated to *Bharat Mata*, who is another name of our trinity of deities, i.e. *Lakshmi, Durga* and *Saraswati*. A few lines from *Ananda Math* deserve to be quoted:

Tumi Durga dasprahar dharinim,
Kamla kamal dal viharinim,
Vani vidhya dayinim,
Namami twam,
Namami kamlam,
Amalam atulam, mataram,
Vande mataram.[16]

Dwijendra Lal Roy is another name who inspired nationalistic fervour in Bengal. He was so popular that his musical songs were sung for almost half a century in every household in Bengal. Dinabandhu Mitra wrote a stirring drama, *Nil Darpan*, exposing inhuman atrocities of the British Indigo-planters.

Rabindranath Tagore has been a towering personality in Bengal. His genius had a hundred facets, one of these being his deep compassion for the down-trodden; they found voice in some of his powerful poems. Bengal has also been the land of extremist movement; hundreds of youths vowed to the use of violent methods against the British government. We have the depiction of this stern reality in contemporary Bengali literature. The poems of Nazrul Islam such as *Bidrohi* (The Rebel) are fire-blazed.

And then comes the age of Gandhi with his message of '*Satyagraha*'. *Satyagraha* Movement (1931-32) brought Gandhi closer to Bengali writers. His impact on them, however, was strongest in the last ten years of his life. Tarashankar Bandhyopadhyaya was one of the top ranking novelists of Bengal. He not only actively participated in the freedom movement, but lived up to the Gandhian ideals as well. Naturally, it found creative expiration in some of his best works. His novel, *Dhatridevata,* deserves to be mentioned. Its hero proclaims:

> *This struggle is, indeed, unique. You don't have to kill, you will have to die. This is a war without arms. Bare-handed, you stand fearless before the guns pointed at your body.*[17]

Other important novels of Tarashankar Babu include *Ganadevata*, *Panchagram*, *Sandipan Pathasala* and *Bicharak.* All these novels are based on Gandhian humanism. Satinath Bhaduri's novel, *Jagari*, is entirely based on Quit India movement. The duration of the action is one night in a central jail in Bihar. Bilu, a Congress worker, has been sentenced to death. The workings of his mind in the cell of the condemned just before the execution have been beautifully portrayed in the novel.

Lila Ray, who translated this novel into English under the title, *The Vigil,* writes in the 'Introduction':

> *The Vigil is the first novel in Bengal to be written against the political and social background of the 1942 movement. It was written in 1944, the year Gandhi was released from prison, and published in 1946, a few months before India was formally declared a free and independent nation. It is apt to say that a novel of this kind could not have been either written or published earlier.*[18]

Mahatma's personality has left strong impact on several other well-known novelists in Bengal. Anand Sankar Ray's *Satyasatya* is concerned with different ideologies including Gandhism, which had had a powerful influence on him. Monoj Basu, Navendu Ghosh, Sumanthanath Ghosh, Gagendra Kumar Mitra and Subodh Ghosh have depicted different aspects of freedom movement in their works.

Gandhian Spirit in Tamil

Let us move to the South again. It is a pleasure to have a dip into the ocean of Tamil literature. The Gandhian impact on Tamil began in the twenties with C. Rajagopalachari, Tiru V. Kalyanasundaranar and P. Varadarajulu Nayudu. It deserves to be mentioned that Tamilians played a major role in the *Satyagraha* movement in South Africa. The struggle has found expression in Tamil songs. M.R. Jambunathan stated at the P.E.N. All-India Writer's Conference, 1947:

> *The rise of Gandhism has infused fervour and virility in the thoughts and expressions of present - day Tamil authors... The Quit India Movement has opened the floodgates of the suppressed and oppressed talents. He makes special mention of Ramalingam, a Gandhian poet, whose verses on Satyagraha landed him in prison. His poem on the spinning-wheel stirred Tamil Nadu. With his words on their lips, thousands of men and women heroically faced lathi charges and bayonet thrusts.*[19]

It is interesting to note that C. Rajagopalachari's works have a bearing of Gandhi's ideas on them, directly or indirectly. And they have helped the Tamil readers to have an intellectual grasp of what Gandhi stood for. Tiru V. Kalyanasundaranar (or Tiru Vika) wrote under Gandhian influence for more than thirty years, and his ideas percolated to a later generation of writers. Andal estimates that in a period of ten years at least a thousand books inspired by Gandhism were published in Tamil. These writers were of 'Monikkodi group' under the leadership of Va Ra, who was himself dedicated to Gandhian reform. V.M. Kodainayaki Ammal, a woman writer wrote more than a hundred novels in which the Gandhian inpact is obvious. The list of the poets under Gandhian influence is long one. Ramalingam Pillai, Pir Mohammad Pavalar and Sankar Das, deserve to be noted. Ramalingam Pillai contributed a remarkable essay on Gandhi to the Tamil Encyclopaedia. R. Krishnamurti (or Kalki) popularised Gandhism in Tamil country not only through many translations of Gandhi's works but also through novels, short stories and plays.

Andal, in an assessment of modern Tamil literature, talks with great warmth of K.S. Venkataramani and his two major novels written in English, *Murugan the Tiller* and *Kandan the Patriot:* "To my mind his novels remain still the best expression creatively of the Gandhian spirit in Tamil."[20] Venkataramani expressed Gandhian ideas in essays, stories and sketches. We have made a detailed discussion of Venkataramani's contribution in another part of the chapter.

Desika Vinayakam Pillai's *Gandhi Charita Kathai* and poems by A.L. Valliappa deserve mention. The abolition of untouchability and the upliftment of women were the ideas that appealed the southern mind. Translations of Gandhi literature occupy a vast field. *The Harijan* had a Tamil edition. Kalki's translations are outstanding, particularly his rendering of Gandhi's *Autobiography*. A ballad biography of Gandhi composed by Kottamangalam Subbu has been sung to audiences for well over a decade.

Gandhian thought as Projected in Marathi

Maharashtra, the land of Shivaji Maharaja and Lokmanya Tilak, has been the land of renaissance. Marathi literature has been as deep and as broad as ocean itself. Kaka Kalelkar, Vinoba Bhave, Dada Dharmadhikari, S.D. Javdekar and S.J. Bhagwat are the writers who not only projected Gandhian thought to the people but also gave it a new dynamism. The drama holds the foremost place in Marathi literature. K.P. Khadilkar, the outstanding dramatist, was a co-worker of Bal Gangadhar Tilak. He was the editor of *Nava Kal* (New Age). After Tilak's death he came closer to Gandhi. He wrote powerful political allegories out of mythological themes. *Savati - matsar Satva Pariksha, Savitri* and *Menka* are among his noted works. B.V. Warerkar, an equally talented dramatist, has based his plays on the foundation of Gandhian thought. *Apurva Bangal* is his most notable work. Its action takes place in Noakhali in 1946, the scene of communal horrors and the effect of Gandhi's appearance in the doomed region.

Among his other plays, *Turungachya Darat* is concerned with untouchability, *Kordi Karamat* with prohibition and *Satteche Gulam* with rural upliftment.

Noakhali with its terrible tragedies appears also in the *Fifteenth of the August* by Madhusudan Kalelkar. And untouchability is again the theme of D.N. Shikhare's *Vaishnav Jan*. S.R. Bivalkar, too, depicts Noakhali under the pressure and counter-pressure of Gandhi's peace mission as he was present on the scene.

Among the Marathi novelists, Sane Guruji and Prema Kantak actively participated in the freedom movement. *Kranti* (Revolution), *God Shevat* (Happy End), *Astik* (Theist) and *Nava Prayog* (New Experiments) are his most notable novels. Gandhian teachings predominate in all these works.

Gandhi has been ranked with the Buddha and the Christ by the author. Prema Kantak dedicated herself to the national movement. *Kam ani Kamini* and *Agni-Yan* are her well known novels. Among other Marathi novelists whose writings reflect the impact of Gandhian ideals are B.V. Warerkar, Pendse, Dandekar and Vibhavari Sirurkar.

The peace mission in Noakhali as well inspired the Marathi poets. Vasant Bapat wrote *Mahayan*. Gorkar and Marngesh Padgaonkar, respectively, composed *Amar Jivan* and *Amar Kahani*. B.B. Borkar wrote a monumental epic titled *Mahatmayan* depicting Gandhi's life in 18,000 stanzas. D.N. Shikhare remarks:

> *It (Mahatmayan) is more the journey of a high soul towards Divinity than mere narration and ornamental adulation of Gandhi's life.*[21]

Other poets where Gandhian ideology found expression are D.G. Kelkar, B.R. Tambe, M.T. Patwardhan and V.W. Shirwadkar. Shirwadkar pays rich tribute to Gandhi thus: "O Prophet! thou hast lit the lamp to illumine/ the darkness around."[22]

Gandhi's Impact on Malayalam

Let us take a view of the literature of the southern tip of India, i.e. Kerala. Vallathol Narayan Menon (or simply Vallathol) was the poet laureate of Malayalam since independence until his death in 1957. Gandhi's impact on Malayalam literature is felt predominantly through his works. A large number of his poems, published in an eight-volume collection titled *Sahitya Manjari,* are inspired by the 'freedom movement' under Gandhi's leadership and dwell on '*Ahimsa*', '*Satyagraha*' and the '*Khadi movement*'. *My Master* is perhaps the most impressive piece among them. To quote the English rendering of some of its beautiful lines:

The power of sacrifice of Jesus Christ,
The zeal of Lord Krishna in defending Dharma,
The non-violence of the Buddha,
The vigour of intellect of Sankara,
The intense compassion of Ranthideva,
The truthfulness of Harishchandra
The courage of prophet Mohammed,
If you want to see all these blended in one man,
Go to my Master and view him close
Or else, peruse the story of his life.[23]

G. Sankara Kurup, an equally powerful poet as Vallathol, has been profoundly influenced by the social and economic urge of the modern world. Like Vallathol he has sought to rouse national consciousness and has extolled India's cultural heritage. Many of his poems have Gandhian ideals for their theme. Let us see the lines from his poem entitled *Do You Remember?* eulogising Mahatma's '*Dandi March*':

He, the gentle-souled,
Walked over arrogant imperialism,
Which raised its angry name in sten-guns,
And stopped to feel his pot with brine to make a pinch of salt,
And at the instant India stood erect in history.[24]

Vennikulam Gopala Kurup, another outstanding poet, has written a book of lyrics titled *Swarajyagita* (The Sacred Song of National Freedom) based on Gandhi's life and work. Pamanna in his poem titled *The Heavenly Voice* sees the Buddha and the Mahatma side by side as 'the purest expressions of the conscience of man.'

We find the spirit of non-violence and Gandhian humanism glorified in Malyalam prose. The name of Keshava Dev may be specially referred. This is equally true in the case of Malyalam plays. N. Krishna Pillai, K. Surendran and E. Govindan Nair are the celebrated playwrights. Several collections of Gandhi's writings and speeches have been rendered into Malyalam, including *The Story of My Experiment with Truth.* K.P. Kesava Menon and P.K. Parameswaran Nair have written biographies of Gandhi. Sukumar Azhikode's analytical work, *Mahatmavinte Margam* (The Mahatma's Way) published in 1959, has been stated to be the most valuable work on Gandhian thought so far written in Malayalam.

Punjab : The Land of Martyrdom

Our discussion will be incomplete if we don't talk the contribution of Punjab in our freedom movement. Punjab : the word is made up of *'Panch'* and *'ab'* that means the land is nourished or watered by the five rivers i.e., Ravi, Chenab, Sutlej, Jhelum and Beas. Punjab is the land of bravery and martyrdom. To quote the lines of a Hindi poet it is *panth khalasa guru putron ki, balidani yeh punya dhara.*

Punjab has played very significant role in our struggle for Independence. The data says that 87 per cent of the sacrifices in the freedom movement were from the land of Punjab. Here it deserves to be mentioned that Sikh brothers are only two per cent of the total population of India. Out of the 121 patriots executed to death, 93 (76 per cent) were

Sikh. Out of 2,646 patriots sentenced to life imprisonment, 2,147 (81 per cent) were Sikh. Out of 1,326 patriots who got martyrdom in Jallianwala Bagh massacre in 1919 majority of them were from Punjab. Out of 113 martyrdom at Bajbaj Ghat 67 were Sikh. In Kuka Movement, 91 Patriots got martyrdom and all of them were Sikh. 500 people got martyrdom in Akali Movement and all of them were Sikh.

Kuka Movement of *Namdharis* in April 1857 was led by Satguru Baba Ram Singh. It was the first Non-Cooperation movement against the British Empire. What does this *Kuka* and *Namdhari* connotates for? I asked this question from Shri Indar Singh Namdhari; one of the learned politician of our time and then officiating speaker of our Lok Sabha told me that *kuka* like *Koel* connotates for enchanting the morning Prayers and *Namdhari* connotates for the person who swears to bear the name of the supreme Lord i.e. *Parampita, Akalpurush etc.*for a noble cause.

It is said that the Namdharis set up and managed their schools, *lungurs, goshalas,* post-offices, warfares etc. and boycotted all the foreign goods, the courts and started wearing the *khaddar* as a mark of *swadeshi*. Namdhariji said Mahatma Gandhi was deeply impressed with this doctrine of Non-Cooperation and later adopted it in his era.

Kukas were the staunch upholder of the Indian values especially the protection of the cows. Once they saw the butchers taking the cows for the slaughter houses, they slaughtered the butchers. Inder Singhji, tells the story of bravery and martyrdom that it was the malign motive of the Britishers to harm the sanctity of the *Harmandir Sahab*. So they used the butchers as an instrument in their hands. Innumerable butcheries were set up in and around Amritsar. The eagles used to pick up the blood stained flesh from the butcheries and drop them into the holy premises of the shrine. This was unbearable for the lacs of devotees visiting Golden Temple daily. The *Namdharis* took it as a challenge to stop this sin. They urged to stop the slaughtering of the cows. When their prayer was declined, they started slaughtering the butchers. The British government was already shaken with the Non-Cooperation of the *Namdharis*. Now with this incident, the government lost its temperament. Malerkotla massacre was the result of this temperament. In January 1872, 65 *Namdharis* were blown out through the canons. Mr. Cowan, the Deputy Commissioner of Ludhiana was the villain of this massacre. Inder Singhji especially mentions the bravery of Bishan Singh; the daring young adolescent boy of 14-15, who had hardly grown his moustache and beard. It is said that when he did not reach to the mouth of the canon; he was made to stand on a height to reach the mouth of the canon to be blown out. The boy was asked to say his last wish. He wanted to say something in the ears of Mr. Cowan. Cowan, having a long beard, knelt down. Bishan Singh caught hold of long beard of Mr. Cowan so tightly that he started crying. Ultimately both the arms of Bishan Singh were mercilessly detached from his body and he was blown out by the canon. Baba Ram Singh was sent to *Kalapani* at Cellular Jail where he breathed last. *Kukas* spreads at different places were bitterly tortured and their property was confiscated. Inder Singhji says that in the history there is no such example where thousands of people were severly punished without any trial in the court.

Madan Lal Dhingra was executed to death in 1909 for killing Curzon Wyllie. Bhai Bal Mukund was sentenced for throwing bomb on the procession of Viceroy Lord Hording in 1912. Here, it deserve to be mentioned that Bhai Bal Mukund was from the family of Bhai Mati Das who got martyrdom with Guru Shri Teg Bahadur ji at Delhi. The *Shishganj Gurudwara* at Chandi Chowk in New Delhi is the monument that says the great sacrifices of Guru Teg Bahadur ji along with his colleagues.

Baba Sohan Singh Bhakhna founded *Gadar* Party in America and gave the slogan of complete freedom from the shackles of Britishers. It was an open challenge to Britishers on the international level. Hundreds of people were caught, hanged and *Kalapani* was given to innumerable patriots. Then came Jallianwala Bagh massacre in 1919. General O'Dyer opened fire on the big mass of people. Thousands of people were killed and there were dead bodies from everywhere to everywhere. More than 120 dead bodies were recovered from the big well in the premises. I would like to quote the very popular song of Kavi Pradeep i.e. Ram Chandra Dwivedi that appeared in the film *Jagriti* (1954):

Jallianwala Bagh ye dekho, Yahin chali thi goliyan,
Ye mat pucho kisne kheli, Yahan khoon ki holiyaan,
Ek taraph banduken dandan, Ek taraph thi toliyaan,
Marnewale bol rahe the, Inquilab ki boliyaan,
Yahin laga di bahano ne bhi baazi apni jaan ki,
Is mitti se tilak karo ye dharti hai balidaan ki.[25]

The whole of the nation stood with Punjab against the British rule. The Martial law was imposed on whole of the Punjab. Hundreds of people were either shot, or hanged, or given life imprisonment, or *Kalapani*. Approximately, three thousand people were sent to jails. In Gurudwara *Sudhar* Movement at *Shri Gurudwara Nankana Sahib*, 130 Sikhs were burnt alive. In Babbar Akali Movement 27 *babbars* were given life imprisonment.

Bhagat Singh, Rajguru, and Sukhdev were executed to death on 23rd of March 1931 for throwing bomb in the Central Assembly. Bhagat Singh was only 24. One of the great poet of Punjabi pays homage to Bhagat Singh:

Desh kaum nu lor bari hai, Bhagat Singh sardara di,
Aao ral ke kami bharyea, ohna diyan vichara di,
Aje na pahunchi saryan tihar, milijo ke han azadi ae,
Desh nu lutt lutt khai jande, Rundli pai barbadi ae,
Hun tan hor lameri ho gai, Lagi line gadaron di,
Desh kaum nu lor bari hai, Bhagat Singh sardara di.[26]

In 1928, Lala Lajpat Rai was leading a protest against Simon Commission and suffered *lathi* charge. He was badly injured in the head and got martyrdom. A young man sardar Udham Singh shot General O Dyer at his home London and took revenge of Jallianwala Bagh massacre. He was caught and hanged. When Netaji Subhash Chandra Bose formed Azad Hind Fauz, General Mohan Singh; a son of Punjab was his right hand. Out of 900 *jawans,* there was good number of soldiers who were from Punjab.

Then came the tragedy of partition. There was mass migration, roits, the murder and the bloodshed, rails running with dead bodies, chaos and confusion running in the air. Punjab faced all this man made tragedy. To quote a visionary poet *Lamhon ne khata ki, Sadiyon ne saza paayi.* It is an irony that our beloved Punjab was doomed to suffer all the consequences of the tragedy of this partition.

But here arises a very important question, What is the motivating force that made Punjab the land of bravery and martyrdom? From where it gets its energy, the immortal drink that enabled it to face these adversities? The answers of all these question lies in the ideology, the vision; the philosophy propounded by a series of *gurus,* rather to say a *Guru-Parampara,* especially the last guru-Guru Gobind Singh jee who gave the philosophy of *Khalasa.* So it is our imperative to view, What this *Khalasa* is? What is its contribution to humanity? What is its relevance today? How it linked the past, the present and the future? And why we must inculcate its values to the generations to come?

The concept of *khalsa* that Guru Gobind Singhjee propounded on *Baisakhi* 1699 is a Universal Philosophy. His words *manas ki jaat sabai ekai pahinaba* is I think the basic principle of unity and integrity of the nation. It is no less relevant today than that time. Acharaya Hazari Prasad Dwivedi in his book *Sikh Guruon ka Punya Smaran* writes:

"Guru Govindji with his khalasa has played very crucial role in the protection of our nation. He fought many wars against the forced conversion and gave a sharp contest to the tyrannical Mughals. He was a great statesman. The human values that he set up through khalasa are very much relevant today. By saying 'khalasa meri jaan ki jan' he has given a wide perspective of his personality."[27]

The word *khalasa* is made up of *khalis* that means pure, sacred, *nirmal,* benign. It is a significant path to lead human life. Here we have the reflection of the *Parampita Parmeshwar, Akalpurusha;* the supreme father, that bears different name in different religion. It is a means of manifestation of natural perfection already in man.

In *khalasa* we have the life and the works of all the former *gurus* blended together. It is the *sangam* of the devotion and the strength. It is the incarnation of the great lives of Guru Govind Singhjee himself. It urges to sacrifice the life to fight against the injustice and the tyranny. It mirrors all the great values that Guru Nanak Devjee, Guru Angad Devjee, Guru Amar Dasjee, Guru Ram Dasjee, Guru Arjun Devjee, Guru Hargovindjee, Guru Har Raiee, Guru Harikrishanjee, Guru Teg Bahadurjee and Guru Govind Singhjee taught and lived. Gurujee himself offered *amrit* to the *'panchpyare'*, himself saluted them and enchanted the hymm;

"Wahe Guruji ka khalasa, Vahe guruji ki fateh"[28]

Guruji acknowledged them as the *khalasa* or the 'lions'. "They are the incarnate children of *akalpurush*." Guruji himself knelt down and saluted them as his *guru*. To quote his beautiful lines from Guru Granth Sahib :

Khalasa mero rup nai khas, khalasa me haun karun nivasa,
Khalasa mero mitra sakhai, khalasa mata pita sukhdai,
Khalasa mero priyu pran, khalasa mero jaan ki jan.[29]

According to Guru Govind Singh this *khalasa* is the new incarnation of all the nine generations of *gurus*. He interpreted, "we are just means in the hand of the supreme Lord." Dr Gokul Chandra Narang says that the confidence that one is a means in the hand of Lord and the reverence for that are the guarantee to win and through *khalasa* Guru Govind Singh has ensured this guarantee to his disciples.

Dr Mahip Singh; one of the authority of Sikh history in one of his book writes that there has been no example in the history when any great men would have been so humble to uphold the dignity of his disciples.

What was the impact of *khalasa* on the socio-political scenario? Dr Cunningham, in his book *History of Sikh* writes:

"Guru Govind Singhji, the last guru of the Sikh awakened the defeated races, motivated them and in their psyche filled up enthusiasm, a sense of freedom and ardent nationalism. This school was associated with the Bhakti cult of Guru Nanak Devjee."[30]

Shri Murli Manohar Mishra; the columnist writes, it was a social revolution as the Guruji urged to forget the differences of caste, colour and creed.

According to Sir Macaliff, approximately twenty thousand people immediately accepted this faith. Dr Harbans Singh; an authority of Sikh History thinks that the *khalasa* propounded by Guru Govind Singhji was the logical culmination of the *Bhakti* cult of Guru Nanak Devji running since two hundred and thirty five years.

To conclude it is apt to say that in the concept of *khalasa* we have a notion of model state. It is an expression of what Goswami Tulsidasji wrote in his *Ram Charit Manas* : *Daihik, daivik, bhoutik tapa, Ram rajya kahu nahi byapa.* Really Guru Govind Singhji like Lord Shiva *Jag ko kalash amrit ka dekar swayam hi wish ka pan kiya* and like Maharshi Dadhichi *manavta ke liye harsh se ashthi vajra ka daan diya.*

Ardent Nationalism in Odiya Poetry

Odisha; in our ancient literature has well been referred as Kalinga, Utkal, Koushala, Kongada etc. It has its glorious history, with its territory normally spreading from the *Ganges* in the north to the *Godavari* in the south. In British India its different parts were kept under the Madras Presidency, the Central Presidency and the Bengal Presidency. In 1912, a separate province in the name of the Bihar and Odisha was set up and was being administered from Patna. It was 1936 when modern Odisha was born.

Madhusudan Das; the great oldman of Odisha has aptly been bestowed as *Utkal Gaurav*. In 1903, he founded *Utkal Samilani* and kept spearheading national renaissance throughout his life. In 1887, he attended Madras Session of Congress. He always advocated that there is no difference between the National Movement for freedom and a strong Utkal Movement because a strong province will naturally strengthen the nation. Shri Aurobindo Ghosh; the great nationalist leader at that time appreciated this point of view. In Congress session at Kolkata in 1928, a representation from Ganjam district raised the question of Odisha and it was strongly supported by Netaji Subhash Chandra Bose. It is to be kept in the mind that Netaji was born and brought up at Cuttack in Odisha.

When Gandhiji launched *Dandi March* and observed *Salt Satyagraha* as a mark of protest, thousands of people disobeyed the British Rule in all the districts of Odisha especially the Bhadrak and the Ganjam districts. At Irom in Bhadrak, there was a police firing and many people were killed in it. Gandhiji himself visited Odisha in 1931 and again in 1932. Pandit Gopabandhu Dash, Rama Devi, Sarala Devi, Gopabandhu Choudhary, Kalindi Charan Panigrahi, etc. played crucial role in mobilising the people to support freedom movement led by Gandhiji. They were arrested and sent to jail many times.

Odiya; the very language of Odisha well mirrors these spirits of the land. There is a galaxy of the poets who have sung the song of nationalism. Of all the litterateurs who actively participated in the freedom movement in the leadership of Mahatma Gandhi, the names of Pandit Gopabandhu Dash, Madhusudan Das, Rama Devi, Kalindi Charan Panigrahi, Sarala Devi, Gopabandhu Choudhary, etc., are eminent one.

Gopabandhu Dash; an eminent nationalist of Odisha was closely associated with Gandhi. In his personality we have an educationist, a political activist, a social reformer, a freedom fighter and a great poet of Odiya blended together. In his poetry, we have an advocacy of ardent nationalism. The poet loves his country so much that he wishes that after his death his body i.e., his flesh and bones to be mingled with the soil of his motherland so that his countrymen may tread on the same. Let us see the lines from his poem titled *Bandire Atmakatha* i.e., soliloquy of a prisoner:

Mishu mora deha e desh matire,
Deshabashi chali jaantu pithire,
Deshera swaraj pathe jete gada,
Puru tanhi padi mora mansa hada.[31]

The poet wishes that not only his life but his death in the prison, too, may inspire his countrymen to move for the freedom movement. To quote lines:

Swadhinta pathe tile hele nara,
Mora jivan dane heu agrasara.[32]

What is the objective of the human life? The poet creates awareness amongst the people of Utkal as to what is their imperative for their country. The poet thinks that the whole human life gets fruitful if it is laid for the cause of motherland, for the protection of the cremation ground of the ancestors, the holy places and the grand heritage of the nation. To quote lines:

Purva purushara, pavitra smashan,
Deshera jatira gaurava gaan,
Punya janmabhumi, punya devalaya,
Udhariba pain kale tanukshaya,
Manaba jivana huai safala,
Ek maha diksha ki bujhiba utkala.[33]

Gopabandhu elsewhere says:

Nija swarth lagi jata nahine Hindu,
Viswa hite Hindu prati rakta bindu.[34]

The poet means to say that the objective of the Hindu is not to be confined within his self but each drop of his blood is designed for the welfare of the whole humanity. The poet has a very broad concept of Hindu and Hinduism. By Hindu he does not mean any creed, religion, or a community. The fact is that Hinduism is our nationalism as Shri Aurbindo Ghosh advocated. It is derived from the name of our land, nation *Sindhu,* which is pronounced as a *Hindu*: the name of our rich heritage, its culture and its way of our life. Late Md. Karim Bhai Chagla; Hon'ble justice of Supreme Court of India once said:

All the Muslims and the Christians living in India are Hindu by race.

Dr Smt. Annie Besant, the great Indian nationalist and a great leader of 'The Theosophical Society of India' said, Hinduism is the soil, in which India's roots are and so let us make no mistake that without Hinduism India has no future.

To conclude our review of 'An Ardent Nationalism in Odiya Poetry', it is apt to say that Gopabandhu is not only the '*Utkalmani*' but a '*Rashtramani*' i.e., the gem of the nation, i.e. one of the greatest laureate of Indian poetry who deserves to be kept in the line of Rabindranath Tagore, Sarojini Naidu, Subhramanyam Bharti, Maithili Sharan Gupta and Ramdhari Singh Dinkar.

Gandhi: A Sindhi

Gange cha Yamune chaiva, Godavari Saraswati,
Narmade Sindhu Kaveri, jalesmin satnidhim kuru.
Pushkardhyani tirthani, Gangadhyah saristastatha,
Aagachantu pavitrani, snankale sada mama.[35]

After the critical appreciation of depiction of the nationalistic spirit especially the Gandhian movement in approximately all the languages of our country, let us move into *Sindhi*; the language of *Sindh*; that we have lost into the hand of Pakistan in the tragedy of our partition. '*Jana gana mana adhinayak jaya he, Bharat bhagya vidhata*' in our national anthem we sing '*Punjab, Sindh, Gujrata, Maratha, Dravida, Utkal, Banga*'. But have we ever thought that Sindh is no longer with us. It is in our national anthem, only where our beloved Sindh exists.

Shri Lalkrishna Advani; one of the towering personality of our contemporary Indian politics gets nostalgiac when he talks on Sindh. It was 2nd of January 2013, when Shri Advaniji on my request consented to talk to me at his residence 30, Prithvi Raj Road, New Delhi.

Shri Advani talked to me the glorious history of Sindh, its unbreakable bond with India since the dawn of its civilisation and its role in our freedom movement. Shri Advani gave me some of his beautiful books including *My Country, My Life*. I think this memoir of Shri Advani is more about our country than about his life. I express my gratitude to Shri Advaniji for providing all the matter with the help of which I could write this article.

Sindh has been the very identification of our Indian Nationalism. Verbally it means the land that is nourished by the great river *Sindhu*. The beautiful *shlokas* from our scriptures quoted at the beginning simply means that without invoking *Sindhu* along with *Ganga, Yamuna, Saraswati, Godawari, Kaveri, Narmada* etc. none of our *pujas, yagyas*, marriages, funeral, or either of our rites could be performed. This is why our the national sages say that the seed of our nationalism lies in our cultural heritage. Now it is *Sindhu* or Sindh from which the name of the nation Hindu or *Hind* or *Hindustan* or even India is derived. It is fact that the Persians or the people of Arabian countries in the medieval ages whose traders and ambassadors usually visited India uttered '*ha*' instead of '*sa*'. So in their travelogues they used the words *Hind* or Hindu or *Hindustan* i.e. the land of Hindus. This is why it is said that Hindu or Hinduism connotates for our land, the nation and not the religion like other creeds e.g. Muslims or Christians. With the passage of time our nation was called India as the Greek people uttered '*aa*' in place of '*ha*'. Megasthanese; the famous Greek ambassador in India named his book '*Indica*', i.e. story of India, thus it is proven that India, i.e. the modern popular name of our country is originally derived from *Hindu* or *Sindhu* only.

Sindh or the *Sindhus* has been the land of great Indus Valley Civilisation. In the beginning of the twentieth century whole of the western intelligentsia got astonished to view the great excavation of Mohanzodro and Harrapan. It has been the Kingdom of Maharaj Dadir; the bravest of the brave who gave a strong protest to Mohammad Bin Qasim; the first

Muslim invader in India. Karachi; the capital of Sindh has been the centre of the trade in the medieval age.

Sindh has played a significant role in getting our independence. Lal Krishna Advani writes :

> *"When Bal Gangadhar Tilak was sentenced to six years of imprisonment in Mandalay in Burma (Myanmar) in 1908 many Sindhi youths slept on the road in protest. When he visited Sindh in 1920 women came out of their seclusion and offered aarti to him."* [36]

Sindh has been the pioneer in expression of the national spirit. Even before the Indian National Congress was born, let us see one of the editorial of *Sindh Times* published on May 20th, 1884:

> *"Nadir Shah looted the country only once, but British loot us every day. Every year to the tune of 4.5 million dollars is being drained out, sucking our very blood, Britain should immediately quit India."*[37]

Dr Choithram Gidwani (1889-1957) was one of the greatest young nationalist of Sindh. Lokmanya Tilak was very much impressed with his dedication to the nation. Tilak writes in his journal *Kesari*:

> *"If every province had men like Dr Choithram we could break the chains of bondage in no time."*[38]

Mahatma Gandhi also pays an affection tribute to him in his '*Young India*' in 1924:

> *"Choithram has sacrificed everything for the cause of his country and has turned into a faquir."*[39]

And it is an irony that after the tragic partition when Jawaharlal Nehru was reluctant to compensate the Hindu refugees for the property losses, it was Choitram who convinced him to do so. The stream of nationalism in Sindh ran throughout the freedom movement. Not a single public turned up in the reception when Prince of Wales visited Karachi in 1922. Contrary to this when Gandhi launched *Satyagraha* in 1932 there was a peaceful protest on the road followed by a police firing on it and two *satyagrahis* got martyrdom. Jairamdas Daulatram Alimchandani; an eminent Congress leader was also injured. He was shot in his thigh. The whole of the nation was shocked at this. Gandhiji in a message said:

> *"I have not known anyone more pure hearted than Jairamdas. The temple of Swaraj will be built with the blood of such Indians."* [40]

About Jairamdas (1891-1978) it deserves to be mentioned that he became the General Secretary of Congress. And after independence, he served as the editor of "*The Complete Works of Mahatma Gandhi*".

Acharya Kriplani (1888-1982); one of the best known freedom fighter from Sindh was one of the most trusted follower of Mahatma Gandhi.

Prof N.R. Malkani (1860-1974) another great congress leader from Sindh renounced his professorship in the university under Gandhi's influence and joined freedom movement. Prof Malkani helped Gandhi to set up a *Harijan* colony in Delhi.

Allah Bux Soomro (1900-1943); one of the most respected premier of Sindh was the champion of Hindu-Muslim Unity. He strongly countered Muslim League's claim of being the only representative of Muslims in India. Unfortunately he was assassinated in 1943.

Annual session of the AICC was held in Karachi in 1931. In the presidentship of Sardar Vallabh Bhai Patel the resolution was adopted promising the Universal adult franchise in the free India.

Netaji Subhash Chandra Bose was warmly respected and loved by the people of Sindh. K.R. Malkani, younger brother of Prof N.R Malkani and the editor of *The Organiser* in his book titled '*The Sindh Story*' narrates an interesting incident to show the warm affection that the Netaji had in the hearts of the *Sindhis.* When Netaji was leaving Hyderabad by train, one of the Sindhi gentlemen suggested him to marry a Sindhi girl he would then donate a handsome dowry for his national cause. Netaji with humour replied he would marry if Dr Choithram would lead the way. Needless to say that most of those statesmen were unmarried. Netaji further added; Let us form a party of bachelors of India with Choithram as a president and myself as a secretary. We would call it 'Jai Hind Party'. Our objective will be to sacrifice married bliss for the joy of serving the country. The story concludes that the Netaji had the word "Jai Hind" in his mind long before he founded the Indian National Army (INA) in 1942.

Mahatma Gandhi visited Sindh seven times 1916, 1917, 1920, 1921, 1929, 1931, 1934. In one of his article in 1929, Gandhi writes:

"Everything in India attracts us, but when I first visited Sindh in 1916, it attracted me in several ways and a bond was established between the Sindhis and we that has proved capable of bearing severe strains"[41]

Shri Lal Krishna Advani says:

"Of all the leaders of freedom movement Sindhis have the greatest respect for Gandhiji. When the Sindhis were subjected to the untold travails of Partition, it was Gandhiji, who more than any other leader stood by them."[42]

When Sindhi Hindus were doomed to flee from their forefather's land Gandhiji wrote:

"If even a single Sindhi leaves Sindh, it will be a matter of shame to Mr. Jinnah as a Governer General." [43]

On May 27th 1947 Gandhi told in his prayer gathering:

"The people of Sindh want me to go to them. I have not been to Sindh for many years, but I have maintained such close relations with the people of Sindh that one time I used to call myself a Sindhi." [44]

Gandhi constantly urged Government of India and the British authorities to do everything to Sindhi refugees. He even talked to Maharao of Kuchh and got land in Kandla for Sindhu Resettlement co-operation.

It was 30th of January, 1948, the last date of Gandhi's life. A Sindhi delegation led by Dr Choithram met Gandhi. When he listened the tales of killing and looting of the refugees, his eyes filled with tears. He said:

"If there can be a war for Kashmir, there can also be a war for the rights of Sindhis Hindus in Pakistan."[45]

K.R. Malkani writes in his book that his brother Prof N.R. Malkani met Mahatma only an hour before he was assassinated. Prof Malkani was appointed by the Government of India as Additional Deputy High Commissioner in Karachi to organise orderly migration from Sindh. Giving his blessings to him Gandhiji's advised;

"Take out everybody. See that you are the last person to come out. And tell khushroo[46] *I want to visit Sindh to re-establish peace. Let him consult Jinnah and inform me telegraphically"* [47]

It is irony that Gandhiji couldn't visit Sindh as after an hour he was assassinated.

To conclude my article, Gandhi; a Sindhi, I would like to quote Shri Lal Krishna Advani again:

"Sindh is now a part of Pakistan; an independent and sovereign nation, a fact that is to be accepted. But from a civilisational perspective, neither the Sindh can be separated from India nor can Indian forget Sindh." [48]

Gandhian Impact on Indo-Anglian Fiction

The survey of Gandhi's influence on the Indian regional literature measures the height and fathoms the depth of the Mahatma's personality. But this is not the essence of our study; it is simply the background designed with a purpose to assess Gandhian impact on Indian fiction in English. With regard to the Gandhian influence on it, Dr K.R. Srinivasa Iyengar observes:

The stress was on simplicity and clarity and immediate effectiveness rather than on ornateness or profundity and artistry, and this has been as marked in English writing as in writing in the regional languages. As regards the choice of theme and portrayal of character, the Gandhian influence has been no less marked.[49]

It should, however, be kept in mind that these were not the Gandhian trends in particular. In Europe and elsewhere literatures were coming out of grooves and certain literary qualities used by the authors were being subject to ridicule. This new track was to be followed in Indian literature also. Bhabani Bhattacharya has written in this regard:

Gandhi acted as a pioneer. He strengthened the impact of the world trends on India. Under his influence, as much as under the influence of the west, Indian creative thought was being centred increasingly on the life, the joys and the sorrows of the common man.[50]

Gandhian Spirit in the Novels of K.S. Venkataramani

K.S. Venkataramani holds a high place among the early Indian writers in English. His works are clearly influenced by Gandhian ideas. *Murugan, the Tiller* and *Kandan, the Patriot* could have only been written after the emergence of Gandhi on the Indian horizon, for the former dramatises Gandhian economics and the latter, Gandhian politics. The same influence is visible in Venkatramani's another novel, *Jatadharan*, and also in his collection of short stories, *The Next Rung*.

Murugan, the Tiller (1927) is the first novel to reflect on aspect of freedom movement under the leadership of Mahatma Gandhi. It deals with the Gandhian ideals of rural reconstruction as a step towards attaining *swaraj*. The novel is not, therefore, directly political. To its critics and appreciators it is political only remotely. It is mainly a documentary novel depicting south Indian life and manners.

Manjeri S. Isvaran has appreciated the inclusion of *Murugan, the Tiller* in *The Overseas Empire in Fiction,* and does not fail to recognise the political aspect of the novel and thus writes:

The novel affords the author with ample scope for description of scenery for delineation of national types and characters, for reflections of social, political and economic problems.[51]

To the other critics this novel of rural India is unmistakably a novel depicting the "back to the village movement" of the Gandhian era. K.R. Srinivasa Iyengar, in *Indian Writing in English*, has discussed the novel under the heading *Gandhi Literature* and has dubbed *Murugan, the Tiller* as the titular hero of the novel, "an exponent of Gandhian economics." H.H. Anniah Gowda observes:

Living in stirring times, Venkataramani in this novel concerns himself with agrarian problems, highlighting the evils of Western education, the Rule of Law and the racial difference in the country.[52]

In the novel we have beautiful description of Indian life and manners, but these are only designed to expound the main theme more markedly; and the main theme here undoubtedly is the rural reconstruction of India after the ideals of Gandhi. Let us have a brief look into the novel to make the point clear.

Ramchandran *alias* Ramu, the western educated young man is the central character. The novel depicts the conflict that goes on in his mind. The conflict is between the two pulls; one of them being the city life of Madras and another, the rural life of village Alavanti. Meenakshi represents the two pulls, the city bred lady, mother-in-law of Ramu, and Murugan, the son of the soil, his most faithful servant. Ramu, who was primarily appointed as an office clerk in the city, attains the post of Deputy Collector by virtue of his sincerity, honesty and dedication.

In this way the author portrays Ramu as an ideal character who builds India of Gandhi's dream – a rural India where "none slaved for other." It is in the sense that the novel *Murugan, the Tiller* has a nationalistic theme. The Gandhian idea of going 'back to village' was very much prevalent at the time throughout the country and this is why K.R. Srinivasa Iyengar calls it 'a tract for the times.' The context of the novel and the dialogues, too make the novel purely Gandhian. Let us see a dialogue between Ramu and his British officer, Mr. Cadell:

We are powerless in our land. Just see what happens in a village. By direct taxation, Government takes one-third of the gross produce, and yet another third goes in the wake of civilised needs, cloth, kerosene, coffee and sugar, and both one-third is left in the village. The rest we have to export. We need shelter both from the howling trade winds of civilisation and enormous cost of Government. No wonder we are ill fed. And the lands don't yield well. A hungry man is no thinker. He does not and cannot plan his future. [53]

Beyond doubts, such an opinion is purely Gandhian. That the novelist intends to give a Gandhian tinge to the character of Ramu is evident when we find him talking to Kedari, his friend:

The glory of nation will be nourished on a painless and non-violent food, dripping from nature as sunlight drips from the sun. The soul of Science is ahimsa, the redemption of all sentient life from violence to others and to itself and from the dull pain of muscular labour.[54]

Ramu, in the same conversation, later says:

Kedari, half of our misery is self-inflicted and man-made. It springs from lack of courage to utter the truth in thought, word and deed.[55]

These are unmistakably Gandhian ideas. To quote G.P. Sharma:

Murugan, the Tiller is thus a novel depicting primarily the Gandhian ideal of going 'back to the village' and, secondarily, emphasising the need for the traditional Indian way of living.[56]

K.S. Venkataramani's next novel, *Kandan, the Patriot* (1932), is on the other hand, a novel depicting the political aspect of the national struggle of India of the same period. K.R. Srinivasa Iyengar writes, "Murugan is an exponent of Gandhian economics as Kandan is an exponent of Gandhian politics."[57]

It reflects the national movement for political freedom under the leadership of Gandhi, but Gandhi himself is not introduced as a character. And the novelist seems to have done it with a purpose. He wants to show that during the freedom movement there was one Gandhi in every village or town to lead the people by staying in their midst. It gains strength when we hear Kandan, the hero in the novel, addressing Rajeshwari Bai, a dedicated freedom fighter, thus:

Men like Gandhiji, instead of being a world phenomenon to be worshiped like the sun, must grow on every hedge like blackberries. At least every cottage must have one Gandhiji working for its renovation till it is restored to healthy life and needs one Gandhi for a trumpet call to pure, selfless public work.[58]

Let us have a dip into the story of the novel. Kandan, as the very title of the novel suggests, is the leader of the freedom struggle in a village called Akkur. He gives up his ICS to join India's national movement. He is Gandhi for the villagers, an embodiment of honesty and saintliness. They cannot disobey him and have given up taking liquor. Rangan, an Oxford educated young man, is another parallel character in the novel. He, too, being an ICS officer has deep sympathy for national freedom struggle. As a punitive measure against him he has been transferred to Tranquebar. Rajeswari Bai, a Marathi girl and daughter of a Bombay millionaire, whom Rangan loved at Oxford, joins the national movement actively and postpones marriage. She urges Rangan to give up ICS to join national movement. She says only then she would be his. On appeal of Rangan they move to Tranquebar to discuss the national and the personal issues.

At Akkur station Rangan is persuaded by the *Mirasdar*, the landlord of the place, to get down from the train to solve the conflict between *Mirasdar* and the villagers led by Kandan.

It was the charismatic influence of Rangan that the problem was solved and *Mirasdar* was won over and he turned to be a nationalist. Peace was restored in the estate. All the people including *Mirasdar* move to Tranquebar to spend a week there. In the course of a public meeting and consequent *lathi*-charge Kandan was badly injured and breathed his last preaching the people to devote their life for nation's cause and upliftment of the poor. The people assure him, "We will think of no earthly pleasures till the freedom of the country is won."[59]

Parallel to the main story of the novel, the sub-stories are also equally inspiring. Padma and Raghu, the two brothers, leave their studies and government job respectively to serve the nation by joining the freedom struggle. Raghu says to his mother informing her of his resignation:

> *Yes mother, drunk with wine of freedom, no more am I a slave at the desk grinding accounts for an alien rule to keep a pampered system going. Truth nothing but truth, mother. Are you not proud of me today that I have won my freedom so that I may work for public cause? Mother, the thing is in the air, who can escape it?*[60]

Sundaram and Saraswati, the railway stationmaster and his wife, join freedom struggle actively, leaving the government service. Saraswati says to her husband:

> *... in these glorious days when a new India is in the making, you and I must do some noble work for the country.*[61]

Kamakshi, a poor helpless village maiden, and Ponnan, a British government spy, turn nationalists to be active freedom fighters.

At every step in the novel the Gandhian impact is clearly discernible. The character of Kandan and Rangan are weaved with the thread of Gandhian ideals. Kandan's view about *Swaraj* is yet another indication of it:

> *We must build our swaraj in such a way we produce no brokers at the top, like worms in cheese, who deal carelessly with the lives of the millions. The tyrant and the coward shall not flourish in this ancient land of courage and love. The difficulty is not in getting swaraj; for we are surely getting it. For ours is a fight to the finish; to live or die as a nation. The test of our new life is not in winning*

freedom; but in applying it selflessly and courageously to the freedom of all, even to the humblest in the land.[62]

Mulk Raj Anand and his Novels

Mulk Raj Anand's *Untouchable* (1935) and Raja Rao's *Kanthapura* (1938) are excellent works wherein we have an elaborate treatment of central concept of Gandhian philosophy.

In *Untouchable,* we find Anand diagnosing the disease of untouchability and recommending the solution as offered by Gandhi. Anand was deeply impressed by Gandhi's ideals; he had himself stayed with Gandhi in his *Sabarmati Ashram*, and this intimacy had not only enriched his creative vision but also filled up his heart with the Buddhist *karuna* and compassion. As a result we find *Untouchable* a very sensitive, compassionate and realistic portrayal of the humiliations and indignities suffered by the untouchables. At the same time, it is a relentless exposure of the Hindu caste sytem and the theory of *Karma* which perpetrate inhuman atrocities against the downtrodden people like Bakha. Anand confesses in the author's note of the novel:

I am sure, however, that the warmth towards Bakha which has made this character lovable to so many people may, to some extent, have emerged from my warmth towards the person of Gandhi.[63]

Gandhi has himself been introduced as a character in the novel, and the novelist has excellently and vividly drawn the pen-portrait of the Mahatma, seated like a child huddled up between two women, Kasturba Gandhi and Miraben.

He also powerfully demonstrates the electrifying impact of Mahatma on the minds of the people through Bakha:

He (Bakha) had not asked himself where he was going. He hadn't paused to think. The word 'Mahatma' was like a magical magnet, to which he, like all other people about him, rushed blindly.[64]

The entire speech made by Gandhi is a collage of his actual statements about untouchability, which makes his picture authentic. Bakha is intrigued and mystified by Gandhi's speech: "The Mahatma seemed to have touched the most intimate corners of his soul."[65]

Momentarily, he even forgets the fact of his own untouchability. The Mahatma had left a 'glow of brotherliness and humanitarianism'.[66]

There was only one strange voice of dissent in the entire crowd, the voice of a '*desi sahib*', who decried the Mahatma by saying:

Gandhi is a humbug, ... a fool. He is a hypocrite. In one breath he says he wants to abolish untouchability, in the other he asserts he is an orthodox Hindu. He is running counter to the spirit of our age .... He is in the fourth centry BC with his swadeshi and his spinning-wheel .... [67]

However, the sympathy exhuded by the Mahatma unfortunately seems too abstract to significantly change Bakha's immediate world. Anand seems to be saying that high moral principles, by themselves, cannot provide the change that is needed for men to be free. Such provision can only come through action. And a Marxist revolutionary poet (Iqbal Nath Sarashar) suggests the action. The proposed action, while sounding strange coming from the lips of a poet, is lyric in its simplicity:

Remove the basis for the demeaning labour that provokes the need for the untouchables by installing the modern sanitary system — the flush system. The proposal, if carried out, immediately provides relief for Bakha's plight – or does it?[68]

There is a physical side to each man's need for salvation, but man also dwells in the world of abstract ideas and belief. Centuries of piling customs and beliefs have created indelible marks on man's psyche — marks that a simple mechanical solution cannot by itself eradicate. Bakha might be relieved of his demeaning labour, but it does not follow that he would feel equal to those whom he formerly served.

Thus Bakha's need for salvation, a need triggered by centuries of tradition and oppression, can only be met by an all-compassing solution that takes into account all facets of man's existence: physical, social, and spiritual. As Anand told Gandhi, he was interested in posing the question rather than answering it. So he has chosen to demonstrate his answer by giving each speaker–the padre, the Mahatma, and the poet–a germ of truth in his response.

In another novel of Gandhian era titled *The Sword and the Sickle* (1942), Anand has dramatised the conflict between the Marxist and the Gandhian ideologies in the soul of its protagonist, Lal Singh, a Punjabi youth who has returned to India after being released from a German prison camp during World War I. Lalu gets involved in a peasant movement in U.P., led by Kunwar Rampal Singh, an avowed Communist who frequently quotes Lenin and Marx and celebrates the anniversary of the Russian Revolution with the peasants of Ramgarh. When the peasant movement receives a setback, Lalu seeks an interview with Gandhi at Anand Bhawan, Allahabad, in the hope that the Mahatma would help him alleviate the sufferings of the peasants. He is, however, bewildered to hear the Mahatma talk about the spiritual significance of suffering, self-sacrifice and non-violence. He is also disillusioned to see Gandhi much preoccupied with the protection of the cow and the values associated with the *Sanatan Hindu Dharma.* When Gandhi refuses to go to Ramgarh at Lalu's request, Lalu and his party lose their faith in the Mahatma and become critical of Gandhi's words and deeds in their later conversation. It is only at the end that Lalu finally realises the truth of Gandhi's faith in the futility of violence. Anand's attitude toward Gandhi remains one of artistic detachment. The Gandhian image projected by the novel is neither romantic, nor eulogistic. Gandhi is mostly seen through the eyes of Lalu and other peasant workers who feel the magical pull of the Mahatma's personality but fail to understand the meaning of his ideas and ideals.

In another novel titled *The Big Heart* (1945), we find Anand challenging Gandhi's attitude towards machines and industrialism. The Gandhian view is represented by Mahasha Hans Raj, an *Arya Samaji* leader, who through his supporters, particularly Satyapal, a student leader, and Professor Majid, spreads the gospel of Gandhi's *swadeshi* and pleads with the jobless *thathiars* (coppersmiths) to boycott machines. The *thathiars* are persuaded that the machines are not only the cause of their massive unemployment but they are also against the teachings of Gandhi who thought that the introduction of machinery in India was a symbol of the imposition of British civilisation in India that it also led to the exploitation of poor workers by the rich capitalists. The champion of machines is the novel's protagonist Ananta, who not only wants to usher in the 'Age of Machine' but also trade unionism to better the lot of the working class. He has a strong supporter in Puran Singh Bhagat, a Marxist poet, who repudiates the Gandhian system of values. Their effort to form a union of unemployed coppersmiths is, however, foiled by Mahasha Hans Raj. Professor Majid, a powerful orator, sways the jobless *thathiars* against Anant and the factory owners by persuading them "that the real enemy is hidden here, the factory which is going to convert you all from feudal slaves to wage slaves."[69]

One jobless worker gets out of hand and he forces his way into the factory and starts smashing the machine with a huge hammer. Anant comes forward to protect the machine and is killed with a smash. Anand's attitude toward Anant and the machine remains ambivalent. Perhaps it was best expressed through Iqbal Nath Sarashar in *Untouchable*:

I hate the machine. I loathe it. But I shall go against Gandhi there and accept it. And I am sure in time all will learn to love it.[70]

Mulk Raj Anand had a pronouuced Marxist bias. His fictional treatment of Gandhian ideology shows considerable artistic detachment. Though he challenges some of Gandhi's ideas and attitudes, he has never questioned their underlying sincerity and humanism.

The Road (1961) is the next Gandhian novel by Mulk Raj Anand. Here the novelist regrets that though the Government of India has officially abolished the untouchability, Gandhi's dream of *swaraj* still remains unfulfilled because the Hindus continue to persist in their attitudes of bigotry and prejudice against the *Harijans*. The image of Gandhi is porjected in the novel through Dooli Singh, the villege headman, who champions the cause of the untouchables against the cruelty of the caste-Hindus like Thakur Singh. Bhikhu, the young protagonist, is an untouchable like Bakha, but he is more sensitive and more conscious of his need for freedom and the human dignity than Bakha. Bhikhu's dicision to leave the village for Delhi 'where there would be no caste or outcaste'–despite the local Gandhi's memorable sacrifices and support for the *Harijan* community–clearly reminds the reader that the struggle for the Gandhian values has not yet ended.

The images of Mahatma Gandhi as projected in different novels of Mulk Raj Anand are authentic, objective and free from the emotional adoration of the Mahatma. It is interesting to study and analyse the works of Anand in the light of the objectivity with which he portrays Gandhi in his works.

Raja Rao and *Kanthapura*

Raja Rao's *Kanthapura* (1938) is one of the most celebrated novels wherein we have the treatment of Gandhi's ideals at its best. Here the author seems to have captured the heart of entire Gandhian movement by depicting the emergence of national consciousness in a village. The novel is full of Gandhian references, thoughts and imagery, and the theme is tied with Gandhian life and philosophy. Here we find Gandhi eulogised, romanticised and mythologised. There is a beautiful blending of myths, legend, religion, poetry and politics here and *Kanthapura* has become throbbing heart of India responding to the call of Mahatma. Here we have all social and political activities of thirties associated with Gandhi beautifully depicted, e.g. '*Dandi March*', 'Civil Disobedience Movement' '*Satyagrah*', '*Harijan*- upliftment', '*Swadeshi*', '*Swaraj*', 'propaganda against liquor addiction', 'fasting' and 'wheel spinning', 'police- atrocities', 'Gandhi-Irwin Pact', 'Second Round Table Conference', etc. The major focus of the novel is on the electrifying zeal with which the villagers of Kanthapura rises to the call of the Indian nationalist movement led by Mahatma Gandhi. The image of the Mahatma is projected through Moorthy, the pivotal character in the novel, who is rightly described as 'a Gandhi man'. Moorthy is a true *satyagrahi*, dedicated to all Gandhian ideals, i.e. 'self-purification', 'self-sacrifice', 'non-violence', 'truth' and the ideal of *swaraj*. He is a true humanist who chooses to do the *Pariah* work. He carries the dead body of the wife of Puttaya. The people of Kanthapura say:

> *He is our Gandhi. The state of Mysore has a Maharaja, but the Maharaja has also another Maharaja who is in London, and that one has another in Heaven, and so everybody has his own Mahatma, and this Moorthy who has been caught in our eyes playing as a child, is now grown up and great, and he has his wisdom in him and he will be our Mahatma.*[71]

Moorthy, like Mahatma, is persecuted and excommunicated by the orthodox people, the Swami and Bhatta, who in him see not a saviour of the lowly and the lost but a menacing threat to their age-old religious and social traditions. In the entire novel we have the spirit of Gandhi pervaded and most of the villege people continue to pledge their support for the Mahama, Moorthy begins to show impatince with Mahatma's policies in the end.

He seems to be drifting towards Nehru. He writes to Ratna:

> *Things must change. Jawaharlal will change it. You know Jawaharlal is like a Bharatha to the Mahatma, and he, too, is for non-violence and he, too, is a satyagrahi, but he says in swaraj there shall be neither the rich nor the poor. And he calls himself an 'equal-distributionist', and I am with him and his men.*[72]

Narayan's *Waiting for the Mahatma*

R. K. Narayan's *Waiting for the Mahatma* (1955) is the next work for our consideration in this category. Narayan has himself described it as a novel of Gandhi. Gandhi himself occupies a pivotal position in the novel, and the love story of Sriram and Bharati revolves around him. Here the image of Gandhi is that of a warm, loving, and good-humoured Bapu and the portrayal is authentic. Actually Narayan had written a story titled '*Gandhi's Appeal*' before independence; dealing with nationalistic theme, i.e. irresistible appeal of Gandhi on the masses. Thematically, *Waiting for the Mahatma* can be described as an extension of this story. Narayan calls it 'a novel of Gandhi'. We see Gandhi in person staying at Nallapa's Grove in Malgudi and years later in Delhi on the fatel day of his assassination. Narayan's picture of Gandhi's activities and his daily routine is authentic.

Through Gandhi's words and actions, he brings out the major concepts of Gandhian philosophy such as spinning on the *charkha*, the practice of absolute truth and non-violence, the idea of purity, self - discipline, and self-reliance, and the removal of untouchability. He also shows how Gandhi, through his personal example, touches and transforms the lives of the common people, including Sriram and Bharati.

Khwaja Ahmed Abbas's *Inquilab*

Khwaja Ahmed Abbas's *Inquilab* (1955) can be studied with Narayan's *Waiting for the Mahatma.* Both the novels were published in the same year (1955). In *Inquilab* also we find Gandhi portrayed as a prominent national leader and the novel covers the political events of nearly two decades beginning with Jalianwala Bagh massacre of 1919 to the Gandhi-Irwin Pact in 1931. It is at Dr Ansari's house that Anwar sees Gandhi first: "A thin spindly-legged man in coarse *dhoti* and *kurta*, playing a *charkha*".[73] Later, he has an emotional interview with Gandhi at the house of Muhammad Ali, and at that time he suddenly understands the secret of Gandhi's greatness:

> *Now he knew why they called him Mahatma — a Great Soul. On his face was a look of suffering, kindness and pity, as if he personally felt the misery of every single human being. But there was also infinite calm and serenity and the boy's spirits revived as he looked into those gentle eyes.*[74]

This meeting of Anwar with Mahatma Gandhi enables him to develop a "total vision" of the Indian political scene.

In the preceding discussion we have seen a benign and complimentary image of the Mahatma as portrayed by some Indian fiction writers of English. But after the national Independence and subsequent disappreance of Gandhi from the national scene, however, things began to change. Because of the corruption and moral degradation of his unscrupulous followers the image of Mahatma was also tarnished. Some novelists have also presented this phase of diminishing popularity of the Mahatma in their works.

Khuswant Singh and his Works

Khuswant Singh has been a very celebrated journalist of our time. *Train to Pakistan* and *We shall Not Hear the Nightingale* are his famous novels. In *Train to Pakistan* the image of Mahatma is that of a religious man:

> *Look at Gandhi! I hear he reads the Koran Sharif and the Unjeel along with his Vedas and Shastras. People sing his praise in the four corners of the earth... Even the English respect a man of religion.*[75]

The author severely attacks the disciples of Gandhi in the government:

> *Ask anyone coming from Delhi and he will tell you that all these Gandhi disciples are minting money. They are as good saints as the crane. They shut their eyes piously and stand on one leg like a yogi doing penance; as soon as a fish comes near - hurry up.*[76]

Mr. Singh holds the miscalculation of 'Baniya' politician at Delhi (an obvious reference to Gandhi) responsible for India's partition resulting into mass massacres of 1947.

Chaman Nahal in *Azadi* (1975) projects a similar view. The person of Sialkot had a perfect faith in Gandhi's determination to keep the nation united. Lala Kanshi Ram cannot even imagine how the 'Partition' could happen:

> *The Congress had a promise to keep with the people. For the last thirty years, since that wizard Gandhi appeared on the scene, it had taken the stand that India was a single nation, not two. And Gandhi was not only a politician, he was a saint.He had his inner voice to satisfy, too. Would that nagging voice of his let him accept the slaughter of so many? That's what it would mean, if Pakistan did come into existence and Gandhi was shrewd — surely he saw it all. He wouldn't give in to such butchery.*[77]

But, 'Partition' was like a bombshell that fell too suddenly on the people of Sialkot, and their faith in Mahatma got shattered.

Manohar Malgonkar's *A Bend in the Ganges*

In Manohar Malgonkar's *A Bend in the Ganges* (1964) we have two-pronged apporach to Gandhism. The author simultaneously exposes the hypocrisy and emptiness of Mahatma's disciples and probes into the Gandhian philosophy of non-violence posing the question- 'Could it ever serve as a philosophy of life itself?' Gandhi himself appears in the novel briefly but his creed of non-violence has been attacked severely throughout the novel. The story has been told through the viewpoint of an extremist group, who are thorough bred nationalists but believe in active militant action against the Britishers. These members of extremist group, obviously, have no faith in Gandhian ideology of *Ahimsa*, and openly they hold Gandhi responsible for the atrocities committed during India's partition.

Basu, a character in the novel, denounces Gandhi's philosophy of non-violence:

Non-violence is merely a pious thought, a dream of the philosophers. I shudder to think what disillusion confronts them; what Gandhi will feel when he sees the holocaust that will engulf this country. He will die a thousand deaths, I tell you, he will suffer for each single man that suffers, Hindu or Moslem, but will he ever recognise that mankind is not prepared for true non-violence — will never be prepared?

No! No! He will go on living and preaching his dream.[78]

Basu is a revolutionary by creed. He capitalises on the fact that Gandhi himself had doubts about the efficacy of non-violence. He quotes Gandhi. This quotation, in fact, has been used by the author (Malgonkar) as an epigraph to the novel:

This non-violence, therefore, seems to be due mainly to our helplessness. It almost appears as if we are nursing in our bosoms the desire to take revenge the first time we get the opportunity. Can true, voluntary non-violence come out of this seeming forced non-violence of the weak? What if, when the fury bursts, not a man, woman, or child is safe and every man's hand is raised against his neighbour?[79]

In this epigraph lies the very tone of the novel. Gian, who has been an admirer of the Gandhian creed of non-violence, discovers that the *Ahimsa* cannot serve as a philosophy of life. To quote Tekchand, the great industrialist in the novel, who expresses the similer view, i.e. inefficacy of Gandhian philosophy:

Now he could see that as the people of India were concerned, Gandhi's message was merely a political expedient; that for the bulk of them, it had no deeper significance. At best, they had accepted it as an effective weapon against British power. It seemed that the moment the grip of British power was loosened, the population of the sub-continent had discarded non-violence overnight and were now spending themselves on orgies which seemed to fulfil some basic urge.[80]

The very '*Author's Note*' of the novel deserves our special attention:

Only the violence in this story happens to be true; it came in the wake of freedom, to become a part of India's history. What was achieved through non-violence was brought with it one of the bloodiest upheavals of history: seventeen million people had to flee, leaving their homes; nearly half a million were killed; over a hundred thousand women, young and old, were adbucted, raped, mutilated.[81]

This does not mean that the author recommends the violence as a way of life in preference to the Gandhian principle of non-violence; he simply exposes the hypocrisy of followers of Gandhi. The author's attitude, perhaps, is best reflected through the words of the extremist leader, Devidayal, uttered on August 12, 1947:

Yet what was the alternative? Would terrorism have won freedom at a cheaper price and somehow still kept Hindus and Moslems together? Perhaps not. But at least it would have been an honest sacrifice; honest and manly — not something that had sneaked upon them in the garb of non-violence.[82]

When we attained our freedom we took a pledge to run the administration of the country in accordance with the ideals and principles of Mahatma Gandhi. But when the diplomatic and the complicated political problems were encountered it was felt that the said principles were not of much help. This phase of our national life has been expressed by the novelists of our time. Nayantara Sahgal's *This Time of Mourning* and Bhabani Bhattacharya's *Shadow from Ladakh* are within the purview of our consideration.

Nayantara Sahgal's *This Time of Mourning*

Nayantara Sahgal's *This Time of Mourning* (1965) deals with the power politics in the last days of Nehru's prime ministership. The protagonist, Kailash Vrind, a veteran Gandhian, doubts the creed of non-violence. We are told:

He accepts non-violence as the finest way for India at that moment in the history of freedom movement; but he never accepts it as a philosophy of life and it could apply to sovereign state which has to maintain armed strength for its defence.[83]

He also believes that many of Gandhian ideals, e.g., prohibition of liquor, cow protection, sexual abstinence, aversion to science and industrialisation are out of tune with the twentieth century. The image of Gandhi is pervasively felt in the reflection of Kailash Vrind. In fact, in his moment of retrospection, the entire history of Gandhi and his involvement with the country's progress to self government, beginning with Gandhi's experience in the train from Durban to Pretoria in 1893, has been recapitulated by Kailash Vrind. Here we have almost one chapter devoted to this purpose. The author seems to affirm Gandhian values by showing the moral degeneration and eventual downfall of a power-mongering politician. Kalyan Sinha, who represents this attitude, sees in Gandhi only the history of India's decay:

> *... decay and decline, culminating fantastically in the person of a man acknowledged saint and leader who had believed that liberating the Untouchable from the job of cleaning a latrine was more important than liberating a people from foreign rule.* [84]

That, the question — "Can a sovereign state which has to maintain armed forces for defence live up to the ideal of Gandhi's principle of non-violence?"- had actually become crucial during the Chinese invasion on India in 1962. Perhaps it is the question that the author has posed in *This Time of Mourning*, and in this way has reflected the true spirit of the age. Gandhian philosophy was found inadequate to meet the new challenges that the nation faced.

Bhabani Bhattacharya's *Shadows from Laddakh*

Shadow from Ladakh (1966) by Bhabani Bhattacharya is the next novel within our purview. It is proper to study this novel in the light of the context we have just discussed. Here the author has powerfully expressed the conflict between Ghandhism and industrialism. After independence it was felt that if India wanted to strengthen its defence power and become economically self-sufficient, it has to accelerate its pace for industrialisation and technological advancement. The author has described this conflict figuratively: "... the frail old world wheel of wood set against the giant machines of the modern age."[85]

The novel is full of Gandhian thought and symbology. Gandhi's words reverberate throughout the book. The scene is set in Gandhigram, a replica of Gandhi's *Sevagram* that embodies rural India of Gandhi's dreams representing the Gandhian way of life. The image of Gandhi is projected through Satyajit, a staunch Gandhian, dedicated to the life of austerity and high principles. He expects the same kind of rigid self-discipline from his wife, Suruchi, and his daughter, Sumita, that he has imposed on himself. When there is Chinese invasion on India he faces a great dilemma:

> *India was under invasion, and what could the answer be? Armed resistance. Violence against violence. Had he, Satyajit, a second answer? Had he a clear alternative to conflict ?*[86]

The question, "What would Gandhiji have done this time?",[87] is asked by Satyajit again and again. He remarks:

Gandhi had summoned its [India's] people more than once to meet brute force with soul force in a struggle against the mightiest of empires.[88]

Yes, he would act like Gandhiji and take a *Shanti Sena,* a Peace Mission, to Laddakh: "Satyajit follows the footprints left by Gandhi on history, and history will repeat itself."[89] And then, "Today the ground was ready again for Gandhi."[90]

Satyajit is so steeped in Gandhian thought that he has come to look upon himself as another Gandhi. And he is confronted with another problem. He thinks that Lohapur or Steel town run by Bhaskar Rao, a young engineer who has received his training in the United States, seriously threatens Gandhigram. To Bhaskar Rao, the expansion of factory is the need of the hour, the target of the nation to produce more and more steel for defence purpose. Satyajit and Bhaskar Rao are two poles representing the opposite ideas. This conflict reaches its climax. It is not a clash of personalities but a conflict between two ways of life.

By dramatising the conflict between Gandhigram and Steel town, between Gandhism and industrialism, Bhattacharya seems to have brought a synthesis, an integration of Tagorian ideals:

... integration of the simple and the sophisticated; the ancient and the modern; city and village; East and West.[91]

Suruchi, Satyajit's wife, suggests this ideal of integration:

There was one way left for Gandhigram. It must make readjustments. That would mean acceptance of life in its totality. But not the Steel town way; that also was denial of life deep under the surface. Let licence be chastened by restraint. Let restraint find its right level by a leavening of freedom. Let there be a meeting-ground of the two extremes; let each shed some of its content and yet remain true to itself. [92]

The resolutions to the conflict come through the fusion of the two ways of life. The union between Sumita, Satyajit's daughter, and Bhaskar has suggested this symbolically. Finally, Bhaskar decides not to annex. Gandhigram and Satyajit also soften his attitude towards Steel town. Sumita feels at home at both places. In this way steel town becomes a symbol of new India incorporating the best qualities of the old and the new. The other conflict also is resolved automatically when the Chinese forces withdraw ultimataly from the Indian territory.

Eternity of Gandhian Values

So, *Shadow from Laddakh* offers a revalidation of Gandhian philosophy in the context of the new challenges faced by free India. And Bhabani Bhattacharya puts a stamp over it when he says:

Gandhi, gone nearly three decades ago from the Indian scene, is as vivid a presence today as before in tens of millions of minds. More so, in a way. For, guiltily conscious of our utter incapacity to live up to his ideas, we strive to redeem ourselves by dedicating to him attractive shrines — constructed not only out of tangible materials like brick and concrete, but out of words — that glow. The measure of our deification is that we try to invest the Mahatma fondly with every worthwhile attribute we can envisage.[93]

References

1. Anand, Mulk Raj. *Apology for Heroism*. New Delhi: Orient Paperbacks. p. 19.

2. Iyengar, K. R. Srinivasa. *Indian Writing in English*. New Delhi: Sterling Publishers Pvt. Ltd, 1962. p. 252.

3. Dinkar, Ramdhari Singh. "*Bapu*". Allahabad: Lokbharati Prakashan. p. 47.

4. Gupta, Maithili Sharan. *Gandhi Marg*. pp. 44-45.

5. Dwivedi, Sohan Lal. *Gandhi Marg*. p. 56.

6. Bajpayee, Atal Bihari. *Jagriti ke Swar*. Lucknow: Lokhit Prakashan, 1969. Reprint *Meri Ekyavan Kavitayen*, New Delhi: Kitab Ghar.

7. Vatsyayan. Qtd. in *Contemporary Indian Literature*. New Delhi: Sahitya Akademi, 1959.

8. Bhattacharya, Bhabani. *Gandhi the Writer: The Image as it Grew*. New Delhi: National Book Trust, 1969. p. 236.

9. *Contemporary Indian Literature*. pp. 62-63.

10. Kamlesh, Padma Singh Sharma. *Gujarati Aur Uska Sahitya*. New Delhi: Rajkamal Prakashan, 1960. p. 88.

11. Thakore, Dilip. Qtd. in *Gandhi the Writer: The Image as it Grew*. p. 236.

12. Gandhi, M. K. *Gandhi Marg*. October 1963: pp. 279-283.

13. Sitaramayya, K.V. *Gandhi Marg*. September 1968: p. 282.

14. Yamunacharya, M. *Gandhi Marg*, July 1959: p. 214.

15. Das, Omeo Kr. *Gandhi Marg*, January 1959.

16. Chattopadhyaya, Bankim Chandra. *Anand Math*. p. 84.

17. Bandyopadhyay, Tarashankar. *Dhatridevata*.
18. Ray, Lila. '*Introduction*'. The Vigil.
19. Jambunathan, M.R. PEN All India Writer's Conference, 1947.
20. Andal. Qtd. in *Gandhi the Writer....* p. 243.
21. *Ibid*, p. 244.
22. Shirwadkar, V.W. *Indian Litreture Today*. p. 156.
23. Menon, Vallathol Narayan. Qtd. in *Gandhi the Writer...* p. 245.
24. Kurup G. Sankara. Qtd. in *Gandhi the Writer....* p. 247.
25. Patriotic Songs, Film: *Jagriti*,
26. *Patriotic Songs of Punjab*.
27. *Complete works of Hazari Prasad Dwivedi*.
28. Hymns from *Guru Granth Sahib*.
29. *Ibid*.
30. *History of Sikh*, Dr Cunningham.
31. Gopabandhu Dash, Bandire Atmakatha, p. 2-4, Published by Lok Sevak Mandal, 1941, Cuttuck, Reprint by Satyabadi Press, 1957, Puri, India.
32. Gopabandhu Dash, *Abakash Chinta*, p. 17, Odisha Sahitya Akadami, 1951, Bhubaneshwar.
33. *Ibid*, p. 21.
34. Gopabandhu Dash, *Bandire Atmakatha*, p. 7, Published by Lok Sevak Mandal, 1941, Cuttuck.
35. A morning prayer from our scriptures that invokes the ideas of National Integration
36. Advani, L.K. *My Country My Life*, Rupa & Company, p. 22. New Delhi.
37. *Sindh Times*, May 20th 1884.
38. Qtd. by L.K.Advani, *My Country My Life*, Rupa & Company, p. 22.
39. *Ibid*. p. 23.
40. *Ibid*. p. 23.
41. *Ibid*. p. 24.
42. L.K. Advani, *My Country My Life*, Rupa & Company, p. 25.
43. Qtd. by L.K. Advani.
44. Qtd. by L.K. Advani.
45. *Ibid*.
46. Mohammad Ayub Khushro; the Chief Minister of Sindh at the time of Partition.
47. Qtd. by L.K. Advani.
48. L.K. Advani, *My Country My Life*, Rupa & Company, p. 26.
49. Iyengar, K.R.S. *Indian Writing in English*. p. 228.
50. Bhattacharya, Bhabani. *Gandhi the Writer*. p. 249.
51. Iswaran, Manjeri. *S. Venkatramani: Writer and Thinker, An Appreciation*. Madras: The People's Printing and Publishing House, 1932. p. 5.

52. Gowda, H.H. Anniah. '*East West Encounter*'. Qtd. in Fiction and the Reading Public in India. Ed. C.D. Narasimhaiah. University of Mysore, 1967. p. 57.

53. Venkatramani, K.S. *Murugan, the Tiller.* New Delhi: Orient Paperbacks, 1927. p. 175.

54. *Ibid*. p. 286.

55. *Ibid*. p. 289.

56. Sharma, G.P. *Nationalism in Indo-Anglian Fiction*. p. 194.

57. Iyengar, K.R.S. *Indian Writing in English*. p. 228.

58. Venkatramani, K.S. *Kundan, the Patriot*. New Delhi: Orient Paperbacks, 1932. p. 249.

59. *Ibid*. p. 280.

60. *Ibid*. p. 224.

61. *Ibid*. p. 84.

62. *Ibid*. p. 246.

63. Anand, Mulk Raj. *Untouchable*. New Delhi: Orient Paperbacks, 1935. p. ii.

64. *Ibid*. p. 149.

65. *Ibid*. p. 165.

66. *Ibid*. p. 149.

67. *Ibid*. pp. 166-67.

68. *Ibid*. p. 172.

69. Anand, Mulk Raj. *The Big Heart*. Orient Paperbacks, 1945. p. 204.

70. Anand, Mulk Raj. *Untouchable*. p. 167.

71. Rao, Raja. *Kanthapura*. New Delhi: Orient Paperbacks, 1938. p. 74.

72. *Ibid*. p. 181.

73. Abbas, K.A. *Inquilab*. New Delhi: Orient Paperbacks. p. 49.

74. *Ibid.*

75. Singh, Khushwant. *Train to Pakistan*. New Delhi: Orient Paperbacks, 1948. p. 14.

76. *Ibid*, p. 20.

77. Nahal, Chaman. *Azadi*. New Delhi: Orient Paperbacks, 1975. pp. 48-49.

78. Malgonkar, Manohar. *A Bend in the Ganges*. Orient Paperbacks, 1964. p. 14.

79. *Ibid*. p. 24.

80. *Ibid*. (Epigraph). p. i.

81. *Ibid*. (Author's Note). p. 39.

82. *Ibid*. p. ii.

83. Sehgal, Nayan Tara. *This Time of Mourning*. New Delhi: Orient Paperbacks, 1965. p. 46.

84. *Ibid*. p. 218.

85. Bhattacharya, Bhabani. *Shadow from Laddakh*. New Delhi:Orient Paperbacks, 1966. p. 59.

86. *Ibid*. p. 127.

87. *Ibid*. p. 151.

88. *Ibid*. p. 208.

89. *Ibid*. p. 214.

90. *Ibid*. p. 322.

91. *Ibid*. p. 215.

92. *Ibid*. p. 221.

93. Bhattacharya, Bhabani. *Gandhi the Writer*. p. 270.

2

Gandhian Impact on the Thematic and Stylistic Pattern

Literature that can speak to Millions

The impact of Mahatma Gandhi on Indo-Anglian fiction is beyond the fictional representation of his own image and philosophy. He gave a new direction for Indian writers in matters of both style and subject- matter. He was not a man of letters himself in strict sense of the term, but he wrote frequently in the leading English weeklies of the period - *Indian Opinions*, *Young India* and *Harijan* - to spread his message. His style was simple, clear, direct and free from the flamboyant rhetoric characteristic of many Indo-Anglian writers of the time. He wrote in the editorial of one of his journals: "I want art and literature that can speak to millions."[1]

Gandhi did not believe in the theory of 'art for art's sake', nor did he care for fictional form. He says:

> *For me, all arts must be based on truth. I reject beautiful things, if instead of expressing truth they express untruth. Whatever can be useful to starving millions, is beautiful to my mind; let us give today first the vital things of life, and all the graces and ornaments of life will follow.*[2]

Gandhi counters the Foreign Influences

Gandhi's insistence on truth in literature and his pragmatic approach pioneered realism in fiction. The vogue of writing historical romances, adventure, or mystery novels, or those dealing with exotic religious cults, came to an end. Instead, the novelist turned to the living reality of the contemporary socio-political scene for inspiration. That was also the time when many young writers were beginning to feel the impact of Marx and Freud. Gandhi's message of peace and non-violence, his ethical idealism and the saint-like austerity of his personal life, counter-balanced these foreign influences and awakened among Indian writers a new sense of national pride and purpose. Bhabani Bhattacharya aptly remarks:

> *Inspired by him (Gandhi), they (the Indian writers) turned towards the depiction of the life of the common man, the poor and the illiterate, particularly in the villages. Their prose style became less ornamental, less designed for the highbrow scholar. Simple, direct, natural, the literature of the Gandhian era aimed at appealing not to the classes alone, but to the masses as well... There was a reaction against obsolete values. The writers drew largely on life for their themes and new horizon opened up before them.*[3]

M.K. Naik, in a similar vein, remarks:

> *Gandhiji's greatness was an unusual greatness in the sense that some men are great at small things; some others are great at one great thing; but Gandhiji belonged to that giant race of great men who are great at a great many things and whose greatness embraces large areas of human experience.*[4]

Indo-Anglian fiction has also felt the impact of Gandhian spirit in more than one way. As Falstaff describes himself: 'not only witty in myself, but the cause that wit is in other man', Mahatma Gandhi is not only an Indo-Anglian writer in his own right but also a colossus who bestrides almost over the entire field of Indo-Anglian writing in several forms, appearing either as a character, or a subject-matter, or a pervasive influence upon the socio-political scenes depicted by the writers.

Gandhian Age in Literature

As referred to earlier, the period between the two world wars is generally taken as the Gandhian age in India. C.R. Reddy has rightly described it as our modern 'Heroic age'. There was a feeling of frustration throughout the world in general and India in particular at the end of the First World War because of unrealised hopes. The Montague-Chelmsford Reforms seemed to many a shell without substance, and people felt that it would be futile to find the seeds of self-government. There was an air of disappointment everywhere. The muslims were disappointed with the treatment they got from the Britishers in Turkey at the Versailles Peace Conference. The Jallianwalla Bagh massacre of people poured fresh oil on the flame of discontent. This burst into a blinding blaze of national agony and resentment. Dr K.R. Srinivasa Iyenger observes:

It was the phoenix hour and Gandhi the Mahatma gave the signal, and a whole nation awoke from its suspended animation and felt the blood-streams of a new life coursing through veins.[5]

At this crucial hour Mahatma Gandhi pronounced:

Awake, arise, and realise this truth. I give you 'abhaya', fearlessness. You are slaves no more. Awake and realise the truth that you are free.[6]

What were its consequences? To quote C.F. Andrews: "... in a sudden movement', her (India's) fetters began to be loosened, and the pathway of freedom was opened."[7]

Dr Iyengar put it thus:

Life could not be same as before and every segment of our national life, politics, economics, education, religion, social life, language and literature – acquired a more or less pronounced Gandhian hue.[8]

Gandhi : The Writer

Thus Gandhi exercised a potent influence on our languages and literature, both directly through his own writing in English and Gujarati, and indirectly through the movements he generated by his revolutionary thought and practice. Several regional languages acquired a new versatility and power, and many of the political leaders of the Gandhian age – for example, C. Rajagopalachari (Rajaji), N.C. Kelkar, Abul Kalam Azad, Rajendra Prasad, Pattabhi Sita Ramaiyya, Jawahar Lal Nehru, Vinoba Bhawe, Jai Prakash Narayan, were themselves thinkers, writers, agitators and social reformers rolled in one. Dr Iyengar emphatically says:

No apology is needed, therefore, considering Gandhiji as a writer and as a formative influence on writers of his time.[9]

When we talk about the acheivement and greatness of Gandhi, we are reminded of the beautiful stanza of H.W. Longfellow:

The heights, by the great men reached and kept,
Were not attained by sudden flights.
But they, while, their companions slept,
Were toiling ahead in the night.[10]

This is exactly true in the case of Gandhiji. The greatness and achievement of Gandhiji was not the result of sudden flights but that of a long process of trial and error, aspiration and endeavour, indubitably his own. The story of his '*Experiments with Truth*' is actually the unfolding of this process, and Sri Iyangar has rightly described it as an 'imperishable classic' of our time. Originally it appeared in his journals, *Navajivan*, the weekly in Gujarati, and *Young India*, published in English. It was published in book-form in 1925. Gandhi said in its '*Introduction*':

"My experiments in the political field are now known, not only to India but to a certain extent to the 'civilised' world. For me they have not much value and the title of 'Mahatma' they have won for me has, therefore, even less. Often the title has deeply pained me; and there is not a moment I can recall when it may be said to have tickled me. But I should certainly like to narrate my experiments in the spiritual field which are known only to myself, and from which I have derived such power as I possess for working in the political field."[11]

Gandhi : The Journalist

To appreciate Gandhiji critically as a writer in English we find him mostly as a journalist. *The Autobiography*, which was originally written in Gujarati, and later translated into English by Mahadeobhai Desai, cannot, therefore, be considered as an original contribution to Indian writing in English. Gandhiji as a journalist in English has a very long career of almost half a century. It starts from 1903, when he started *Indian Opinion* in South Africa, and runs upto his death in 1948, when *Harijan* was still appearing. Gandhiji had an exalted conception of the role of a journalist. He condemned yellow journalism and is reported to have once described a journalist as 'a walking plague'. The story is told of a journal which Gandhiji's fellow passengers started in a ship destinated for England. The journal was called *Scandal Time*. The editor brought the first issue of it to Gandhiji who quietly took out the pin with which the sheets of the journal were fastened and returned the rest saying, 'I have taken from your journal the only thing that is worthwhile.' It was this type of journalism that he had in mind when he declared, 'If I were appointed dictator for one day I would have stopped all newspapers'.

What was his motive in taking journalism as a career? Let us see what Gandhi himself had to say on it:

> *I've taken up journalism not for its own sake, but merely as an aid to what I have conceived to be my mission in life.*[12]

He goes on to say that as a journalist he has been very careful in remaining true to his mission - 'truth and non-violence'. He cannot write in anger or malice, or even idly; cannot write to excite the passions. In his choice of subjects and of words he has to exercise the greatest restraint. It is a terrible ordeal for him when his 'vanity dictates a smart expression', or his 'anger a harsh adjective', but it is a fine exercise for him to remove the offending words and phrases. To his self-appointed task of journalism with a mission, Gandhiji was always faithful. Let us see what he says about his first journal, *Indian Opinion*, which was launched in 1903:

> *Week after week I poured my soul into its columns. I cannot recall a word in these articles set down without thought or deliberations, or a word of conscious exaggeration or anything merely to please.*[13]

This claim of Gandhiji is really justified in the case of all the journals, which he launched and successfully managed over a considerably long period.

It is this exalted idea of the role of the journalist that makes Gandhiji's journalism more than mere journalism. Schopenhauer described the newspaper as the 'second hand on the dial of world history,' and it is obvious that while most journalism is for the day, true literature is for all times. It is rightly said, "Literature that does not last is journalism, and journalism that lasts is literature."[14] Judging by this *dictum*, most of the Gandhiji's journalistic writings qualify as a literature, for to him the 'newspaper' was always a 'views paper'; it was a vehicle for the expression for his ideas. This is why many of his articles on education, language-problem, social reform, religion, ethics and numerous other subjects, are serious prose which, both in terms of his thought and the style, have a perennial appeal to the student of literature.

Gandhiji's thought had roots in his Hindu ideology though we find in his person numerous influences of the thoughts of Tolstoy, Ruskin, Thoreau and others. But his greatest strength lies in his utter sincerity and transparent honesty. It is possibe to differ with Gandhiji's view on several controversial questions such as language-problem in India or education; but it is impossible for any reader to finish reading anything written by him and go away umimpressed by the authenticity of his convictions. It is this authenticity that makes Gandhiji a master of English prose style, though he had no pretensions to be a writer. He has himself said:

> *My writings should be cremated with my body; what I have done will endure, not what I have said or written.*[15]

The spirit behind what he said and what he wrote was too great to be expressed in a manner, which has the hallmark of authentic literature in it. Dr K.R. Srinivasa Iyengar observes:

Gandhi the speaker, the writer, used language – be it Gujarati, English or Hindi – as a necessary tool, just as he used his spectacles, his walking stick, or his safety razor. Writing with him was not for writing's sake, nor speaking for speaking's sake, but rather for achieving communication, for conveying information, for converting people to his point of view. [16]

All the journals, that Gandhiji edited, were just his mouthpiece and engine of action. *Indian Opinion* served this purpose in South Africa, and *Young India* (and later *Harijan*) played the same role in India. Beginning, Gandhiji took it over, *Young India* reached the circulation nearly 40,000 at the time of his arrest in March 1922. This circulation was achieved without any aid of advertisement. But neither this five-figure circulation of the journal nor the crowds that always gathered around him give the correct index to the magic power that was behind his words. Gandhiji had no time, no inclination to cultivate the so-called art of wrting, or speaking. His writings, his words that he spoke are straight and when we read them today, the words seem to be often insipid or anaemic without any straining after imphasis having no colour, or irradiating brillance. But these words are Gandhiji's words and their very bareness is their strength. Words by themselves are nothing just as the rows of numbers are nothing unless the decimal point is placed; it is the decimal point which yields the power of the personality of the writer, or the speaker.

Gandhi: The Speaker

With the advent of Gandhi, there was a break with the old Macaulayan tradition of public speaking and formal writing. But Gandhiji's mastery of language, though very simple and unornamented, was never less adequate to the place, mood, or occasion. Let us see the very celebrated Benares Hindu University speech delivered on February 4th, 1916, evidently spoken extempore; it is:

I want to think audibly this evening. I do not want to make speech, and if you find me this evening speaking without reserve, pray, consider that you are only sharing the thoughts of a man who allows himself to think audibly... [17]

Let us see how Gandhiji targets hypocrisy, exploitation - physical and mental both. The elaborate security regulations seem to have irked and exasperated him:

All of us have had many anxious moments while the Viceroy was going through the streets of Benares. There were detectives stationed in many places. We were horrified. We asked ourselves: 'why this distrust? Is it not better that even Lord Hardinge should die than live a living death?[18]

What a way of presenting things! Let us see one more example, equally unconventional and explosive:

We may foam, we may fret, we may resent, but let us not forget that India of today in her impatience has produced an army of anarchists. I myself am an anarchist, but of another type. But there is a class of anarchists amongst us and if I am able to reach this class, I would say to them that their anarchism has no room in India.[19]

Gandhiji's words are like Gandhiji's only. He speakes like him only: the great patriot, the great humanitarion, the apostle of *Ahimsa*, and the prophet of *Satyagraha.* But his words cause a flutter on the platform and thrill the student congregation. Mrs Annie Besant as President tries helplessly to steer the speaker of the dangers. But Gandhiji goes his own way. He will not spare anybody. In an earlier part of the speech he refers to the condition of Benares temple:

It is right that lanes of our sacred temple should be as dirty as they are? The houses round about are built anyhow. The lanes are tortuous and narrow. If even our temples are not models of roominess and cleanliness, what can our self-government be?[20]

The change that Gandhiji effected in the prose style of Indian writing in English is his most single contribution to it. With Gandhian revolution in our political life there came about a revolution in our writing also. Gandhiji was not in sympathy with the view that our literature was absolutely autonomous and was far more inclined to make it a hand made to life. In a conversation with Dilip Kumar Roy he once remarked:

Life must immensely exceed all the arts put together. For what is this hot-house art-plant of yours without the life-soul and background of a steady worthy life? ... What after all does this fussing with art mount to; it all the time stultifies life instead of elevating it?[21]

Tolstoy and Gandhi on Art

Tolstoy and Gandhi have similar views on 'Art'. Both have erred in denying particular autonomy and prominence of it. The views of both these thinkers have been a corrective to the aberrations of those who hold that art is for art's sake alone, or even that life itself is only for art's sake.

Apart from their doctrines on 'Art', both these thinkers have a 'sense of awe' for 'Art'. Tolstoy himself was the creator of a world of imperishable values, while Gandhi responded readily to the mystic poetry. One of his favorite poems was *The Hound of Heaven* to which Chakravorty Rajagopalachari prepared a gloss. Gandhiji loved poems and songs too much. This aspect of his life has been discussed elsewhere in the book.

Bilingual Writing in English

Since the days of Raja Rammohan Roy, Indian publicists have had the necessity to be bilingual. Raja Rammohan Roy wrote in Bengali as well as in English. Lokmanya Tilak edited the *Kesari* in Marathi and the *Mahratta* in English. Sri Aurbindo's *Bandemataram* and *Karmayogi* were edited in English, and *Dharma* in Bengali. Gandhi likewise wrote both in Gujarati, his mother-tongue, and in English. Dr K.R. Srinavasa Iyengar observes:

> *Under the influence of his (Gandhi's) example, writing in the various regional languages flourished as never before during the twenties and after, acquired a modern incisiveness and force and went all out to reach the masses.*[22]

But it is interesting to note that along with the Indian regional languages, Indian writing in English also flourished. Gandhiji's own weekly papers, *Young India* and *Harijan* were among the most widely read and discussed organs of public opinion. Gandhiji, not a great scholar though, knew very well the *New Testament* in English and his writings in English had the characteristic feature of simplicity, pointedness and clarity.

This deserves to be stated that this was in contrast to the heaviness, eloquence, elaboration and exuberance of the earlier writers. Gandhian writing was recognisably functional. The age-old Macaulayan amplitude and richness of phrasing and the weight of miscellaneous learning was gone. Like his life itself Gandhian writing was as bare and austere, but it never lacked the fullness of fulfilment.

Gandhi Pioneered Clarity and Brevity in Language

Since the Gandhian revoulation, Indian writing and speaking in English have tended to be wisely utilitarian. It has the virtues of clarity, directness and brevity rather than eloquence and elaboration and exuberance. Here we find a world of difference between the sonorous period of Bipin Chandra Pal, Madan Mohan Malaviya and Surendranath Banerjee, or the editorials in *The Hindu*, *Amrita Bazar Patrika* and the leaders of some decades ago, and the speeches of Gandhiji, Rajaji and Subhash Chandra Bose.

Liberal School of Oratory

I would like to quote two extracts randomly chosen to show this change in the habits of thinking, writing and speaking.

Let us see the presidential address of Ambika Charan Mazumdar in the Lucknow session (1916) of the Indian National Congress:

> *There are, however, those who say 'not yet'. Not yet! Then 'when'? - asks the Indian nationalist. But here the oracle is dumb and echo only answers -'when'! Edwin Bevan's parable of 'The Patient and the Steel Frame' is cited and the people are strictly enjoined to lie in peace and possess their souls in patience until their political Nirvana is accomplished. Simile and metaphor are not safe guides in practical life, for all fables are but fallacies clothed in equivocal language, which captivates the imagination and deludes the reason. For even the patient in the 'steel frame' requires a gradual relaxation and occasional readjustment of his splints and bandages and, above all, a steady, substantial improvement in his dietary arrangements, as after all it is the food and nourishment and not the splint and bandages, that are calculated to give him strength and cure him of his injuries. You cannot indefinitely keep him on milk and sago to help either the 'knitting of the bones' or the 'granulation of the flesh'. Our critics however would enjoin 'perfect quiet and repose' without prescribing any kind of diet until the people shall have, in their spirit of quiescence, fully recovered themselves in their steel frame. If any illustration were actually needed, one might fairly suggest that the case of either the swimmer or the rider would probably furnish a more apposite object lesson. You cannot expect the one to be an expert jockey without training him on the back of a horse, as you cannot expect the other to be an expert swimmer without allowing him to go into the water. There must be repeated falls and duckings before any efficiency can be attained by either... There is a school for the lawyer, the physician, the educationist and the engineer where he can obtain his passport and begin his profession; but is there any school or college where an aspirant can be admitted to his degree for self-government? Is it through self-government that the art of self-government can be either taught or acquired ... in the words of Mr. Gladstone it is the institution of self-government which constitutes the based training-ground for self-government...*[23]

This is a typical example of the old 'liberal' school of oratory: The speaker being a scholar, a lawyer, addresses the educated, the intellectuals who are expected to follow a laborious smile, to recognise a quotation, to relish a reference to a British statesman.

The speaker in his elaborately wrought language means to say, "The British say that the time for transfer of power is 'not yet', beacause we are not experienced in the art of self-government but unless we are first trusted with this responsibility how can we gain the experience?"

Robust Commonscene and Steely Strength

Let us see another passage. This is also a presidential address, made during the Karachi session (1931) of Indian National Congress. Here the speaker is Sardar Vallabhbhai Patel, Gandhi's 'sword-arm' in the Congress, a formar Ahamadabad lawyer. Vallabhbhai was essentially a peasant leader with a peasant's common sense and sturdiness of character. The theme of the speech is the future of India as a federation of the Indian provinces and the native princely states. The address goes as follows:

> *There is no receding from the Lahore resolution of complete Independence. This independence does not mean, was not intended to mean, churlish refusal to associate with British or any other power. Independence therefore does not exclude the possibility of equal partnership for mutual benefit and dissolvable at the will of either party...*
>
> *Federation is a fascinating idea. But it introduces new embarrassments. Princes will not listen to severance. But if they will come in the true spirit, it will be a great gain. Their association must not impede the progress of democracy. I hope therefore they will not take up an uncompromising attitude that may be wholly inconsistent with the spirit of freedom. I wish they would without any pressure give us an earnest of their desire to march abreast of the time-spirit. Surely the fundamental rights of their subjects should be guaranteed as of the rest of the inhabitants of India...*[24]

As a matter of fact, this is a business-like, cold and colourless language, but after having a closer scructiny one can realise that not a single point has been missed. In this bare, bloodless passage we have the robust commonsense and steelly strength that stood India in good stead during the dark days of 1947 and after. The Sardar not only agreed to the Indian Republic remaining with the Commonwealth but also repeated the feat of Bismark. This resulted into the integration of the 600 scattered princely states with the Indian Union.

Gandhi Pioneered Change in the Style

This is the change in style that Gandhian impact brought in on the language of Indian writing in English. This change in style was from the elaborate to the simple, from the ornate to the plain, from the opulent to the pointed. This change in style, to some extent, was a global phenomenon. Even in England we witness a pronounced change from the massive Victorian oratory of Gladstone during his Midlothian compaign to the packed urgencies of Churchill's speeches during the Second World War.

Laboured Tone at High Seriousness

Let us see another passage, a *peroration* in the old style. Here the speaker is Surendranath Banerjee, '*the Thunderer of Bengal*'. The speech was delivered at the occasion of unveiling ceremony of the portrait of Dadabhai Naoroji in the Cowasji Jehangir Hall, Mumbai, in the year 1919:

> *The truest memorial that we can have of the illustrious dead is to raise tabernacles in our hearts in their honour, to devote ourselves to the worship of those principles which were theirs, and to the furtherance of those aims which were their life work.*
>
> *Then will these great men, emancipated from the fetters of flesh and blood, live in our midst in a higher form of existence and be imperishable guides in our out-ward march, which must lead to the accomplishment of our highest destinies. Dadabhai Naoroji will be one of such leaders. You may have your busts, your statues, and your portraits. They serve a useful purpose; they remind us of their mortal existence and of their imperishable work. But let not our reverence, our affection and our esteem be confined to mere dead forms, but let them be a living source of inspiration to us. Let them raise us to the higher atmosphere fragrant with the breath of these immortals and inspire us with a resolve to incorporate into our daily life the ideals, which they have left for our instruction and guidance. Let us imprint upon our minds the lessons of sobriety, moderation, of lifelong devotion to the Mother Land, which Naroji has taught us. Then we shall have raised in his honour a memorial more lasting than brass or marble, a memorial transmissible from age to age, that will become the lasting heritage of our people in the rich possession of those moral qualities which are the truest guarantees of continued and undying national progress.*[25]

Let us see the features of this passage: The laboured tone of high seriousness draws our attention, the exhortation has rounded fullness amplitude, and the sentiments are turned to the occasion solemnly. But when we turn to another *peroration* by Rajaji, the *Socrates of Tamil Country*, the change is marked. This speech was delivered in the Convocation of Madras University in 1948:

> *I have told you enough about the sacred duties that now devolve on you. Daily an earnest prayer and honest effort will enable one to acquire two great qualities, a sense of responsibility and an affectionate temperament. These best adorn citizenship. If our youth acquires these virtues, India will be happy and great. External courtesies will help the growth of corresponding internal feelings. Restraint in behaviour and consideration for the feelings of others are what distinguish a man of culture. Be patient and kind always. Do not give way to jealousy or desire to boast. Be not rude. Do not always insist on having your own way. Do not allow you to be irritated or be resentful. Do not rejoice at wrong. Rejoice in the right. Try to bear misfortunes bravely. Show trust in others and have faith that love will prevail. This is what Paul said. This is what Gandhi said. May God bless you!*[26]

Here we have no style at all. The sentences are short; they come sharply one after another like a series of brushstrokes, and the last three sentences link up Paul, Gandhi and God building up revelation and a benediction, almost *Upanishadic* in tone.

Sri Aurobindo: Global Sweep in Thought and Expression

Apart from this we have the colourful poetical, polyphonic prose of Sri Aurobindo and the Aurobindionians having a global sweep in thought and expression. However, even among the exact contemporaries, who shared much common features, the 'style' must vary from individual to individual. This is better illustrated by having a subtle observation of the obituary tributes to Gandhiji paid by Nehru, Sarojini Naidu, and Rajaji, all of whom had long known and loved Mahatmaji.

Nehru's Obitury Tribute: Sensitiveness of a Humanist

Let us first see Pundit Nehru's speech delivered in the Constituent Assembly:

> *We praise people in well-chosen words and we have some kind of a measure for greatness. How shall we praise him and how shall we measure him, because he was not of the common clay that all of us are made of... How can we praise him, we who have been the children of his, and perhaps more intimately children of his than 'the children of his body, for we have all been in some greater or smaller measure*

the children of his spirit.The glory has departed and the Sun that warmed and brightened our lives has set and we shiver in the cold and dark. Yet he would not have us feel this way. After all, the glory that we saw all these years, that man with the divine fire, changed us also, and such as we are, we have been moulded by him during these years and out of that divine fire many of us also took a small spark which strengthened us, made us work to some extent on the lines that he fashioned. And so, if we praise him, our words seem rather small; and if we praise him, to some extent we praise ourselves.[27]

In these words we have expression of anguish, purifying an exalting emotion, the feelings of the bereaved orphan, the words of a responsible statesman and a literary artist.

Mrs Naidu's Homage: Tidal Wave of Imagination

Now let us see Mrs Naidu's broadcast, especially the *peroration* that was somewhat different:

"Some of us are indeed dead, with him. Some of us, indeed, have had vivisection performed on us by his death, because the fibres of our being, our muscles, veins and hearts and blood were all inter-twined with his life ..."

... *May the soul of my Master, my Leader, my Father, rest not in peace, not in peace. My Father, do not rest. Do not rest. Keep us to our pledge. Give us the strength to fulfil our promise, your heirs, your descendants, your students, guardians of your dreams, fulfillers of India's destiny.*[28]

How audacious the imagery is! 'Our fibres muscles veins hearts blood were intertwined with his life'. Nehru also says the same thing, "This man of divine fire managed lifetime to become enmeshed with millions and millions of heart so that all of us became somewhat of the stuff that he was made of "Our hearts were intertwined with his life," says Mrs. Naidu. "His life was enmeshed with our hearts," says Nehru. Really these are the words expressing love and anguish that made both the authors say almost the same thing and in almost the same way.

Rajaji's Homage: Ethical Earnestness of steady Wisdom

Let us see what Rajaji spoke in Kolkata ten days after the Mahatma's last rites were performed:

Even now our grief tends to find solace and shape in anger and violence. Eternal must be our vigilance against this original sin, which poisons our natures. Suppression and State coercion cannot be avoided in this imperfect world. But let us clearly and once for all realise that ill-will cannot be overcome except in the way our beloved leader taught. There is much warlike talk about peace and much belligerent demand for goodwill. But fire cannot be quenched by pouring oil on it... Do not demand love. Love is never obtained that way. Begin to love and you will be loved. Increase your love and more love will be induced and will flow towards you. This is the law and no statute or logic can alter this.[29]

In Nehru's words we have all-sufficing simplicity and sensitiveness of a humanist; in Sarojani Naidu's opinion there is force of tidal wave and poet's frenzy of imagination, and in the words of Rajaji we have exhortation, the urgency and ethical earnestness of a man of steady wisdom.

Gandhi's Prose Style: Directness, Simplicity and Clarity

Indo-Anglian prose style before Gandhi, as examplified in Srinivasa Sastri, Surendranath Banerjee and others, was apt to be rhetorical and periodical, *á la* Macaulay and Newman. It was a style characterised by balancing and skilful marshalling of clauses, learned quotation and classical allusion, dignified oration and sonorous peroration. The shadow of Victorianism loomed large over it. Gandhiji ushered in a style which is surprisingly modern – modern in its being completely functional, a style remarkable for its directness, simplicity and clarity. Let us consider a passage from *Harijan*:

Light used to come out from the East. If the Eastern reservoir has become empty, naturally the East will have to borrow from the West. I wonder if light, if it is a light and not a miasma, can ever be exhausted. There is nothing to prevent me from profiting form the light that may come from the West. Only, I must take care that I am not overpowered by the glamour of the West. I must not mistake the glamour of the true light.[30]

What a capital opportunity did the author of this passage have to be eloquent over the theme of 'East *versus* West', a theme with which its ready-made facile dichotomy seems to invite effusive, rhetorical treatment. Gandhiji avoids the temptation and pursues his argument with relentless and clear-eyed single-mindedness.

Gandhi: Master of English Prose

However, this does not mean that Gandhiji deliberately eschewed all graces of a style, or that his style is, therefore, non-descript or undistinguished. Just as his own single loin-cloth was ever spotlessly cleaned and its folds were always adjusted with meticulous tidiness, so his style also makes occasional use of simile and metaphor in projecting his meaning effectively, though his similes and metaphors are never decorative but strictly functional.

For example, he calls *charkha* 'no new invention' but a 'rediscovey, like the discovery of its own mother by a strayed child'.[31] He talks about 'the white ant of untouchability' which is 'eating into the foundations of the nation';[32] and decribes the pilgrimage to *swaraj* as 'a painful climb.... It will not spring as the magician's mango. It will grow almost unperceived like the banian tree!'[33] He characterises prayer as 'the key to the morning and bolt of the evening'[34] and his pain is also capable of throwing up pithy, memorable sayings like: 'To enjoy life one should give up the lure of life'[35] and 'three parts by Bible and one part Shakespeare'[36] is the description of the English language. His pages are lit up with stray flashes of humour, too; for instance, 'The woes of *Mahatmas* are known only to *Mahatmas*.'[37] Gandhiji's autobiography also shows that he can be skilful narrator, with a keen sense of dramitic incident. Let us consider how he describes the incident in South Africa when after a violent quarrel with Kasturba he dragged her to the door and wanted to push her out.[38] His pen-portraits of many people are extremely vivid, as already pointed out. The Autobiography cannot, however, be considered strictly a piece of Indian writing in English, but we find here the evidence to reveal the literary power of its author–the power which could be utilised fully because Gandhiji was committed to produce not so much 'literature of power' but 'literature of knowledge'. Even then the old adage that 'knowledge being the power' is true in a different sense in the case of Gandhiji's writings, because what he intended to be merely 'literature of knowledge' has also become the 'literature of power'. Dr M.K. Naik observes:

> *As a writer of English prose, Gandhiji lacks the rhetorical amplitude of Sastri and Dr Sarvapally Radhakrishnan, the poetic splendour of Sarojini Naidu, the burning zeal of Swami Vivekanand, the imaganative and emotional overtones of Nehru and the idol-breaking ardour of Nirad C. Chaudhury. But the athletic vigour of his direct, simple prose establishes him as a prose writer distinct among Indian Masters of English.*[39]

Gandhi's Pervasive Influence on Literature

Gandhi's influence on Indo-Anglian literature has been so extensive that even if he had not written a single line in English, he would still have had a secure place in Indian writing in English.

Gandhi has inspired a whole library of books in various languages – books describing his life, discussing his ideas, and the books of creative literature. Homer A. Jack, in ***Wit** and Wisdom of Gandhi* (Bombay, 1961), estimated that there were 'more than 1400 books on Gandhiji in English alone'; but this was an estimate made almost five and a half decades ago, and now the number of books must have multiplied many times. Indian fiction in English, especially, owes far more to Gandhiji than it is generally recognised. Truly speaking, before the thirties there was no school of Indian fiction in English. Toru Dutt's *Bianca* or *The Young Spanish Maiden* (1878), the first novel in English by an Indian that remained incomplete; R.C. Dutt's *The Lake of Palms* (1902), *The Slave-girl of Agra* (1903), and Rabindranath Tagore's *The Home and the World* (1919), *The Wreck* (1921), etc., were translations from Bengali into English. Therefore, they do not legitimately belong to the history of Indian writing in English. To quote Rabindrnath Tagore, 'Whatever else a translation may retain; the vitamins are inevitably destroyed in the process.'[40]

It is not mere coincidence that there came a sudden flowering of Indian fiction in English in the 1930s – a period during which the star of Gandhiji attained its meridian on the Indian horizon. The Indian struggle for independence, under the leadership of Gandhij, became thoroughly democratised for the first time, to the very grass-roots of Indian society, and revitalised it to the very core. It is possible to see a close connection between this development and the rise of Indian novel in English. Of all literary genres, the fiction is most vitally concerned with social conditons and values. Indian society, galvanised into new social and political awareness, was bound to seek creative expression for its new consciousness and the novel has, in all ages, been a handy instrument for this purpose. Mulk Raj Anand, Raja Rao and R.K. Narayan, the pioneers of Indian fiction in English, started writing during the 1930s, and the very first novel of each of the first two novelists demostrated the Gandhian impact convincingly.

Gandhi Pervades the whole Narratives

There are a number of Indian novels in English in which Gandhiji appears as a character or as a pervasive influence on the social and political scene. Actually he appears in the novels like Anand's *The Untouchable* and *The Sword and the Sickle*, Narayan's *Waiting for the Mahatma*, K.A. Abbas's *Inquilab, Nagrajan's The Chronicles of Kedaram*, etc., while in a host of other novels like K.S. Venkataramani's *Kandan, the Patriot*, and

Raja Rao's *Kanthapura*, though he does not appear in person, his spirit pervades the whole narrative. Mulk Raj Anand's two presentations on Gandhiji, *The Untouchable* and *The Sword and the Sickle*, are complementary to each other. The former depicts the impact of Gandhiji on the mind of a sweeper boy, 'Bakha', who does not fully understand what the great man is saying in public speech, but is nevertheless impreseed by the 'something beautiful and saintly in the face' of the Mahatma, and 'something intimate and warm about him.'[41]

In the latter novel, Gandhiji is observed through the eyes of a young revoulationary who feels the power and the sincerity of the Mahatma and also discovers that he has a keen sense of humour, but nevertheless concludes that the great man was set in his own ideas, that he was full of himself, that he wanted complete submission to his capricious will.'[42] In Abbas's *Inquilab*, Anwar, the Muslim boy (who in the end is revealed to be the illegitimate son of a Hindu), reacts thus with the *sympathetic* touch of Gandhiji : 'Now he knew why they called him Mahatma – a Great Soul. On his face there was a look of suffering, kindness and pity, as if he felt personally the misery of every single human being. But there was also infinite calm and serenity. Here was someone who understood him without the need of explanations'.[43] K. Nagrajan's The Chronicles of Kedaram (1961) shows Gandhiji coming to the town, to Kedaram, and among other things, composing the long standing differences between two factions in the Aiyangar community by adopting the bold gesture of mounting the disputed Rangaswami stone platform and chanting 'Hare Ram' from it, thus illustrating the truth that all Gods are one and all kinds of worship run to the same God.[44]

The one major Indian novel in English in which Gandhiji figures far more prominently is R.K. Narayan's Waiting for the Mahatma. The modern critics have not rated this novel very high. Professor Srinivasa Iyengar, in his monumanal history, calls it an 'ambitious effort', but feels that in it 'Narayan's art – now denied the security of Malgudi and catapulted into Gandhian or terrorist political action – betrays unsureness and perplexity'.[45] Professor C.D. Narasimhaiah, in *The Writer's Gandhi*, rightly points out that Narayan has got his facts wrong when he shows Gandhiji standing on the dias with his palms brought together in a 'salute', and when he describes the Mahatma's voice as 'booming in the amplifire'.[46]

It is also easy to say that the hero of the novel seems to be waiting not so much for Mahatma Gandhi as for Mahatma Kamadeva, the god of love; that he seems to be more interested in Bharati than in '*Bharatmata*.' In saying all these, however, the critical opinion has perhaps unjustly neglected a significant aspect of the novel. In *Waiting for the Mahatma* we have a complimentary picture of Gandhiji. Here the author seems to have highlighted Mahatma's concern for truth, his simplicity, his sense of discipline, his dignity, his love for children, his sense of humour.

It seems that the real focus of the novel is the ironic portrayal of the response of various Indians to Gandhiji's thought and philosophy. The irony in the Municipal Chairman's ridiculous attempts to bask in the borrowed limelight of the Mahatma is of course too obvious to be missed. There is subtle irony in the picture of the impact of Gandhiji on the hero, Sriram. The critics usually miss this irony. That Sriram is an unheroic hero is a universally agreed concept. He has become a typical specimen of the common educated Indian in his response to Gandhiji. Sriram feels the magnetic pull of Gandhiji and joins the freedom-struggle, but it is clear, right from the beginning, that he has not understood Gandhi or Gandhism properly; so that he only becomes a blind follower of a leader whose methods and policies are too subtle for his limited comprehension. When Gandhiji is put into prison, Sriram starts taking orders from Bharati; and when she, too, is jailed, he becomes 'a blind slave of Jagdish', under whose leadership he indulges in terroist activities defying all Gandhian principles. The author's suggestion in this picture is very simple. Narayan perhaps wants to suggest that a large section of the Indian public could not understand Gandhism properly at all. There seems a fleeting touch of irony in the portrayal of Bharati – a far more devoted and disciplined follower of Gandhiji, but once again a follower whose extreme devotion to the master makes her little more than a puppet and all her actions are manipulated by the strings in the master's hands.

In Raja Rao's *Kanthapura,* we have the finest fictional presentation of Gandhiji's impact on rural India. Here Gandhiji himself does not appear, but his influence is so powerful that his spirit goes marching along the whole narrative. *Kanthapura* shows the other side of the shield and provides a useful corrective to the *Waiting for the Mahatma*. The novel beautifully depicts how the whirlwind of the Gandhian revolution shakes a little south Indian village to its very roots.

To see the reasons which have made this picture utterly authentic, guarding it against dreamy-eyed sentimentality that is always round the corner when such themes are dealt with, we have to turn to M.K. Naik. He observes:

> *Raja Rao goes to the very roots of the transformation, by demonstrating how the new nationalistic flavour in Rural India in*

the 1930s blended completely with the age-old, deep-rooted spiritual faith and thus revitalised the spiritual springs within and helped rediscover the Indian soul.[47]

Let us have a peep into other novels of Gandhian age. This authenticity for one reason or other is missing in many other novels of this age. K.S. Venkatramani sentimentalises the whole issue. His hero makes a long speech of exhortation; as he lies dying, from each of his near and dear ones he takes leave ceremoniously. In Kamala Markandaya's *Some Inner Fury*, we find much of the fury of the freedom-struggle lost owing to the prominence enjoyed by the love affair between Mira and Richard. In Nayantara Sehgal's *A Time to be Happy* we have much grace and charm but it has been merely a stereotyped picture of the stock theme of East-West encounter.

Gandhi in the Short-Stories

If we take a glance over the other genres of literature, we find that Indian writer's acheivement in the field of short story in English has been less significant than that in the field of the novel. We have not many short stories by Indian writers in English where the Gandhian impact has memorably been depicted. Raja Rao's solitary collection of short stories, *The Cow of the Barricades and Other Stories*, is once again the best example for our purpose. 'Narasiga' is an evocative picture of how the national consciousness roused by Gandhiji percolates into the mind of a small, illiterate, South-Indian orphan, though in that process, ancient myth and legend also get mixed with it so that Narasiga can see Gandhiji only as an *avatar of Rama* 'going in the air, with his wife Sita… in a flower chariot drawn by sixteen steeds'. '*The Cow of the Barricades*', the title story, illustrates the same Indian synthesis, which Nehruji describes in *The Discovery of India* (p.7) as 'India's power of carrying on the old tradition and yet ever adopting it to changing times'. The cow is named *Gauri* after the goddess, and is a holy cow representing an age-old Indian tradition. She dies of a bullet fired by a British officer during the freedom riots and in that process saves the lives of many in the village. The holy cow has thus become doubly holy and has created a new myth grafted on an old one.

Gandhi in the Indian Plays

When we consider the Indian drama in English for our purpose, the immediate reaction is that of agreement with the epithet, 'sick man' of Indian writing in English. Here we have not many noteworthy representations of Gandhian impact. Bharati Sarabhai's *The Well of the People* is outstanding among the few. The play is based on a true story published in *Harijan*. An old lady saves money to go to the *Kumbh Mela*, but later, when she finds herself unable to undertake the journey she spends her savings in digging a well for the poor in her village. The playwright makes the story even more 'Gandhian' by making a significant change – her protagonist decides to dig a well for the *Harijans*. Here also, like *Kanthapura* and *The Cow of the Barricades*, we see how the true secret of the Gandhian impact is mingled with the traditional religious consciousness. The effective use of chorus and the verse, which T.S. Eliot praised for its 'strikingly original English idiom', has made the technique of the play equally striking. Sheela Puri in *The Little Colossus* has failed to transmute her biographical material into adequate dramatic terms. K.S. Rangappa also marks this flaw to a greater extent in another 'Gandhian' play, *Gandhiji's Sadhana*. Bhaskar Rao, another playwright, is reported to have won an award in the Gandhi centennial play-writing competetion sponsered by Southern Illinois University for a play on Gandhiji. This play unfortunately has not yet been published.

Gandhi in the English Poetry

Of all genres of litereture, poetry is the most sublimate expression of man. But it is an irony that we find very little genuine poetry written on Gandhiji and Gandhism in Indian poetry in English. Furthermore, a genuine 'tribute' poem is a very difficult acheivement. Perhaps the finest example of the tribute poem in English are those by W.H. Auden, in particular his poems on W.B. Yeats and Freud. In contrast with this, the 'Gandhi' poems like *A Light unto our Path* by R.R. Seshtha; The *Lotus* by Sarojani Naidu; *Mahatma* by Humayun Kabir, appear to be mere catalogues of commonplaces full of cliché-ridden cocophonies, rhetorical effusions and sentimental outpourings, some telling illustrations of which are perhaps like Seshtha's 'weep, orphaned children,' Sarojani Naidu's 'thy glorious heart' and 'thine ageless beauty', Kabir's 'Gandhi breaks the charm of the magic sleep' and 'A lone figure stands upon the sands of time'.

Sarojani Naidu and Humayun Kabir are writers of some distinction. In this context it deserves to be mentioned that countless Indian versifiers have written poems on Gandhiji but they hardly deserve to be discussed. At the same time it needs to be stated that our survey does not consider the numerous biographies, critical studies, historical accounts, memoirs and such other 'Gandhian' things in Indian writing in English.

Now the question that crops up is whether the Indian writing in English has done justice to Gandhiji and Gandhism? This question needs to be answered before we conclude the chapter. The answer is definitely negative, with the exception of fictions. But writers are not to be blamed for this. M.K. Naik analyses it thus:

> *Perhaps our writers are too near Gandhiji and Gandhism to understand both completely and what is even more important – to transmute this understanding into art. Critics have noted that Tolstoy's War and Peace came fifty years after the Napoleonic invasion on Russia.*[48]

Let us, therefore, hope that an epic on Gandhi and Gandhism, whether in prose or in verse, may be written in future.

References

1. *Young India*, July 25, 1928.
2. *Ibid*. p. 2.
3. Bhattacharya, Bhabani.*Gandhi the Writer,The Image as it Grew*. pp. 228-229.
4. Naik, M.K. *"Gandhiji and Indian Writing in English"*, The Banasthali Patrika, July 1970.
5. Iyengar, K.R.S. *Indian Writing in English*. p. 248.
6. *Ibid*.
7. *Ibid*.
8. *Ibid*. p. 249.
9. *Ibid*.
10. Longfellow, H.W. "*A Psalm of Life*", Anthology of Poems. New Delhi: NCERT, 1996.
11. Gandhi, M.K. '*The Preface*', The Story of my Experiments with Truth. Navajivan Publication, 1925.
12. *Young India*. 2 July, 1925.
13. *Indian Opinion*. 1903.
14. *Gandhiji and Indian Writing in English*. p. 371.
15. *Harijan*. May 1st, 1937.
16. Iyengar, K.R.S. *Indian Writing in English*. p. 263.
17. *Young India*. March 1916.
18. *Ibid*. p. 2.
19. *Ibid*. p. .3.
20. *Ibid*.
21. *Ibid*.

22. Iyengar, K.R.S. *Indian Writing in English*. p. 272.
23. Majumdar, Ambika Charan. Qtd. in *Indian Writing in English*.
24. Patel, Ballabh Bhai. Qtd. in *Indian Writing in English*. pp. 273-74.
25. Nauroji, Dadabhai. Qtd. in *Indian Writing in English*.
26. Rajgopalachari, Sri Raj. Qtd. in *Indian Writing in English*.
27. Nehru, Jawahar Lal. Qtd. in *Indian Writing in English*.
28. Naidu, Mrs. Sarojini. Qtd. in *Indian Writing in English*.
29. Rajgopalachari, Sri Raj. Qtd. in *Indian Writing in English*.
30. Gandhi, M.K. *Harijan*. Jan. 13th, 1940.
31. *Ibid.*
32. *Ibid.*
33. *Ibid.*
34. *Ibid.*
35. *Ibid.*
36. *Ibid.*
37. *Ibid.*
38. Gandhi, M.K. *The Story of My Experiments with Truth*.
39. Naik, M.K. Qtd. in *The Banasthali Patrika*. p. 273.
40. Tagore. Rabindra Nath. Qtd. in *The Banasthali Patrika*. p. 274.
41. Anand, Mulk Raj. *The Untouchable*. p. 142.
42. —. *The Sword and the Sickle*. p. 208.
43. Abbas, K.A. *Inquilab*. p. 111.
44. Nagrajun, K. *The Chronicles of Kedaram*. p. 32.
45. Iyengar,K.R.S.Qtd.in *Gandhi and Indian Writing in English*.The Banasthali Patrika, 1970. p. 293.
46. Narasimhaiah, C.D. *The Writer's Gandhi*.
47. Naik, M.K. Ed. *Gandhiji and Indian Writing in English: Critical Essays*.
48. *Ibid*. p. 381.

3

The Core of Gandhian Philosophy

Vaishnava jana to tene kahiye
je peer parayi jane re,
par dukkhe upakar kare soye,
man abhiman na aane re.
Sakal lok ma sahune bande,
ninda na kare keni re,
vach kach man nischhal rakhe,
dhan dhan janani teni re.
Samadristi ne trishna tyagi,
par stri je ne mata re,
jihva thaki asatya na bole,
para dhan nav jhae hath re.
Moha maya byape nahi jene,
driha vairag jena manma re,
Ram nam su tali lagi,
Sakal tiratha tena tanama re.
Van lobhi ne kapat rahit chhe,
kama krodh nivarya re,
bhan narsaiyon tenu darshan karta,
kul aekoter tavya re.[1]

The rationale behind beginning the chapter with this well-known hymn of Narsimha Mehta, the medieval Gujarati saint-poet, is that it seems to be encapsulating the very core of Gandhian philosophy. Mahatma Gandhi was so charmed with it that he usually sang it in his morning prayers and also on other important occasions. The influence of the thematic and poetic beauty of this hymn was so strong that poets of different regions and countries felt inspired to render it into their respective languages. The English rendering of the same reads thus:

Lo! Him we may call a Vaishnava,
who experiences in himself the pain that another feels;
who renders service to soothe another's distress;
who does not import into his mental texture pride of *ego or of deed.*
Who venerates each one in every world;
who speaks ill of none;
whose speech, whose senses and
whose mind are kept under firm discipline
blessed is the mother who gave birth to him.
Him we may call a *Vaishnava.*
Whose sight is equivisual;
whose ambitions have been abandoned;
to whom all women not locked with him
in marriage are as mother;
whose tongue slips not to utter untruth;
whose hand does not stretch forth to touch
what is not his own.
Him we may call a *Vaishnava.*
He does not fall prey to delusion;
he is not overwhelmed by material lures;
his mind is incapable of attachment to things of this world;
he is engrossed in his love for the name of the blissful,
Lord: his person is so cleansed and pure that in it are
centred all the sanctifying places of pilgrimage of this *earth*. Him we
may call a *Vaishnava.*
He cherishes no desires; he knows no tortuous ways;
he has cast off wishful longings, also resentment
and indignation. Says Narasanyo;
seventy-one generations of ancestors pass on to
Paradise on one's attaining a glimpse of such a one
Him we may call a Vaishnava.[2]

Indubitably, this beautiful hymn of Narsi Mehta is so closely associated with Gandhi's life and his ideals that the cohesive whole of Gandhian ideas, conveniently called Gandhism, is depicted here in its best manner.

But the basic question is as to what is Gandhism? What does it stands for? What are its components? What is its relevance for our age and the ages to come? Why do its values need to be inculcated in the mind of the generations to come?

Gandhiji did not build up an original system of thought. Many aspects of Gandhian philosophy are borrowed from popular Hinduism and Jainism. He, however, kept modifying, developing, and amending his own concepts in the light of his experiences from time to time. Nevertheless, the core of his philosophy lies in a few central concepts around which the entire Gandhism revolves. These concepts are: *Satya* (truth); *Ahimsa* (non-violence); *Swadeshi* (indigenous); *Swara*jya (self-rule); *Satyagraha* (truth-force), and *Achhutoddhar* (Upliftment of the untouchable). These concepts, in varying degrees, have found expression in Indo-Anglian fiction of the Gandhian age and have continued to inspire the novelists even after the Independence. The frictional transfiguration of these central concepts underlying Gandhian philosophy is the prime concern of our study here.

From a man of Common Calibre to Towering Heights

Bhabani Bhattacharya, a noted Indo-Anglian novelist and critic, in the '*preview*' of one of his recently published works on Gandhian philosophy, writes:

Gandhi's life from the earliest days to its last phase was marked by certain precise characteristics: constant unfoldment in a wide variety of directions; pauseless evolution; an uninhibited assessment of accepted values; and unceasing self-expansion all through, even up to the last days of his long life.[3]

Mahatma Gandhi, the great political philosopher, did not build his personality in a day or a decade. This is all the more true in the case of his ideas or his philosophy. Plain inconsistencies showed even through the iron restraint of his words. It is not that he wasn't aware of it; he has rather admitted this at many places: "I must admit my many inconsistencies. There is a consistency running through seeming diversity".[4]

And again:

I am not at all concerned with appearing to be consistent. In my pursuit after truth I have discarded many ideas and learnt many new things. Old as I am in age, I have no feeling that I have ceased to grow inwardly.[5]

Gandhi was not born 'great'. He was basically a man of common calibre. To put it cryptically, he was Everyman. As Bhabani Bhattacharya says:

And Everyman has his secret funds of strength besides his overt areas of weakness. Never did Gandhi depart from the grassroots out of which he had grown. However, even in that not-too-fertile soil, he grew steadily to an extraordinary, towering height; feet planted on near-barren earth, his head reached dizzily upward.[6]

Gandhi and Buddha

The passage, that is naturally the inward passage, from a common man to one of the greatest figures of the world history, is full of dramatic overtones. There was no will or conscious effort on the part of Gandhi to find a place for himself among the great ones of the world. Gandhi had not the least longing or even the illusion in this regard. In his fortieth year he was thoroughly immersed in a kind of *nirvana* (passionlessness). In this context, it is apt to draw a parallel between Mahatma Gandhi and Gautama Buddha. A man, who attains absolute control over his inner self, while living in this mundane world, is a rarer phenomenon than one of his kind who lived 2500 years ago. Gautama Buddha and Mahatma Gandhi are the two ends of the same bridge that connect the yester-years and to-day.

The words that came on his lips or flowed through his pen in the last three decades of his life are the living record of the great heights that Mahatma Gandhi attained, whose constant prayer was the great hymn of the *Upanishads:*

Asato ma sadgamaya,
Tamso ma jyotirgamaya,
Mritur ma amritamgamaya.
(From untruth lead me to Truth
From darkness lead me to Light
From death lead me to Immortality).[7]

The heights reached by Mahatma Gandhi are not the outcome of any sudden flight. There came many turns in his life from the day he was born to the day he breathed his last. These turns are the stairs that upheld him to these immeasurable heights. These phases in his life are the factors responsible for shaping his persons and moulding his ideas, commonly known as Gandhian philosophy. The different phases in his life that moulded his personality and strengthened his convictions about his ideas are full of inspirations for the generations to come.

A Staunch Vaishnav Family

Mohandas Karamchand Gandhi was born in a staunch *Vaishnav* family on 2nd of October 1869 at Porbandar, a seaside town of Kathiawar peninsula in Gujarat. The bookshelves of his house contained the exclusive books on *Sanatan Hindu Dharma*. Putlibai, the mother, in whose twenty-fifth year of life Mohandas was born, had religious passion and preoccupation with prayer. She observed long and frequent fast meant to chastise the flesh. She had a strong living influence on her son, Mohandas. The family shifted to Rajkot, comparatively a big town. Here Mohandas happened to view a Gujarati play titled *Harishchandra.* He was strongly stirred when he saw the hero, Harishchandra, in blood and flesh.

The family was a strict vegetarian. The ancient epic, *Ram Charit Manas* of Goswami Tulsi Das, dug deep into his mind; it was a life- long influence about which Gandhi has himself written: "Today I regard the *Ramayan* of Tulasi Das as the greatest book in all devotional litrature…"[8]

To Mahatma Gandhi, God, *Rama* and Truth are synonymous, the interchangeable terms. To quote his words:

> *He is the Eternal, the unborn, the one without a second. Him alone I worship. He belongs equally to all…. Is there one God for the Mussalmans and another for the Hindus, Parsis, or Christians? No, there is only one omnipotent and omnipresent God. He is named variously.*[9]

Gandhi's *Rama*

Gandhi reverenced Lord *Rama*. To utter the hymns dedicated to Him was his second nature. Whenever he found himself distressed he invoked *Rama.* At least two instances could be cited to substantiate this. Once it happened at a South African railway station. Having been beaten brutally by the 'white' police he fell down unconscious with the word *Rama* on his lips.

The second time it happened in a prayer meeting at Birla House in New Delhi when he was assassinated. '*Hey Ram*' were the last words he uttered thrice.

Gandhi's Favourite Books

Of many books on his father's bookshelves that left impression on Gandhi's mind, *Manusmriti,* the Law of Manu, the law-giver of ancient times, deserves to be referred. *Manusmriti* strengthened his conviction that morality was the basis of all things, and that truth was the substance of all morality. Truth in this way became his sole objective. A beautiful stanza of Shamal Bhatt, a seventeenth-century Gujarati poet, became his guiding principle. It reads thus:

For a bowl of water, give a goodly meal;
For a kindly greeting, bow thou down with zeal;

For a simple penny pay thou back with gold;
If thy life be rescued, lives do not withhold;

Thus the words and actions of the voice regard;
Every little service tenfold they reward.

But the truly noble know all men as one,
And return with gladness good for evil done.[10]

The Vegetarian in London

It was decided that he would become barrister-at-law, and, in order to pursue the course he left India for London on September 4, 1888. The dream was about to be fulfilled. For a highly orthodox Hindu it was a bold decision to cross the black waters in those days. His mother reluctantly permitted him for it but only when she got three vows from him: 'that he would never touch wine, women, and meat.' But this was not enough for the orthodox community, and he was declared an outcaste, which he accepted patiently.

On his arrival at London he registered himself at the Inner Temple of the Inns of Court. Later he matriculated from the University of London with French, Latin and Physics as his main subjects. Bentham's '*Theory of Utility*' was a work of English philosophy that he chanced to read on the advice of a friend. In fact, the clever friend had a special purpose behind introducing Bentham to him; it was to make him give up the cult of vegetarianism. He argued: 'What is the value of a vow made before an illiterate mother, in ignorance of conditions here? It is pure superstition to stick to such a promise.' The words made no impression on him. Gandhi replied, 'A vow is a vow, it cannot be broken'.[11]

At the entrance of a vegetarian restaurant he noticed a book titled *Plea for Vegetarianism by* Henry Salt; he read the book from cover to cover. It gave him confidence, and what had begun as a mere sentiment in his mother's wish got crystallised into an intellectual conviction. To quote his impression: 'I blessed the day on which I had taken the vow before my mother.'[12]

The other books that Gandhi studied on vegetarianism were *Ethics of Diet* by Howard Williams and *The Perfect Way in Diet* by Dr Anna Kingsford. He was enlightened to know that all the prophets, philosophers, mathematicians and scientists - from Pythagoras and Jesus down to those of today- had been vegetarians. He also read the writings of Dr T.R. Allison, who prescribed for his patients a strictly vegetarian diet.

Communion with the idealists

A vegetarian society in those days had launched a campaign in England to create awareness about vegetarianism through its weekly journal and illuminating lectures. Due to his inborn *samskar* Gandhi joined the society. Very soon he became the secretary of its executive committee Sir Edwin Arnold, the editor of the daily *Telegraph* and creative translator of ancient Indian classics, was the president of the society. He was one of the pillars of vegetarianism in England to whom Gandhi came into contact with. Gandhi now realised that the real seat of taste was not the tongue, but the mind.

The vegetarian society had close links with other societies of England, e.g. *Thoreau Society, Walt Whitman Group, Socialist League* and *Fellowship of New Life.* These societies were based on the transcendentalism of Emerson, Thoreau and Walt Whitman. Bhabani Bhattacharya writes:

... so it happened that the vegetarianism that Gandhi discovered in England was rooted in the current humanitarian and socialist ideals.[13]

And, Pyarelal writes:

They were Socialists because they were humanitarians, and because they were humanitarians they were drawn into the ferment of the Vegetarian Movement.[14]

Pyarelal emphatically points out that Gandhi was not acquainted with Thoreau's ideas till 1907. To quote him again:

Thoreau's thoughts percolated down to him indirectly through the English vegetarians. The well from which he imbibed was thus the one in which the buckets of both the East and the West had often dipped and grated together.[15]

Edwin Arnold and Annie Beasant

Gandhi's active association with the 'Vegetarian Society' brought him into contact with many celebrities of the time. He met the theosophists who talked about *Bhagavad Gita* to him. Gandhi so far had not read the *Gita* either in the original Sanskrit or in its Gujarati translation. He had the opportunity to first read Sir Edwin Arnold's translation of *Bhagavad Gita* titled "*The Song Celestial*". This left a profound impression on him. To quote his words:

It opened to me a new view of life... I had found at last, as I believed, the light I needed.[16]

Gandhi observes that the verses of second chapter continued to ring in his ears for a long period. To quote the verse:

If one
Ponders on objects of the sense, there springs
Attraction; from attraction grows desire;
Desire flames to fierce passion, passion breeds
Recklessness; then the memory - all betrayed -
Lets noble purpose go, and saps the mind,
Till purpose, mind, and man are all undone.[17]

Esme Wynne Tyson observes:

Arnold's presentation of the purest Indian thought to one who was to be known as the Father of the Indian nation was 'a striking example of the outworking of Karma'. Through him Britain started to pay off a great debt to India. Yet perhaps an even greater Karmic fruit was achieved by these two remarkable men in that they by means of their spiritual sensitivity and sincerity have built a bridge of understanding by means of which East and West could very positively meet.[18]

At this time Gandhi was introduced to Madame Blavatsky as well as Annie Besant. He read '*The Key to Theosophy*'. It stirred in him the longing to read his own religion, Hinduism. Dr Annie Besant said: 'Make no mistake; without Hinduism India has no future'. He became an associate member of the Blavatsky Lodge. He was much impressed with theosophy by its doctrine of universal brotherhood and its religious tolerance.

The Sermon on the Mount

One of the members of the society, a devout Christian by creed, urged him to read the *Bible*. He read it and got inspiration from the Prophets, Psalms and Ecclesiastes. The life of Jesus left immediate impression on him, and when he read the *Sermon on the Mount*, he was intensely moved. To quote his words:

The verses, but I say unto you, that ye resist not evil, but whosoever shall smite thee on the right cheek, turn to him the other also. And if any may take away thy coat, let him have thy cloak too,' delighted me beyond measure.[19]

The words of the *Sermon on the Mount* have shaken the world, and shook the psyche of Gandhi once again. To quote the beautiful words:

Blessed are the poor in spirit: for theirs is the kingdom of heaven.
Blessed are they that mourn: for they shall be comforted.
Blessed are the meek: for they shall inherit the earth.
Blessed are they which do hunger and thirst after righteousness: for they shall be filled.
Blessed are the merciful: for they shall obtain mercy.
Blessed are the pure in heart: for they shall see God.
Blessed are the peace-makers: for they shall be called the children of God.
Blessed are they that are persecuted for righteousness' sake: for theirs is the kingdom of heaven.
Blessed are ye, when men shall revile you and persecute you, and shall say all manner of evil against you falsely, for my sake.
Rejoice, and be exceeding glad: for great is your reward in heaven: for so persecuted they the prophets which were before you.[20]

Gandhi's thoughts were so deeply influenced by *Sermon on the Mount* that many people confuse to say that these are Gandhi's words while the fact is that these are the words of the *Sermon*. To quote these words of the *Sermon*:

Ye have heard that it hath been said, An eye for an eye, and a tooth for a tooth:
But I say unto you, That ye resist not evil: but whosoever shall smite thee on thy right cheek, turn to him the other also.
And if any man will sue thee at the law, and take away thy coat, let him have thy cloak also.
And whosoever shall compel thee to go a mile go with him twain.
Give to him that asketh thee, and from him that would borrow of thee turn not thou away.
Ye have heard that it hath been said, thou shalt love thy neighbour, and hate thine enemy.

But I say unto you, Love your enemies, bless them that curse you, do good to them that hate you, and pray for them which despitefully use you, and persecute you."[21]

Many critics are of the opinion that Gandhi's idea of passive resistance was partly the outcome of the impact of the *Sermon on the*

Mount on him. The revelation of the *Sermon on the Mount* found affirmation later when Gandhi had deep study of the *Bhagwad Gita*. On the philosophy of Mahatma Gandhi the impact of the beautiful blending of the teachings of the *Bhagwad Gita* (Hinduism), *The Light of Asia* (Buddhism) and the *Sermon on the Mount* (Christianity) can well be seen.

A Passage to South Africa

M.K. Gandhi, Bar-at-Law, began to practise law at Rajkot. Expectations led him to move off to Bombay. As he was ignorant of the Indian law his studies began anew. He read Mayne's *Hindu Law, The Civil Procedure Code* and *The Evidence Act.* A decisive turn came in his life at this crucial stage. A wealthy Muslim merchant of Porbandar handed him a complicated law suit in South Africa. South Africa, in those days, was not only known for its geographical distance and rough sea-ways of thousands of miles, but also for its primitive pastime of apartheid where civilised human values had become subject of mockery. It was a big challenge for Mr. Gandhi. In the desert of the civilised human values he was to be an oasis. He was to prove himself a morning sun in the darkness of the human values though he had to pay heavily by suffering.

His South African experiences are the first peak point in his long and steep ascent of spiritual eminence.

The Baits from Christian Missionaries

A.W. Baker, an attorney and a preacher, tried to convert him into Christianity by advocating vehemently that no one can find eternal peace unless he accepts Jesus as the saviour of mankind. Many others made this attempt of conversion. Hundreds of books on Christianity were offered to him to read. Among the eighty books that he read on Christianity were Joseph Butler's *Analogy*, Dr Parker's *Commentary* and Arthur Tappan Pierson's *Many Infallible Proofs.* Despite these efforts Gandhi stood firmly on the Hinduism faith. He doubted Christianity's claim to be the only truth and rejected the idea that it was possible to attain salvation simply by adopting the faith. To quote his words:

> *Philosophically there was nothing extraordinary in Christian principles.... It was impossible for me to regard Christianity as a perfect religion or the greatest of all religions.*[22]

The *Sermon on the Mount* though stood on a different pedestal. It was not a treasure of the Christianity alone; it was universal. Gandhi writes in one of his articles titled '*Truth is God*':

I have not been able to see any difference between the Sermon on the Mount and the Bhagvad Gita... Today, supposing I was deprived of the Gita and forgot all its contents but had a copy of the Sermon, I should derive the same joy from it as I do from the Gita.[23]

The Gospels as an Allegory

Here it needs to be mentioned that during his stay in South Africa his communication with his Christian friends in England also continued. Edward Maitland, the founder of the Esoteric Christian Union, sent him two of his books — *The Perfect Way*, prepared in collaboration with Anna Kingsford, and *The New Interpretation of the Bible*. Here was repudiation of current Christian beliefs, and Gandhi found in them support for Hindu thoughts. Maitland wrote:

Christianity had failed, not because it was false but because it had been falsified. What was needed was not a new religious system but a true interpretation of the religion now existing.[24]

Maitland wrote further:

The Gospels should not be treated as history but as allegory. Jesus was not a real personage but a principle, a process, a system of life and thought by the observance of which man becomes purified from Matter and transmuted into Spirit... And he is a Christ who, in virtue of his observance of this process to its utmost extent while yet in the body, constitutes a full manifestation of the qualities of the Spirit.[25]

The aspirant to Christ-like perfection must accept self-denial for a spiritual purpose, as also vegetarianism and close communion with nature. He should take the vows of Abstinence, Prayer, Meditation, Watchfulness, Self-restraint, Fearlessness and Voluntary Poverty.[26]

Obviously such writings made a strong impact on Gandhi. With Edward Maitland he had a prolonged correspondence. He later applied Edward Maitland's manner interpreting the Gospels allegorically in the case of the *Ramayana*, the *Mahabharata* and the *Gita*. To quote him:

The Ramayana, the Mahabharata and the Gita are not as historical works but philosophical poems presented in a historical setting.[27]

Gandhi learnt with Maitland to have broad attitude on religions. He gave much publicity to Maitland's book in South Africa. In one of his letters to the *Natal Mercury* he states:

The system of thought expounded by (these) books is ... a system of religions which teach Universality.... It reconciles the other religions with Christianity which, in the opinion of the authors, is noting but one mode (among many) of the presentation of the same eternal truth.[28]

In his another letter, written to *Natal Advertiser*, Gandhi writes in a similar vein:

The system (of thought) ... establishes the unity and common source of all the great religions of the world, and points out the utter inadequacy of materialism which boasts of having given the world a civilisation which was never witnessed before, ... all the while forgetting that its greatest achievements are the invention of the most terrible weapons of destruction.[29]

Deeper Study of Hinduism

Gandhi had a comparative study of religions - Christianity, Islam and Hinduism. In India he had met Shri Rajchandrabhai, a Gujarati Hindu sage, who urged him to make a deeper study of Hinduism. Gandhi maintained a close correspondence with him during his stay in South Africa. Gandhi is much indebted to him for the devout ideas, that latter inculcated in him the *Sanatan Hindu Dharma* and the ancient Hindu scriptures. He writes his impressions about Rajchandrabhai:

His burning passion for self-realisation: this was the only thing for which he lived .... I enjoyed the closet association with him .... I have since met many a religious leader or teacher.... I must say that no one else has ever made in me the impression that Rajchandrabhai did; ... his intellect compelled as great a regard from me as his moral earnestness. In my moments of spiritual crisis, therefore, he was my refuge. He advised me to make a deeper study of Hinduism included Panchikaran, Maniratan Mala, Mumukshu Parakaran of Yogavasuntha and Haribhadra Suri's Saddarshana Samuchaya.[30]

In Gandhian ideas we find a broader outlook on religions. Rajchandrabhai inculcated this value in his person. He also taught Gandhi to be firm, to be victorious and to be proud of Hinduism, his own religion. Pyarelal quotes him paying an obligation to Rajchandrabhai in one of his articles titled *Rajchandrabhai* dedicated to him:

Personally I believe that ... all religions are perfect as well as imperfect. For, after one has attained a certain stage of spiritual development, even the prescriptive formulas of the shastras become a fetter on further progress. It is unnecessary for anyone to give up his own religion and adopt another in order to attain liberation by following his own, for liberation means complete freedom from all attachment and hatred and this is the comman goal of all religions.[31]

The contribution of *Dharma Vichara*, a Gujarati work by Narmadashankar, in building up of Gandhian ideas, deservers to be mentioned. About the author, who was a renowned Gujarati poet, and who led a bohemian life and suffered social ostracism, Bhabani Bhattacharya writes:

He had been set on destroying the old order wholesale. Then a great change occurred in his ideas. This was due to his study of Hindu institutions and of national culture. Such a living example of the study of Hindu concepts on an apostle of revolt could not be lost on Gandhi.[32]

Gandhi read Prof Friedrich Max Mueller's *India: What Can It Teach Us?* He also read Sir Edwin Arnold's *The Light of Asia.* In addition to these works glorifying the Indian wisdom Gandhi studied the *Upanishads* and Patanjali's *Yoga Sutra* in translation issued by the Theosophical Society.

The impact of these thought-provoking works was so strong on Gandhian ideas that it counter-balanced the influences that he had from his Christian friends. Gandhi cherishes the memory of his relation with them. To quote his words:

I shall always cherish the memory of their contact. The years that followed had more, not less, of such sweet and sacred contacts in store for me.[33]

In a brief chapter titled *The Magic Spell of a Book* in his *Autobiography* Gandhi writes that the three 'moderns' left a deep impression on his life and 'captivated' him: Rajchandrabhai by his living contact; Tolstoy by his book, *The Kingdom of God is Within You,* and Ruskin by his *Unto This Last.*

John Ruskin : *Unto This Last*

Unto This Last has made a deep imprint on Gandhi's sensibility. It was Ruskin's first book that Gandhi read. To quote his impression:

Of many books, the one that brought about an instantaneous and practical transformation in my life was Unto This Last ... I discovered some of deepest convictions reflected in this great book of Ruskin, and that is why it so captured me and made me transform my life.[34]

Gandhi was so impressed with this book that he translated it into Gujarati with the title *Sarvodaya, i.e.* welfare of all. Here it deserves to be noted that the word *Sarvodaya,* coined by Gandhi, has been one of the most cherished terms of our freedom movement used in all Indian languages. It is because of its meaningful connotation, its depth of humanism, and its wide-ranging implication for India's downtrodden masses.

It is interesting to note the circumstances how this book came into Gandhi's hands. It was 1893; Gandhi was leaving for Durban on a business trip. Henry Polak, his vegetarian friend, an assistant editor of the *Transvaal Critic,* came to see him off at Johannesburg railway station and gave him a book to read during the long journey. This was the book, John Ruskin's *Unto This Last*. Gandhi read the book all through journey and was captivated. Henry Polak writes about the impact of this book:

> *He had come to a firm decision: he would change his entire outward life in accordance with the ideals set forth by John Ruskin. The drastic decision was based on one solid reason: Gandhi found in this book, expressed in clear terms, the innermost echo of some of his own growing convictions.*[35]

John Ruskin with his strident call to mankind for equality and brotherhood had touched upon something that had been latent in Gandhi himself. Mahatma Gandhi later expresses his debt:

> *Great Britain gave me Ruskin, whose Unto This Last transformed me overnight from a lawyer and city-dweller into a rustic living away from Durban on a farm, three miles from the nearest railway station.*[36]

In course of an interview with the Editor of the *Spectator* during the Second Round Table Conference in 1932, in London, Gandhi was asked: 'Did any book ever affect you supremely and was there any turning-point in your life?' Gandhi's answer was: 'Yes, the book that affected me more than any other was by Ruskin… It made me decide to change my whole outward life. There is no other word for it, Ruskin's words captivated me…I lay awake all night and then decided to change my whole life.'[37]

The teachings of *Unto This Last* can conveniently be summed up under three heads: The good of the individual is contained in the ultimate good of all. All men have the same right of making a livelihood from their work, and it made no difference whether the person followed the profession of a lawyer or that of a barber. The life of labour, that is, the life of the tiller of the soil and the handicraftsman, is the life worth living. Gandhi, writing on the thematic aspect of these principles, states in *Harijan*:

I stand by what is implied in the phrase Unto This Last. All must have equal opportunity. Given the opportunity, every human being has the same possibility of spiritual growth.[38]

Ruskin's writings became the guiding principle for Gandhi. What appealed to Gandhi most in his works was the set of economic principles which supported his own concept of an *ashram* organisation. Both sought the conversion of the upper classes by a change of heart. But John V. Bondurant observes a subtle distinction between the two philosophers, Ruskin and Gandhi:

Ruskin could not consider the masses of men as ends in themselves; rather, did he treat them as ends of others. Gandhi conceded the possible result that voluntary transformation might fail. He recognised the power of the common man and placed before him the means whereby he could assure himself the 'justice' about which Ruskin could only speculate. Gandhi believed in the worth of the individual man and considered his welfare the ultimate social goal. The element which distinguished the Gandhian approach is, again, the provision of a means to achieve that end–a technique of direct social action.[39]

It was after all the discrepancy between word, creed and conduct that has been life's deadly venom leading civilisation to its doom. Gandhi with his own example strove to bring a synthesis of thought and conduct, of targets and deeds. Gandhi wrote a few months before he passed away:

If mankind was to progress and to realise the ideal of equality and brotherhood, it must adopt and act on the principle of Unto This Last, a book written with 'blood and tears'.[40]

Gandhi says that Ruskin's *Unto This Last* has been a lesson for Indians no less than for English readers. It is an irony that the British Government along with his own book *Hind Swaraj* banned this book during Gandhi's first *Satyagraha Movement* in India in 1920. Gandhi writes in the Gujarati version of *Unto This Last*:

India must indeed have Swaraj but she must have it by righteous methods. Our Swaraj must be the real Swaraj, which cannot be attained either by violence or industrialisation. India was once a golden land, because Indians then had a heart of gold. The land is still the same but is a desert because we are corrupt. It can become a land of gold again only if the base metal of our present national character is transmuted into gold. The philosopher's tone which can effect this transformation is a little word of two syllables, Satya

> *(Turth). If every Indian sticks to truth, Swaraj will come to us of its own accord.*[41]

Thoreau's Impact on Gandhian Ideas

Henry David Thoreau has been one of the greatest American thinkers of our age. His writings are widely read and deeply pondered over by millions of people. His writings are not mere writings; he practised the ideas that he preached. Mahatma Gandhi has been one of those few persons who have put Thoreau's ideas into practice. Thoreau being impelled by a sense of duty wrote much against his own country.

To him it was a great sin that the Americans kept many people in the bond of slavery. He strove to put an end to this trade. He urged his countrymen not to pay the tax to the State where slavery prospered. He was imprisoned. In imprisonment only he wrote his famous book titled *Civil Disobedience*. It is a unique co-incidence that Mahatma Gandhi chanced to read this book when he was in imprisonment in Volkshurst prison. He was moved with Thoreau's ideas. In Gujarati section of the Indian Opinion, he writes: "Both his example and writings are at present exactly applicable to the Indians ..".[42]

Gandhi presented a simplified summing-up of Thoreau's Civil Disobedience in Gujarati, Hindi and English. To quote him from an article titled '*For Passive Resisters*':

> David Thoreau was a great writer, philosopher, poet and withal a most practical man, that is, he thought nothing he was not prepared to practise in himself. He was one of the greatest and most moral men America has produced. Campaigning for the abolition of Negro slavery, he wrote his famous essay, "On the Duty of the Civil Disobedience". He went to prison for the sake of his principles and his essay is sanctified by his suffering. It is written for all time. Its incisive logic is unanswerable.[43]

Gandhi acknowledges his gratefulness to Thoreau:

> Thoreau furnished me through his es*say on "Civil Disobedience" scientific confirmation of what I was doing in South Africa.*[44]

In many of his writings, we find repetition of this impression. In one of his letters to President Roosevelt he writes: "I have profited greatly by the writings of Thoreau and Emerson."[45]

Gandhi wrote an article on *Voluntary Poverty* in *Young India.* It is a beautiful gospel on *aparigraha, i.e.* non-possession. Gandhi says:

Civilisation in the real sense of the term, consists not in the multiplication, but in the deliberate and voluntary reduction of wants. This alone promotes real happiness and contentment, and increases the capacity for service.[46]

Louis Fischer comments aptly on Thoreau's impact on Gandhian ideas:

There was a Thoreau imprint on much that Gandhi did; as there was an Indian imprint on Thoreau ... Thoreau in Massachusetts borrowed from Gandhi's India and repaid the debt with words that reached Gandhi in a South African cell.[47]

Emerson was a disciple of Thoreau. It is a pleasing co-incidence to note that both, the *guru* and the disciple, were deeply impressed with Indian wisdom. In the writings of both these authors the very echo of Indian wisdom can be viewed. Gandhi in one of the early issues of *Indian Opinion* presents an excerpt of Emerson's *The Over-Soul.* Thoreau and Emerson collectively helped in formation of Gandhian philosophy. But Thoreau's impact was more than that of Emerson's. To quote George Hendrick:

The Walden philosopher was a practical man willing to practise his beliefs .... The Mahatma was especially indebted to Thoreau who defied society and government to follow his conscience.[48]

Thoreau and Gandhi will be remembered for the technique of resistance they applied against a tyrannical state which commanded a great force. However, there was a vast divergence between the two. Thoreau's concern was the individual. It was the individual who had to offer Civil Disobedience in conflict with the State. It is true that Gandhi had great faith in the dignity of the individual. To quote him from one of his articles titled *The Gospel of Freedom:*

If the individual ceases to count, what is left of society? ... Individual freedom alone can make a man voluntarily surrender himself completely to the service of the society. No society can possibly be built on a denial of individual freedom.[49]

Thoreau s revolt was a one-man affair. Gandhi moved a step ahead from Thoreau. Almost a half-century later, he was wholly concerned with the arousal of mass revolt. His gigantic task was to organise the resistance of the oppressed millions against an alien state which had few scruples about the application of naked brute force. It is of significance that on the eve of non-cooperation movement in India the first S*atyagraha* leaflet was simply a reprint of Thoreau's *Civil Disobedience.* To sum up it is apt to say that Thoreau was an ideologue, not a man on the battlefield. In Gandhi we have a blending of both these dimensions. Thoreau was a pioneer of the idea. Gandhi translated this idea into a technique, developed it step by step over a span of forty years, and having won complete command over millions of hearts, he pitched united "soul-force" against relentless brute-force; and, finally, by one of the most astounding feats recorded in world history, he drew conquest from what looked perilously as the chasm of defeat. Bhabani Bhattacharya writes:

> *It may be said that where Thoreau's bridge-building stopped, Gandhi's began. And the Mahatma, walking the bridge to its end, stepped off onto solid earth and still walked on - he walked on and on towards the remote horizon.*[50]

Tolstoy and Gandhi

Gandhi discovered Count Leo Tolstoy, the greatest Russian saint and author. He read his works, *The Kingdom of God is Within You, The Gospels in Brief: What to Do, Reason and Religion, The First Step* and *How Shall We Escape?* and came to realise the infinite possibilities of universal love. It is significant to note that Tolstoy shattered all the delusions Gandhi had about the Christian churches. With Tolstoy Gandhi agreed that the Christian missionaries had perverted the moral and spiritual teachings of Jesus Christ. Tolstoy thus became an influensive force in Gandhi's life. Bhabani Bhattacharya remarks:

> *Ruskin gave him the doctrine of manual labour. Tolstoy, in addition, led him to the avowal of complete non-violence. He taught him strong denunciation of war and all violence, and sanction of resistance to a tyrannical state. Later, it was to provide him material for the ideological aspect of the movement he initiated, and he blended this with that he had learnt from Thoreau.*[51]

Gandhi writes in *Indian Opinion*, "It is believed that in the Western world, at any rate, there is no man so talented as Count Tolstoy."[52]

With some biographical sketches Gandhi formulates the essence of Tolstoy's teachings that impressed him:

1. *Men should not accumulate wealth.*
2. *No matter how much evil a person does to us, we should always do good to him. Such is the Commandment of God, and also His Law.*
3. *No one should take part in fighting.*
4. *It is sinful to wield political power, as it leads to many evils.*
5. *Man must pay more attention to his duties than to his rights.*

6. *Agriculture is man's true occupation. It is wrong to establish large cities, to employ hundreds of thousands in factories so that a few can exploit the poverty of the many.*[53]

Here it deserves to be noted that Tolstoy was himself fascinated by Indian wisdom, particularly the writings and speeches of Swami Vivakanand. He happened to get a copy of Swamiji's *Raja Yoga* in English published in New York in 1996. Gandhi was well aware of this fact. He felt thrilled with A *Letter to a Hindoo*, Tolstoy's comment on the current unrest in India. It was the message of civil disobedience that he read in the lines of this letter. He became impatient to tell Tolstoy about the *Satyagraha Movement* already underway in Transvaal, South Africa. In his letter dated October 1, 1909, he writes:

> *An utter stranger to you, I have taken the liberty of addressing this communication in the interests of truth, and in order to have your advice on problems, the solution of which you have made your life-work.*[54]

Tolstoy promptly answered the letter:

> .... *Your interesting letter gives me great pleasure. May God help all our dear brothers and co-workers in the Transvaal. This fight between gentleness and brutality, between humility and love on one side and conceit and violence on the other, make itself felt even more strongly to us here especially in the sharp conflict between religious obligations and the laws of the state.*[55]

Gandhi mailed Tolstoy a copy of his book, *Hind Swaraj* or *Indian Home Rule*. With Tolstoy's permission, he issued a reprint of *A Letter to a Hindoo*. In its preface he describes himself as a 'Humble follower of that great leader whom I have long looked upon as one of my guides....' And Tolstoy in a letter to a friend writes about Gandhi as 'a person very close to us, to me more should be known about Gandhi's movement'. Tolstoy expressed pleasure on the progress of Gandhi's 'passive resistance movement'. Here it needs to be pointed out that this 'movement', experimented by Gandhi in South Africa, evolved as *Satyagraha Movement* in context of Indian Freedom Movement, and he owes to Tolstoy for the doctrine of the same. Gandhi writes years after the death of Tolstoy:

> *Russia gave me in Tolstoy a teacher who furnished a reasoned basis for my non-violence. Tolstoy blessed my movement in South Africa when it was still in its infancy and of whose wonderful possibilities*

I had yet to learn. It was he who had prophesied in his letter to me that I was leading a movement which was destined to bring a message of hope to the downtrodden peoples of the earth.[56]

Jayaprakash Narayan, speaking at the 'Venice Tolstoy Seminar' in 1960, said:

Tolstoy did not live to witness the Indian Satyagraha Movement, but he had learnt enough of Gandhi's work in South Africa to write to him this long letter, which must have been one of the longest things Tolstoy wrote.[57]

Joan Bondurant remarks on Tolstoy's contribution to Gandhian philosophy:

The influence of Western thinkers - of Tolstoy, Ruskin, Thoreau - has been repeatedly acknowledged by Gandhi himself. But in each case the influence was that of corroboration of an already ethical precept, a crystallisation of basic moral predispositions.[58]

Some critics think that Tolstoy negates the state by non-violent, non-resistant means. So did Gandhi. But, like Thoreau, Tolstoy remained primarily a theorist and had no technique for mass action. Joan Bondurant illuminatingly points out:

The contribution of Gandhi lies in his transformation of just such principles as these into the dynamic techniques of action, Satyagraha.[59]

At Geneva in 1932, Gandhi was asked: "What is the distinction between the Christian doctrine of non-resistance and your resistance without violence? Have you taken your principles from Tolstoy?" Gandhi answered: "It has often been said that I owe my principle of non-violent resistance to Tolstoy. It is not the whole truth."[60]

Gandhi went on to explain that while he had benefited greatly from Tolstoy's ideas, he had developed the method to such an extent that it looked quite different from Tolstoy's. He had acted as a capable pupil who had built upon the foundation laid by his teacher; but had made his own addition to the legacy.

Count Leo Tolstoy was supreme creative artist but his prestige as a social philosopher had greatly suffered. It was Gandhi who is credited to achieve this height. Jayaprakash Narayan in an address at Venice Tolstoy Seminar, 1960 says:

India is the only country in the world where a serious attempt has been made-not by a small group of eccentrics but through mass movements-to put some of Tolstoy's ideas into practice.[61]

And the whole credit goes to Mahatma Gandhi whose experiment in the socio-economic laboratory of the world-history has been unexcelled.

Gandhi was now intellectually maturer for the writings of his own. Two of his pamphlets appeared in 1895 titled *An appeal to Every Briton in South Africa* and *The Indian Franchise.* He logically countered all the objections of the Natal Whites to Indians using the right of franchise. To quote his words:

> *To separate the two communities is easy enough, to unite them by the 'silken cord' of love is difficult. But, then, everything that is worth having is also worth a great deal of trouble.*[62]

The South African press warmly appreciated the *Appeal* though they differed with the views expressed. The *London Times* took good notices of the *Appeal* and in outspoken article strongly supported the same.

The Impact of *Bhagvad Gita* on Gandhi

It was 1897. Gandhi left for India on a six-month tour. He attended a three-day session of the Indian National Congress at Calcutta. His resolution on Indians in South Africa was passed. He tried to meet Maharshi Debendranath Tagore but could not. He went to Belur to meet Swami Vivekananda and again failed as Swamiji was sick and was staying elsewhere. He read Swamiji's *Raja Yoga.*

This was the time when he was drawn closer to *Bhagvad Gita* which now became his 'infallible guide of conduct' offering him a ready solution for all his trials and troubles. It was not merely a book or scriptures. His life was moulded in the light of the values propounded in *Bhagvad Gita.* Mahadev Desai asserts: "Every moment of Gandhiji's life is a conscious effort to live the message of *Gita.*"[63]

The *Bhagvad Gita* played a very important role in building up of Gandhi's personality as also his ideology. He acknowledges his debt to the *Bhagvad Gita* in '*Young India*':

> *When doubts haunt me, when disappointments stare me in the face, and when I see not one ray of light on the horizon, I turn to the Bhagvad Gita, and find a verse to comfort me: and I immediately begin to smile in the midst of overwhelming sorrow. My life has been full of external tragedies and, if they have not left any visible and indelible effect on me, I owe it to the teachings of the Bhagvad Gita.*[64]

Gandhi again observes in *Harijan*:

The Gita has become for me the key to the scriptures of the world. It unravels for me the deepest mysteries to be found in them. I regard them with the same reverence that I pay to the Hindu scriptures.[65]

On the significance of the *Bhagvad Gita* in Hinduism, Gandhi states:

For me, Sanatana Hindu Dharma is the vital faith handed down from generations... and based upon the Vedas and the writings that followed them. For me the Vedas are as indefinable as God and Hinduism... The Vedas are remnants of the discourses left by unknown seers... Then arose a great and lofty-minded man, the composer of the Gita. He gave to the Hindu world a synthesis of Hindu religion, at once deeply philosophical and yet easily to be understood. It is the one open book to every Hindu who will care to study it, and if all other scriptures were reduced to ashes, the seven hundred verses of this imperishable book are quite enough to tell one what Hinduism is and how one can live up to it.[66]

There are hundreds of commentaries and renderings of the *Gita* available. Of all them the works of Sri Aurobindo, Bal Gangadhar Tilak, Dr Annie Besant, Mahatma Gandhi, Acharya Vinoba Bhave, S. Radhakrishnan, Swami Prabhavanand, Christopher Isherwood, and Sri Krishna Prem are the excellent ones. Gandhi's commentary is aptly described as an allegorical interpretation of the *Bhagvad Gita.* Gandhi believes that the *Gita* is an allegory describing the inward conflict in which mankind is perpetually involved. Arjuna, the great *Pandava* warrior, who shrinks from duty in the battlefield, is reminded by *Krishna*, the divine charioteer, that the warrior's duty is to take precedence over all else. Gandhi observes:

Treated as an allegory, Krishna is the Dweller within, the fight is between the baser and the higher impulses in us, our own body being the field of battle. Here is a never- ending struggle between the forces of darkness and of light: not the picture of what happened thousands of years ago, but that is going on today in every human heart. It is the description not of a war between cousins but between the two natures in us—the good and the evil... it is the description of the eternal duel going on within ourselves.[67]

Gandhi says that all our religious endeavours are the means to attain self-realisation. He adds that *anasaktiyoga,* i.e., the doctrine of disirelessness–renunciation of the fruits of action — is the pivot around which the entire *Gita* is woven. He quotes from the *Gita*:

Karmanye wadhikaraste ma phalesu kadachana;
Maa karamaphal heturbu ma sango astkarmani.[68]

The English rendering of the same reads thus: "Do your allotted work but renounce its fruit; be detached and work; have no desire for reward."[69]

The doctrine of *Karmayoga*; the path of action is another great principle that Gandhi derived from the *Gita*. Gandhi has expounded the essence of *Karmayoga* in his discourses on the *Gita*. *Yogah Karmasu Kaushalam,* i.e. the *yoga* adds grace in one's wisdom. Gandhi writes:

> *The success of an act lies in performing it, and not in its result, whatever it is. Therefore be calm and do your duty clear of consequences... Freedom form action cannot be attained without action; wisdom never comes to a man simply on account of his having ceased to act. Man does not become perfect merely be renouncing everything. One who sits with folded hands is a fool.*[70]

The doctrine of *aparigraha*, i.e., non-possession, in the *Bhagvad Gità* fascinated him. But how could he be rid of his possession? Must he give up every thing? In the light of *Gita's* teaching, he realised the meaning of the term *trustee*. He interpreted the doctrine of *aparigraha* to mean that he had to act as a trustee who controlled large possessions but had no right to consider them as his own. In its essence it meant a change of heart a change of attitude. To quote Vincent Sheean:

> *Non-possession, non-attachment, the cardinal rule of the Gita, couldn't be merely a beautiful idea sonorously recited in ancient poetry. It had to be true.*[71]

Like other *pundits* and critics Gandhi is of opinion that more than one interpretation is possible of any literary work however sacred it may be. The meanings of great works are subject to a process of evolution. This is exactly true in the case of *Bhagvad Gita*. Gandhi says:

> *The Gita is not an aphoristic work; it is a great religious poem. The deeper you dive into it, the richer the meanings you get... With every age, the important words will carry new and expanding meanings. But its central teaching will never vary. The seeker is at liberty to extract from this treasure any meaning he likes, so as to enable him to enforce in his life the central teaching.*[72]

Gandhi was back in South Africa. This second visit was for a period of 11 years. This time his intellectual status had undergone a change. In 1893 his Christian friends had tried to baptise him. Now, he was at a firmer ground. His Hindu conciseness was stronger and bolder. Now, he had to give rather than to receive. This change was due to the impact of the

Hindu nationalist ideology on him inculcated by the theosophists, Swami Vivekananda's literature and others.

A Homage to Lokmanya Tilak

Gandhi being the triumphant leader in the struggle against apartheid in South Africa, returned to India. Now India was the stage where he had to play the role in giving a shape to his time. It is to be kept in mind that this was the time when India was the spotlighted corner of a massive world-stage where the destiny of human kind was being determined. Potentially he was to be the greatest leader of the time. Political historians have dedicated the annals - 1915 to 1947 - as the Gandhian era. Lokmanya Tilak, the greatest mass leader, had passed away. Gandhi, being grief-stricken, pays his tributes to Tilak:

> *It is difficult to believe of him as dead. He was so much a part of the people. No man of our time had (such a) hold on the masses. He was unquestionably the idol of his people. A giant among men has fallen. The voice of the lion is hushed... His patriotism was a passion with him. He knew no religion but love of his country. He will go down to the generations yet unborn as a maker of modern India. It is blasphemy to talk of such a man as dead. Let us erect for the only Lokmanya of India an imperishable monument by weaving into our lives his bravery, his simplicity, his wonderful industry and his love for his country.*[73]

We find that whatever he said about Lokmanya Tilak, proved equally true of him. From Tilak, Gandhi learnt to be an ardent nationalist. "*Swaraj* is my birthright", said Tilak. In Gandhi's priority, too, the freedom of the nation was at the top. To quote him:

> *I long for freedom from the English yoke. I would pay any price for it. I would accept chaos in exchange for it. For, the English peace is the peace of the grave. Anything would be better than this living death of a whole people. This satanic rule has wellnigh ruined this fair land materially, morally and spiritually.*[74]

Advocate of the Weaker Races

Gandhi was the advocate of the weaker races of the society. Besides being a nationalist, he was also a great humanist. As he says:

> *My ambition is much higher than independence. Through the deliverance of India, I seek to deliver the so called weaker races of the earth from the crushing heels of Western exploitation in which*

England is the greatest partner. India's coming to her own will mean every nation doing likewise.[75]

Gandhi was not simply a thinker. He was a man of action. In his person there was a blending of a *rishi,* a saint, and a *yoddha*, a warrior. The struggle that he fought in India was two-dimensional. He fought against the British for the freedom of the nation. Simultaneously he kept on his strife against the century-old dogma of untouchability aiming at consolidation of Hindu society.

Satyagraha: A Heritage of Humankind

His struggle was unique in the world history as there was no weapon used in it. It was *Satyagraha,* a unique weapon, now handed over to the humankind as a heritage for generations to come.

Satyagraha is defined as the truth force having the essence of entire Gandhian philosophy and technique of action at its core. The word was coined by him at an early stage of his resistance movement in South Africa. In its original form in 1906, it was a seed. Presently it was a seedling, and when Gandhi finally quit South African land, he kept this plant and planted the same in India. What Gandhi himself thought about *Satyagraha* is imperative to see in his own words:

For me, Satyagraha is not a mere copy-book maxim; it is my very life. To me nothing but truth has any interest. I am convinced that the country can never benefit by untruth. The more we strive to realise an ideal, the farther it recedes. To pursue it the more vigorously is the only object worthy of endeavour. We may stumble and fall, but shall rise again; it should be enough if we did not run away from the battle.[76]

In the whole span of *Satyagraha* movement the vivification of the evolution of Gandhian thought process could easily be viewed. The interpreters have depicted the doctrine when it was in a state of full maturity, complete in every detail. But it had to pass from stage to stage, ideal to ideal, truth to truth. A few trends in the evolutionary path deserve to be noted. When the term *passive resistance* was changed into *Satyagraha* Gandhi declared that the idea was not infliction of suffering on the opponent but on one's own self. Self-suffering is the essence of Gandhian philosophy. Gandhi himself says about its significance:

No country has ever risen without being purified through the fire of suffering. The mother suffers so that her child may live. The condition of wheat-growing is that the seed grain should perish. Life comes out of death. Will India rise out of her slavery without fulfilling this eternal law of purification through suffering?... Progress is to be measured by the amount of suffering undergone by the sufferer. The purer the suffering, the greater is the progress.[77]

The concept of self-suffering had an inseperable corollary: fearlessness. Gandhi stressed that the *Satyagrahi* must not hesitate to place all his trust in the opponent. But the trust that Gandhi shook of could not withstand the shocks that he received from British Government. He called that government *satanic* in extreme provocation. But with the passage of time in calmer circumstances his expression changed, and he wrote:

Satyagraha excluded violence not only in deed but also thought and word. To say a harsh word to an opponent was a breach of Satyagraha.[78]

According to Gandhi, in *Satyagraha* there is no room for hatred or bitterness. It needs to be stated that Gandhi fought against the British Government but he was never wearied of expressing his warmth and admiration for the British people. C.F. Andrews and Mirabehn, the British, not only became his *ashram*-inmates but with him fought for India's Independence. There were numerous English writers and intellectuals who sought India's freedom.

In Gandhian philosophy there is an affinity between ends and means. Equally important, these are convertible terms. *Satya,* the truth, is the framework that contains the picture of all these ideas. It is all-pervasive.

Satya and Ahimsa : The Sovereign Principle

What is *Satya*? Gandhi says that truth is something that the 'voice within' tells us.

But the 'voice within' depends on the evolution of one's mind. It is fact that what may be truth for one may be untruth for another. The disciplined conscience is the key point here, and when it lacks, it brings untruth. Gandhi says: "Everyone should realize his limitation before he speaks of his inner voice."[79]

Truth is the sovereign principle, and numerous other principles are already included in it, Gandhi emphatically says: "I worship God as truth only."[80]

Gandhi repeats this theme in his editorials many times :

Rather than say that God is truth, I should say that truth is God... It is the living embodiment of God, it is the life, and I identify the fullest life... I know that God is neither in heaven, nor down below but in everyone...[81]

God cannot exist away from the humanity. Gandhi says: "I know that I cannot find Him apart from the rest of humanity."[82]

Gandhi loved humanity. He never desired the perishable kingdom of the earth, nor heavenly amenities he ever willed to avail. What did he desire is the redemption of the grief of the grief-stricken humanity. He says:

I recognise no God except the God that is to be found in the hearts of the dumb millions ... and I worship the God that is Truth, or Truth which is God through the service of these millions.[83]

It needs to be stated that it was the multitude, the dumb downtrodden millions, whom Gandhi included in his *Satyagraha Movement*. Before he launched any *Satyagraha* he tried his best to ensure the surety against any outbreak of violence. To quote him again:

Satyagraha... excludes every form of violence, direct or indirect, veiled or unveiled, and whether in thought, word or deed. It is a breach of Satyagraha to wish ill to an opponent. The right of Satyagraha is for the strong in spirit, not the doubter or the timid. Satyagraha teaches us the art of living as well as dying. Birth and death are inevitable among mortals. What distinguishes man from the brute is his conscious striving to realise the spirit within.[84]

Propounding the doctrine of *Satyagraha* Gandhi declares that it is not *a weapon of the weak.* He urges the *Satyagrahis* to develop an immense inner strength and follow a strict discipline embodied in his code of conduct. He adds that they must never embarrass the wrong-doers. To quote him:

The appeal must always be directed not to the opponent's fear but to his conscience... He was to be converted, to be coerced.[85]

Gandhi utters a stern warning against the misuse of the doctrine of *ahimsa.* He states that *ahimsa,* if it is based on cowardice or weakness, is worse than useless. He referred that the mouse that yielded itself to the cat was not committing an act of non-violence. He declares that he would prefer to "risk violence a thousand times rather than risk the emasculation of a whole race."[86]

He says with a stress that if there is a choice between cowardice and violence, he would support violence. Forgiveness has its value only when it comes from one who has the strength to conquer and power to punish. Ramdhari Singh Dinkar, the great laureate of Hindi poetry and an authority on Gandhian philosophy, writes:

Sach puucho to sar main hi basti hai dipti vinay ki
Sandhi wachan sampujya usi ka jisme shakhti Vijay ki
Sahanshilta, kshama, daya ko tabhi pujta jag hai
Bal ka darp chamakta uske picche jab jagmag hai.[87]

Gandhi states that *ahimsa* is meaningless if it proceeds from a helpless creature: "Self-defence ... is the only honorable course where there is unreadiness for self-immolation."[88]

On Divinity of Humanity

The *Vedanta* philosophy pronounces the divinity of humanity. Tolstoy's *The Kingdom of God is within You* (man) is the echo of the same. Gandhi has embraced this value in his ideology. The dignity of man has become the heart of Gandhian philosophy. *Satyagraha, satya, ahimsa, saddhya* and *sadhana* and all other facets of his philosophy took for granted the intrinsic goodness of man. This is why he says that *ahimsa* is the law of the mankind and its vice-versa is that of the brute:

> *Non-violence is the law of our species as violence is the law of the brute. The spirit lies dormant in the brute and he knows no law but that of physical might. The dignity of man requires obedience to a higher law–to the strength of the spirit.*[89]

Untouchablity : Contrarary to the Spirit of Hinduism

Harijan Upliftment is one of the salient components of Gandhian philosophy. Untouchablity has been the curse of *Sanatana Hindu Dharma* for centuries. Gandhi was deeply aggrieved to witness the plight of *acchuts* (untouchables) in our society. He considered untouchablity as a black spot on the face of our society. To quote his words:

> *I am proud to be a Sanatani Hindu. I have read the Vedas, the Upanishads, the Gita, the Bhagawata, the Manusmriti and the Ramayana. I claim to have understood the spirit of Hinduism. I believe that untouchablity is not a part of Hinduism. If it is so, such Hinduism is not for me.*[90]

Gandhi moves a step ahead. He is of the opinion that untouchablity is not a sanction of *Hindu Dharma;* it is contrary to the very spirit of it. He writes in one of his editorials:

> *Vedas are divine. The spirit of the Vedas is purity, truth, innocence, chastity, humility, simplicity, forgiveness, godliness and all that makes*

a man or woman noble and brave. There is neither nobility nor bravery in treating the great and uncomplaining scavengers of the nation as worse than dogs to be despised and spat upon.[91]

Gandhi has pondered much on untouchablity and the *Vedas*. Once a correspondent asked him if he thought the *sins of touch and sight* were of *Vedic* origin. Gandhi's answer needs to be quoted:

I have full confidence in the purity of the Vedas, and therefore have no hesitation in asserting that the sins of touch and sight have no support in the Vedas. I would, however, add that no matter what is credited with Vedic origin, if it is repugnant to the moral sense, it must be summarily rejected as contrary to the spirit of the Vedas, and perhaps what is more, as country to fundamental ethics.[92]

In the contemporary world, religious conversions of the nationals have changed the identification of many of the nations. Prof Madhavarao Sadasiva Golvarkar says that the conversion of Hindus is the denationalisation of Indians. Gandhi being one of the statesmen of the Indian nation was worried on the conversion of his religionist brothers, the untouchables. He wept when he came to know that Dr Bhiamrao Ambedkar embraced Buddhism denouncing Hinduism stating that humanity is demanded in it. Gandhi seems to be an advocate of Hinduism when he defends it. To quote him:

Can a religion that was professed by Chaitanya, Jnyanadeva, Tukaram, Tiruvalluvar, Ramakrishna Paramahamsa, Raja Rammohan Roy, Maharshi Devendranath Tagore, Vivekananda and a host of others who might be easily mentioned, be so utterly devoid of merit as is made out in Dr Ambedkar's address? A religion has to be judged not by its worst specimens but by the best it might have produced. For that and that alone can be used as the standard to aspire to, if not to improve upon.[93]

Gandhi's love and compassion for the untouchables touch our heart. He called them *Harijans*, the children of God, and his campaign for India's independence, therefore, necessarily incorporated his movement for the emancipation of the untouchables. His words impregnated with the empathy for our Harijan brothers need to be quoted:

I do not want to be reborn, but if I have to be reborn I should be reborn as an untouchable so that I may share their sorrows, sufferings, and the affronts levelled against them in order that I may endeavour to free myself and them from their miserable condition.[94]

Some of the angry youngmen of untouchables' community proposed that they would resort to violence if the *savarna Hindus* did not change their attitude towards them. Gandhi suggested them that untouchablity cannot be removed by force.

The amelioration of the untouchables cannot come through these methods. Humble argument and right conduct is the only way through which the *savarna Hindus* may be convinced to discard bigotry. Gandhi shared the sufferings of untouchables. Addressing the delegates of Untouchablity Conference at Belgaum during the Congress Week Gandhi said:

> *You must have the right of worship in any temple in which members of other castes are admitted. You must have the right of admission to schools along with the children of other castes without any discrimination. You must be eligible to the highest office in the land not excluding even that of the Viceroy's. That is my definition of the removal of untouchability.*[95]

Gandhi diagnoses the diseases of untouchability in the manner a physician treats the patient sympathetically. He does not look to the west for the solution; rather he follows the way indicated into Hinduism itself. Gandhi thinks that wiping untouchability from Hinduism is a sacred cause but it is not just to adopt the Satan's method to serve this sacred cause. To quote him once again from his address in Untouchablity Conference at Belgaum:

> *I pray you to dismiss from your mind the idea of ameliorating your condition by brute force. The Gita tells us that by sincerely meditating on Him in one's heart, one can attain moksha. Meditation is waiting on God. If waiting on God brings the highest bliss of salvation, how much quicker must it bring removal of untouchability? Waiting on God means increasing purity. Let us by prayer purify ourselves and we shall not only remove untouchability but shall also hasten the advent of Swaraj.*[96]

To Gandhi, untoucablity was a blot on humanism, and according to him every Hindu must atone for this sin by opening their temples and wells for their *Harijan* brothers precisely on the same terms as other Hindus. To quote his words:

> *Temple-entry is the one spiritual act that would constitute the message of freedom to the 'untouchables' and assure them that they are not outcastes before Gods.*[97]

Goraksha: the Dearest Possession of Hinduism

Goraksha, the protection of cow, is another eminent aspect of Gandhian philosophy. Gandhi believes that it is the dearest possession of *Hinduism*. No one, who does not believe in cow protection, can claim to be a Hindu. It is the noblest belief. Gandhi interprets *go-puja* (cow worship) as the worship of innocence. To quote his words:

> *For me, the cow is the personification of innocence. Cow protection means the protection of the weak and the helpless. As professor Vaswani truly remarks, cow protection means brotherhood between man and beast. It is a noble sentiment that must grow by patient toil and tapasya.*[98]

Gandhi thinks that cow protection is the central concept of Hinduism. It is the most wonderful phenomena in human evolution. It takes the human being beyond his species. The cow to him connotes the entire sub-human world. Through the cow man is enjoined to realise his identity with whole beings. The cow is a poem of pity. She is the mother to millions of Indian mankind. Gandhi says that Hindus will be judged not by their *tilaks*, not by the correct chanting of *mantras*, not by their pilgrimages, not by their most punctilious observance of caste rules but by their ability to protect the cow. To quote his words:

> *Cow protection is the gift of Hinduism to the world. And Hinduism will live so long as there are Hindus to protect the cow.*[99]

Gandhism : A Subset of Hinduism

Hinduism is a deep ocean bearing full many a gem of purest ray serene in it. The deeper one dives the costlier gems he picks up. Like an expert diver Gandhi plunged into the unfathomed caves of Hinduism and picked up the human values inherent in it. These values collected together in an organised shape may be described as Gandhism or Gandhian philosophy today. Gandhian philosophy is the subset whose elements are derived from the universal set, *Sanatan Hindu Dharma.* Here it deserves to be stated that it is a unique characteristic of Hinduism that it embraces whatever good it finds elsewhere. This is exactly true in the case of Gandhism and hence it embraced some of the human values that Gandhi traced in the works of Thoreau, Ruskin and Tolstoy. But Hinduism has been the soul of his ideology. He learnt to be tolerant and liberal from Hinduism. Once an American correspondent asked him as to why his ideas were akin to Hinduism. Gandhi replied:

On examination I have found it to be the most tolerant of all religions known to me. Its freedom from dogma makes a forcible appeal to me in as much as it gives the votary the largest scope for self- expression. Not being an exclusive religion, it enables the followers of that faith not merely to respect all the other religions, but it also enables them to admire and assimilate whatever may be good in the other faiths.[100]

Gandhi's doctrine of *ahimsa*, i.e., non violence, though is common to many religions, it has found its highest expression and appreciation in Hinduism only. Gandhi never believed Buddhism, Jainism and Sikhism as separate from Hinduism. *Isawasam Idam Sarvam, Yatakinchita Jagatyam Ajagata* from the *Upanishad* was his favourite hymn and so he believed that the whole world is the manifestation of the Supreme Lord. As he says:

Hinduism believes in the oneness not of merely all human life but in the oneness of all that lives. Its worship of the cow is, in my opinion, its unique contribution to the evolution of humanitarianism.[101]

Charkha : A Means to Feed the Belly of the Millions

Charkha, the spinning wheel, has been the innovative weapon in the hands of Mahatma Gandhi. It has been the means to feed the belly of the millions. He wanted to see spinning wheel everywhere as he witnessed pauperism. He realised that unless we feed and clothe the skeleton of the masses of India the religion bears no meaning. He is of the opinion that a *Brahmin* is a better *Brahmin*, a *Muslim* a better *Muslim*, a *Vaishnava* a better *Vaishnava* if he turns the *charkha in* the spirit of service. To quote his words:

If it was possible for me to turn the wheel in my bed, and if I felt that it would help me in concentrating my mind on God, I would certainly leave the rosary aside and turn the wheel. If I am strong enough to turn the wheel, and I have to make a choice between counting beads or turning the wheel, I would certainly decide in favour of the wheel, making it my rosary, so long as I found poverty and starvation stalking the land.[102]

The Doctrine of *Swadeshi*

The *Swadeshi* Movement has been one of the most important aspect of Gandhian freedom movement, strengthening our nationalism. It was an economic strategy aimed at removing the British Empire from the power and improving the economic condition of India. The word is derived from Sanskrit *'Swa'* means 'self' and *Desh* means 'country'. So *swadeshi* the adjective means 'of one's own country'. The *Swadeshi* movement was designed to create awareness amongst the people to boycott British Products and the revival of domestic products and production processes. It was strongest in Bengal and it was called *Vande Mataram* Movement.

The *Swadeshi* movement started with the partition of Bengal(1905) by Lord Curzon, then Viceroy of India and continued upto 1911. It was most successful of the pre Gandhian movements. Shri Aurbindo Ghosh, Lokmanya Bal Gangadhar Tilak, Bipin Chandra Pal, Lala Lajpat Rai, V.O. Chidambaram Pillai, etc., were pillars of *Swadeshi* Movement (1905-1911). When Mahatma Gandhi appeared on the national stage(1914-1948), *Swadeshi* was a key focus of his movement. Mahatma Gandhi described *Swadeshi* as the soul of *Swaraj,* i.e. self-rule.

The people around the world give this credit to Gandhi who put an end to the powerful British empire in India, but this is just one aspect of the truth. Satish Kumar; one of the Gandhian scholar and the editor of '*Resurgence*' Magazine in England, in his *Schumacher Lecture Series* says:

Gandhi was not interested simply in exchanging rule by White Sahibs for rule by Brown Sahibs; he wanted the government to surrender much of its power to local villages.[103]

To Gandhi, the spirit and the soul of India rests in the village communities In one of his articles in *Young India*, April 1931, he says:

The true India is to be found not in its few cities, but its seven hundred thousand villages. If the villages perish India will perish too.[104]

So *Swadeshi* is a programme for long time survival. In Gandhi's concept of *swadeshi* his vision of India's future can be clearly viewed. His vision of free India was a not nation-state but a confederation of self-governing state, self-reliant, self-employed people living in village communities deriving their right livelihood from the products of their homesteads. It is the prerogative of the village assembly to decide what will be imported in the village or what is to be exported from the village.

Rajiv Dixit an ideologue of *Bharat Swabhiman* associated with Yogarishi Swami Ramdevji Maharaj, says:

People have lived for thousands of years in a relative harmony with their surroundings living in their homesteads weaving home spun clothes, eating home grown food, using home made goods; caring for their animals, forests and land: celebrating the fertility of soils with feasts, performing the stories of the great epics and building temple. Every region of India has developed its own distinctive culture to which travelling story-tellers, wandering sadhus and constantly flowing streams of pilgrims made their contribution.[105]

Every village community of free India must have its own carpenters, shoe-makers, potters, builders, mechanics, farmers, engineers, weavers, teachers, bankers, merchants, traders, musicians, artists and priests. In other words, each village is supposed to be a microcosm of India; a web of loosely interconnected communities. Gandhi considered these villages so important that he thought they should be given the status of 'Village Republics' Gandhi thinks :

The village community should embody the spirit of home, an extension of the family rather than a collection of competing individuals. His dream was not of personal self-sufficiency, not even family self-sufficiency but the self-sufficiency of the village of communities.[106]

Contrary to Gandhi's concept of *Swadeshi*, the Europeans believed in centralised, industrialised and mechanised modes of production. Gandhi turned this principle on its head and envisioned a decentralised home-grown, hand-crafted mode of production. In his words, "*Not mass production, but production by the masses.*"[107]

Whenever we adopt the principle of production by the masses, village communities, it adds dignity to the work done by human hands; and when we hand over it to the machines we not only use the material benefits but also the spiritual benefits because the work by hand brings with it a meditative mind and self-fulfilment. Gandhi says in his article:

It is the tragedy of the first magnitude that millions of people have ceased to use their hands in hands. Nature has bestowed upon us, this great gift which is our hands. If the craze for machinery continues then a time is likely to come when we shall be so incapacitated and weak that we shall begin to curse ourselves for having forgotten the use of living machine given to us by God. Millions can't keep themselves fit by games and athletics and why should they exchange the useful productive handy occupations for the useless, unproductive and expensive sports and games.[108]

Here we must keep in our mind that 'mass production' is only concerned with the product, whereas 'production by the masses' is concerned with the product, the producers and the process.

What is the driving force behind mass production? It is a cult of the individual. What motive there can be for the expansion of the economy on a global scale other than the desire for personal or co-operative profit.

Contrary to this a locally based economy enhances the community spirit, the community well being, such an economy encourages mutual aid. Members of the village take care of themselves, their families, their neighbours, their animals, lands, forestry and all the natural resources for benefit of present and the future generations.

Industrialisation that yields mass production leads people to leave their villages, their land, their crafts and their homesteads and go to work in the factories. Instead of dignified human beings and the members of self respecting village community, people become cogs in the machine standing at the conveyer belt, living in the shanty town and depending on the mercy of the bases. Industrialists want more and more production and so they prefer more efficient machines working faster and faster. This throws millions of men and women on the scrap heap of unemployment. Such a society exposes with rootless, jobless millions living as dependents of the state or begging in the streets. In Gandhi's concept of *Swadeshi*, the machines would be subordinated to the workers. It would be allowed to become the master, dictating the pace of human activity. In a same way, market forces would serve the community rather than forcing people to fit the market.

Mahatma Gandhi was a man of prophetic vision. He knew that with the globalisation of the economy, every nation would export more and more and import less to keep the balance of payments in favour. Naturally, in this way there would be a perpetual economic crisis, perpetual unemployment and perpetually discontented human beings.

According to Gandhi, communities practising *Swadeshi* economics would not dominate society though it would have its place. The modern world vision is that more material goods one has he will lead a happy life. But Gandhi has a philosophical attitude. He says:

A certain degree of physical comfort is necessary but above a certain level, it becomes a hindrance instead of help. It is delusion to create unlimited number of wants and satisfying them. The satisfaction of ones physical needs must come at a full stop before the physical decadence. Europeans have to remodel their outlook if they are not to perish under the weight of physical comforts to which they have become.[109]

Gandhi says that in order to protect their economic interest countries go in war-military war as well as economic war. Gandhi says that people should live in village communities and simple homes rather than desire to live in palaces.

Millions of people will never be able to live at peace with each other if they are constantly fighting for a higher living standard. Gandhi says:

> We can't have real peace in the world if we look at each other's countries as *sources of raw materials or as markets for finished industrial goods. The seeds of war are sown with economic greed. If we analyse the causes of war throughout the history we find that the pursuit of economic expansion constantly leads to military adventures. There is enough for everybody's need but not enough for anybody's greed.*[110]

Gandhi stresses that *Swadeshi* is thus a pre-requisite for peace. Thus in Gandhi's concept of *Swadeshi* it is apt to say *Swadeshi* is the way to comprehensive peace, peace with nature.

The Global economy drives people towards high performance, high achievement and high ambition for materialistic success, this results in stress, loss of meaning, loss of inner peace, loss of family relationship and loss of spiritual life.

Gandhi realised that in a glorious past life in India was not only happy and prosperous but conductive to philosophical and spiritual development. So *Swadeshi* for Gandhi is our spiritual imperative. To conclude, I would like to quote the famous *Swadeshi* song that Hon'ble Swami Ramdevji Maharaj usually sings in his morning *yoga* conferences:

Mera ho mann swadeshi, mera ho tan swadeshi,
Mar jaun toh bhi mera, howe kafan swadeshi.

Chattan tut jaye, toofan ghumadh ke aaye,
Gar maut bhi pukare, toh bhi lakshya ho swadeshi.

Jo gaon mein bana ho, aur gaon me khapa ho,
Jo gaon ko basaye, wah kaam hai swadeshi.

Jo haath se bana ho, ya garib se liya ho,
Jisme sneh bhara ho, wah chiz hai swadeshi.

Manave ka dharma kya hai, manave ka dard jane,
Jo kare manushyata ki, raksha wahi swadeshi.

Kar shakti ka vibhajan, mite punji ka yeh shasan,
Bane gaon swawalambi, wo niti hai swadeshi.

Mera ho mann swadeshi, mera ho tan swadeshi,
Mar jaun toh bhi mera, howe kafan swadeshi.[111]

The Essence of Gandhian Philosophy

To Gandhi, the spinning wheel, the rosary, and the *Ramanama*, are all the same. They subserve the same end; they teach us the religion of service. He says that he cannot practise *ahimsa* without practising the religion of service, and he cannot find the *satya* without practising the religion of *ahimsa and* there is no religion other than the *satya.* Gandhi says that the *satya* is the *Satyanarayan*, the *Rama*, the *Krishna*, the *Ishwara*, the *Khuda*, the *Allah*, the *God.* To quote the famous hymn sung by him at all ceremonial occasions:

Raghupati, Raghava, Raja Ram,
Patita Pawan , Sita Ram
Ishwara, Allah tere nam
Sabko sanmati de Bhagwan.[112]

Gandhian philosophy is immense. It is broader and deeper than the ocean and higher than the mountain. No author can claim to have grasped it in its full. We have, however, been able to collect only a few gems out of his variegated ideas. In fine, it can be said that *satya;* truth, *ahimsa;* non-violence, *asteya;* non-stealing, *sevabhava;* chastity, *aparigraha;* non-possession, *sarirashrama;* manual labour, *brahamacharya;* control of the palate, *abhaya;* fearlessness, *sarvadharma sambhava;* equality of all religions, *swadeshi, achutoddhara;* discarding of untouchablity, etc., form the very essence of his ideology. Gandhian philosophy has well been summed-up into this hymn composed by Gandhi himself that was a part of his daily prayers:

Ahimsa satya asteya bramhacharya aprigraha
Sariras ama asvada sarvatra bhaya-varjana
Sarvadharma—samantavasvadesi sparsabhawan.[113]

References

1. Kshitiz. Hindi textbook for class IX. Published by NCERT. 2006, p. 87.
2. U.K.Oza, Published in *Gandhi Memorial Peace*, Number. 186.
3. Bhattacharya, Bhabani. *Gandhi, the Writer.* Delhi: National Book Trust. p. 5.
4. *Young India, February 13, 1930*. p. 52.
5. *Harijan*. April 29, 1933. p. 2.
6. *Gandhi, the Writer*. p. 5.

7. Qtd. from the *Upanishad*.

8. Gandhi, M.K. *An Autobiography*. p. 23.

9. Harijan. April 28, 1946. p. 111.

10. *An Autobiography*. p. 25.

11. *Ibid*. p. 34.

12. *Ibid*. p. 37.

13. *Gandhi, the Writer*. p. 13.

14. Pyarelal. *Mahatma Gandhi: The Early Phase, Part I*. Ahmedabad: Navjivan Publishing House. p. 240.

15. *Ibid*.

16. *An Autobiography*. p. 48.

17. Arnold, Sir Edwin. "*The Song Celestial*".

18. Qtd. in *Gandhi Marg*. April 1965. p. 162.

19. *Ibid*.

20. "*Sermon on the Mount*". Qtd. from the Bible.

21. *Ibid*.

22. *An Autobiography*. p. 101.

23. *Young India*. December 22, 1927.

24. Kingsford, Anna and Edward Maitland. *The Perfect Way or The Finding of Christ*. London: John H. Watking, 1923. p. 219.

25. *Ibid*. p. 219.

26. *Ibid*. pp. 223-224.

27. *An Autobiography*.

28. *The Natal Mercury*. December 12, 1894.

29. *The Natal Advertiser*. February 1, 1895.

30. *An Autobiography*. p. 102.

31. Qtd. in Pyarelal. p. 331.

32. *Gandhi the Writer*. p. 26.

33. *An Autobiography*.

34. *Ibid*. p. 224.

35. Polak, Henry. *Mahatma Gandhi*. London: Odham's Press, 1949. p. 48.

36. Tendulkar, D.G. *Mahatma*, Vol. VI. 177.

37. "*Evening with Gandhi*". The Spectator. London, October 24, 1931.

38. *Harijan*. November 17, 1946. 424.

39. Lippincott, B.E. *Victorian Critics of Democracy*. London: Oxford University Press, 1938. p. 56.

40. *Harijan*. August 25, 1946. p. 281.

41. Gandhi, M.K. *Ruskin's Unto This Last, A Paraphrase in Gujarati*. Ahmedabad: Navajivan Publishing House, 1951. pp. 63-64

42. *Indian Opinion*. Gujarati Section. September 7 and 14, 1907.
43. *Ibid*. October 26, 1907.
44. Tendulkar, D.G. *Mahatma,* Vol. VI. p. 177.
45. *Ibid*. p. 179.
46. *Young India*. June 10, 1911 and July 22, 1911.
47. Fischer, Louis. *Gandhi: His life and Message*. p. 38.
48. Hendrick, George. *Gandhi Marg*. July 1959. p. 178. See also his article, "*The Influence of Thoreau's Civil Disobedience on Gandhi's Satyagraha*" in New England Quarterly, Dec 1956, pp. 42-71. Also, "*Emerson and Gandhi*" by the same author in the Emerson Society Quarterly No. 2, 1956. pp. 7-8.
49. *Harijan*. February 1942. p. 27.
50. *Gandhi the Writer*. pp. 67-68.
51. *Ibid*. p. 69.
52. *Indian Opinion*. 1995.
53. *Indian Opinion*. Gujarati Section, September 2, 1905.
54. *Ibid.*
55. Tolstoy, Leo N. Qtd. in *Gandhi the Writer*. p. 71.
56. *Gandhi the Writer.*
57. Narayan, Jai Prakash. Qtd. in *Gandhi the Writer.*
58. *Joan Bondurant*. p. 106.
59. *Joan Bondurant*. pp. 179, 186.
60. *Young India*. October 25, 1921.
61. Narayan, Jai Prakash. Qtd. in *Gandhi the Writer.*
62. *Gandhi Marg*. January, 1961.
63. *Gandhi the Writer*. p. 76.
64. *Ibid.*
65. *Gandhi Marg*. January 1961. p. 161.
66. *Young India*. August 6, 1925.
67. *Mahatma*. Vol. II. p. 181.
68. *Bhagvad Gita*, Chapter-II, Verse-47
69. Gandhi, M.K. *Discourses on the Gita*. Ahmedabad: Navajivan Publishing House, 1960. pp. 12-13.
70. *The Times*, London, January 27, 1896.
71. Sheean, Vincent. "*Lead, Kindly Light*". New York, 1949. p. 100.
72. *Harijan*. April 18, 1936.
73. *Harijan*. October 1, 1925.
74. *Harijan*. August 6, 1931.
75. *Ibid.*
76. *Young India*. August 6, 1951.

77. *Young India*. July 28, 1920.

78. *Young India*. January 12, 1928.

79. *Young India*. January 12, 1928.

80. *Navajivan*. September 7, 1919.

81. *Ibid*. July 16, 1919.

82. *Harijan*. April 15, 1933. p. 8.

83. *Young India*. December 31, 1931. p. 428.

84. *An Autobiography*. p. xv.

85. *Young India*. August 4, 1927. p. 248.

86. *Harijan*. August 29, 1936. p. 226.

87. Dinkar, Ramdhari Singh. *Kurukshetra*. New Delhi: Rajpal and Sons, p. 45.

88. *Harijan*. March 11, 1939.

89. *Harijan*. April 7, 1946.

90. *Harijan*. March 25, 1939. p. 64.

91. *Young India*. August 4, 1920. p. 5.

92. *Harijan*. July 20, 1935. p. 181.

93. *Harijan*. September 1, 1940.

94. *Young India*. August 11, 1920. p. 3.

95. *Young India*. April 4, 1921.

96. *Young India*. January 4, 1921.

97. *Young India*. October 3, 1929.

98. *Harijan*. July18, 1936.

99. *Ibid.*

100. *Young India.* January 19, 1921.

101. *Young India.* July 25, 1921.

102. *Young India.* May 25, 1921.

103. Satish Kumar: *Schumacher Lecture Series.*

104. *Young India,* April 1931.

105. Rajiv Dixit, *Bharat Swabhiman Lecture Series,* available on the website.

106. *Young India,* April 1931.

107. *Ibid.*

108. *Young India,* February 1931.

109. *Young India,* March 1930.

110. *Young India,* January 1938.

111. *Collected songs of Swami Ramdevji Maharaj*, Bharat Swabhimaan Trust.

112. *Harijan.* January 11, 1933.

113. *Young India.* April 3, 1924.

4

Gandhian Philosophy in the Novels of Mulk Raj Anand

Of all the Indian writers in English it is Mulk Raj Anand who has woven his stories around the Gandhian philosophy. The very titles of his novels and some of the short stories are reflective of it; for example, *Untouchable, Coolie, The Cow and the Brricades*, etc.

Untouchable (1935) is an excellent work of art of all Indo-Anglian fictions of the Gandhian era. This novel is excellent in its intrinsic, artistic worth, and also for its elaborate treatment of Gandhian philosophy. Here we find Anand diagnosing the disease of untouchability and recommending the solution as offered by Gandhi. The novelist was deeply impressed by Mahatma Gandhi, and his works unmistakably bear the impact of Gandhian philosophy.

Prior to entering into the world of Mulk Raj Anand's fiction, it would be proper to study the age, and analyse the social and political circumstances that made Anand write this novel.

Anand is a prolific writer

Anand is a prolific writer, writing not only fiction but also dissertations on literature and other arts. G. P. Sharma writes:

> *As a fiction writer, he has always a serious concern with communicating some ideas of his own to his readers, just as a writer of dissertation usually has. And his concern as a fiction writer has been always the redemption of the poor and the oppressed of the society from the clutches of the rich and the oppressor — an objective which he pursues with the zeal of a missionary.*[1]

But it is a fact that the problem of the poor and the oppressed is not only in India but also in other parts of the world; and when Anand writes for their redemption, he, of course, writes not only about the oppressed in Indian society but also about those in other countries. To quote G. P. Sharma once again:

He is, therefore, like all genuine writers, a Universalist as much as he is an Indian nationalist. Of course, as an Indian nationalist writer, the locale of all his novels and stories is India, and the problems in which his characters are involved are always Indian in context, even though all these problems are not always typically Indian.[2]

Anand is a social reformer. He was inspired by the European political ideologies, especially those of Marx and Lenin. To quote the words of Meenakshi Mukherjee in this context: "We're all engaged in trying to find a solution to the world's woes through new political ideologies."[3]

Mulk Raj Anand, as a writer of fiction appeared during pre-independence period and all his best works came during the two most hectic decades of Indian freedom movement, that is, a decade after the victory of Russian revolution. Anand is preoccupied mainly with three problems of society. G. P. Sharma observes:

The problems of oppression and exploitation of the lowest classes by the upper classes; the tyranny and torture by the higher castes of the lower castes of Hindu society; and the ignorance and superstition of the people caused by illiteracy and orthodoxy that are hurdles to the progress of society.[4]

Anand : From Marxism to Gandhism

Anand's move from the Western ideology to Gandhism is an interesting story. Gandhi was a Himalayan figure in the world of spiritualism, socialism and international politics. He was not a mere philosopher to be studied in the books. His massage of peace and non-violence and the saint-like austerity of his personal life counterbalanced the foreign influences on Anand and awakened in him a new sense of national pride and purpose. To quote Anand from Apology for Hiroism:

My initial interest in Gandhian ideas began in 1919 when Gandhi launched a massive Satyagraha movement in protest against the repressive Rowlett Act imposed by the British Government on India. I was particularly impressed by Gandhi's ethics of simple living, the campaign against untouchability, and the great doctrine of ahimsa, non-violence as practised in the liberation movement.[5]

In 1920, at the age of sixteen, Anand joined Gandhi's non-violence movement and was consequently arrested by the British government. In the thirties he found himself attracted to Marxist doctrine, but his acceptance of Marxism was considerably modified by his faith in the ethical idealism of Mahatma Gandhi. In fact, he never became an active Communist party member. To quote him in this regard:

I accepted the Markxist doctrine as the embodiment of an ethical creed in so far as it was a protest against misery, ugliness and in-equality.[6]

He states that his humanism was different from what he called the mystical humanism of Gandhi:

Under Gandhi's influence, it was necessary for the artist to link himself with the disinherited, the weak and the dispossessed, as a human being; and as an artist, with special talents, to transform society.[7]

Anand in Sabarmati Ashram

With this mission in mind Anand went to live with Gandhi at his *Sabarmati Ashram* in 1921. It was a necessary preparation for his novel, *Untouchable*. He took vows to clean lavatories, to abstain from wine and woman, and to abide by the rigorous discipline of the *Ashram*. He read the back numbers of *Young India*, and was greatly touched by Gandhi's love and compassion for the untouchables. Gandhi called them *Harijans*, the children of God. In one of his editorials Gandhi writes:

Swaraj or independence is a meaningless term if we desire to keep one-fifth of Indin under perpetual subjugation.[8]

Gandhi's programme for India's independence, therefore, necessarily incorporated his movement for the emancipation of the untouchables; he wishes to identify himself as one with them:

I do not want to be reborn, but if I have to be reborn I should be reborn as an untouchable so that I may share their sorrows, sufferings, and the affronts levelled against them in order that I may endeavour to free myself and them from their miserable condition.[9]

Untouchable : A Relentless Exposer of the Hindu Caste System

Anand's close contact with Gandhi not only enriched his creative vision but also brought to his heart the Buddhist *Karuna* or compassion. As a result, *Untouchable* remains a sensitive, compassionate and realistic portrayal of the humiliations and indignities suffered by the untouchables.

It is a relentless exposer of the Hindu caste system and the theory of *karma* which perpetuate human atrocities against the downtrodden people like Bakha. It has thus been a mirror reflecting the sordidness of the Hindu society suffering from the cancer of untouchability. G. P. Sharma writes:

Anand has depicted the problem of untouchability, suggesting the magnitude of the harm it has done by impeding the harmonious growth and development of society as a whole while violating the sense of humanity in a most brutal manner. The oppression and tyranny of the high-cast Hindus all vividly shown here — their ruthlessness, their cruelty, their hypocrisy, and their love for mastery and dominance over the low casters. Against this is shown the sad and passive suffering of the low castes with all their agony and pain.[10]

In the preface to the novel, Anand confesses:

I am sure, however, that the warmth towards Bakha which has made this character lovable to so many people may, to *some extent, have emerged from my warmth towards the person of Gandhi.*[11]

Bakha, an eighteen-year-old sweeper boy, who is not only an individual but also a type, represents millions of his brethren. C.D. Narasimhaiah is quite justified in his observation that through the depiction of Bakha's life, the author shows very clearly and appealingly his '... sympathies for this character because of the centuries of exploitation and suffering that has been his lot'[12] as well as his 'indignation at the society that so treats a fellow human being.'[13]

The bitter experiences of Bakha make him realise: 'they think we are dirt because we clean their dirt.'[14] With a feeling of irredeemable humiliation and servility, Bakha goes out in the afternoon to a solitary place, 'utterly given up to despair.'[15]

In the very beginning of the novel the author gives a grim picture of the surrounding in which 'the outcastes of the Hindu society'[16] live. Indubitably, this life is against the norms of hygiene and, therefore, most unsuitable for human habitation. To quote from the novel:

The absence of a drainage system had, through the rains of various seasons, made the quarter a marsh which gave out the most offensive skin. And altogether the ramparts of human and animal refuse that lay on the outskirts of the colony, and the ugliness, the squarer and the misery which lay within it, made it an uncongenial place to live in.[17]

Bakha is at home. His sister Sohini goes to fetch water from the well that belongs to caste-Hindus. The outcastes are too poor to have a well of their own. As a consequence their women folk have to:

Collect at the foot of the caste-Hindu well and depend on the bounty of some of their superiors to pour water into their pitchers... The outcastes had to wait for a chance to bring some caste-Hindu to the well, for luck to decide that he was kind, for Fate to ordain that he had time to get their pitchers filled with water.[18]

The outcastes are not allowed to fetch water from the well themselves because from their very touch the water would be polluted. Sohini waits, and somehow manages to get her pitcher filled with water by a *Brahmin pundit* of the temple. She comes back. The *pundit* helps Sohini not for any kindness to her but for his attraction towards her blooming youth. He invites her at his temple house for cleaning. Sohini goes to the *Brahmin's* house. Bakha also goes to the temple to sweep its courtyard. He meets there the school-boys of rich upper class family. His long subdued desire for learning flares up to see them:

His uncle at the British barracks had told him when he first expressed his wish to be a sahib that he would have to go to school if he wanted to be one. And he had wept and cried to be allowed to go to school. But then his father had told him that the schools were for the babus, not for the lowly sweepers. He hadn't quite understood the reason for that then. Later at the British barracks he realised why his father had not sent him to school. He was a sweeper's son and could never be a babu. Later still he realized that there was no school which would admit him because the parents of other children would not allow their son to be contaminated by the touch of the lowcaste man's son.[19]

Walking in the way towards the temple he accidentally touches a caste-Hindu. Its result is horrible. He is beaten badly besides being abused and crushed. Bakha weeps bitterly in horror, rage, humility and helplessness. He proceeds to his duty with all cautiousness not to touch any caste-Hindus. In the temple the priests are observing religious rites. The castes-Hindu devotees have thronged into it for their noon-time *pranam*. Bakha, standing on the stairs of the temple, is moved profoundly to hear the chanting of hymns. But he is shocked to hear the disturbing shouts, "polluted, polluted", made by the caste-Hindus. He is driven away to a distance when he hears another shouts, "polluted, polluted" by a priest. This priest in none but the same who had invited Sohini to clean his house. Rushing to the temple he informs his brethren that the sweeper-girl had touched and defiled him when she went to his house to clean it. What an irony! The reality was that it was he, who was the culprit. While the girl was cleaning the house he was enamoured of her, made indecent suggestions to her, and when she declined to yield to him, he raised hue and cry. Bakha is stunned when he learns the fact from his humiliated sister. In anger, he rushes towards the temple to teach those caste-Hindu hypocrites a lesson. People disperse in fear and he comes back vexed.

Bakha has a bitter experience of his lowly existence. Narrating everything to his father he gets advice from him what he should do against all those injustices of society. His father, however, having life-long experience as an untouchable, suggests him to tolerate all those passively for their own safety. He says:

> *They are our superiors. One word of theirs is sufficient to over-balance all that we might say before the police.*[20]

There is one more incident that deserves to be mentioned. It is late afternoon and Bakha is playing hockey with other children. The game ends in pandemonium when a stone hurts a little boy watching the game. Out of love and the sense of duty Bakha carries the child to his high-caste parents, who are supposed to be obliged to him for saving their child. But Bakha is stunned when he is cursed and expostulated by them for defiling their child and house. Bakha is tired of such treatments meted out to him at every step of his life. He feels himself lowly, miserable, as he is untouchable, neglected and unwanted in this world. In this mental status, he leaves his house for a solitary place where he can enjoy the peace of mind being out of human touch. This is the climax of his misery.

He finds then hundreds of people going to a public meeting to be addressed by Mahatma Gandhi. He at once starts moving towards the meeting ground. The author shows in this context the influence of Gandhi on the people of the time. Bakha forgets he is untouchable, neglected and unwanted. Let us see how powerfully the author demonstrates the electrifying impact of Mahatma on the minds of the people through Bakha:

> *He (Bakha) had not asked himself where he was going. He had not paused to think. The word 'Mahatma' was like a magical magnate, to which, he like all other people about him rushed blindly.*[21]

On the way, in his attempt to take a short cut to the meeting place, Bakhà perhaps jumps a fence into a garden when hundreds of others all mesmerised like him by Gandhi's influence follow him. While straightening their way over the garden they damage 'the beautiful garden bowers planted by the ancient Hindu king and since then neglected.'[22]

Anand thinks that it had a symbolic significance:

> *It was as if the crowd had determined to crush everything, however ancient or beautiful, that lay in the way of their achievement of all that Gandhi stood for. It was as if they knew, by an instinct surer than that of conscious knowledge, that the things of the old civilisation must be destroyed in order to make room for those of the new. It was as if in trampling on the blades of green grass, they were deliberately, brutally trampling on a part of themselves which they had begun to abhor, and from which they wanted to escape to Gandhi.*[23]

Arriving at the meeting place, Bakha, being an untouchable, waits for Gandhi in a less crowded part at one end of the ground:

> *He was in the midst of a humanity which included him in its fold and yet debarred him from entering into a sentient, living, quivering contact with it. Gandhi alone united him with them, in the mind, because Gandhi was in everybody's mind, including Bakha's, Gandhi might unite them really.*[24]

When Bakha waits, he hears people around him talk about Gandhi. Gandhi was to them, 'a legend, a tradition, an oracle.'[25]

> *Only recently he heard that a spider had woven a web in the house of the 'Lat Sahib' (Viceroy) at Dilli (Delhi), making a portrait of the sage, and writing his name under it in English. That was said to be a warning to the sahibs to depart from Hindustan, since God Almighty Himself had sent a message to a little insect that Gandhi was to be the Maharaja of the whole Hindustan.*[26]

To the majority of these people, Gandhi was a saint like Guru Nanak, or 'an *avatar* of *Lord Vishnu* and *Krishna*.'[27]

Bakha further remembers how people say that, *no sword can cut the Mahatma's body, no bullet could pierce his scheme and no fire could scorch him.*[28] Bakha hears then a 'rustic' ask a 'Babu' if Gandhi will be able to overthrow the government to which the Babu's reply is:

> *He has the shakti (power) to change the whole world. The British Government is nothing.*[29]

When Gandhi comes, the flower petals are showered upon him, garlands hung around his neck, amidst cries of:

Mahatma Gandhi Ki-jai
Hindu-Mussulman-Sikh Ki-jai
Harijan Ki-jai.[30]

As the meeting begins, the Mahatma raises his right arm from the folds of his shawl and blesses the crowd. The author writes:

> *... the babble of voices die out, as if he had sent an electirc shock through the mass of humanity gathered at his feet.*[31]

On the electrifying impact of Mahatma on the masses Anand remarks:

> *This strange man seemed to have the genius that could by a single dramatic act, rally multi-coloured, multi-tongued India to himself.*[32]

So far as Gandhi's topic of discussion in the meeting was concerned it was untouchability. Apparently this was a harmless topic for the British Government. But he touches upon this social subject against the background of contemporary Indian politics:

> *As we know, while we are asking for freedom from the grip of the foreign nation, we have ourselves for centuries, trampled underfoot millions of human beings without feeling the slightest remorse for the iniquity.*[33]

In this speech we find Gandhi talking of Hindu society. This is introspection inside the Hindu society. Strictly speaking, untouchability is a curse of Hinduism. Gandhiji was proud of great ideals of Hiduism, but what he thinks and categorically speaks is an imperative that every Hindu is supposed to think and introspect. Let us see what Gandhi says:

> *The fact that we addresse God as 'patitpawan', i.e 'the purifier of the polluted souls' makes it a sin to regard any one born in Hinduism, as polluted - it is satanic to do so.*[34]

Gandhiji was emotionally moved to see the sordid plight of untouchables. His speech reflects it clearly:

> *I do not want to be reborn. But if I have to be reborn, I should wish to be reborn as an untouchable, so that I may share their sorrows, sufferings and affronts leveled at them, in order that I may endeavor to free them and myself from their miserable condition.*[35]

Gandhi intends to bring a revolution against untouchability. Elsewhere he says that it is a sin against humanity and God. He makes the people realise this from within. Summing up his speech at the end he says:

> *All public wells, temples, roads, schools, sanatoriums, must be declared open to the untouchables. And if you all profess to love me, give me a direct proof of your love by carrying on propaganda against the observance of untouchability. Do this, but let there be no compulsion or brute force in securing this end. Peaceful persuasion is the only means. Two of the strongest desires that keep me in the flesh are the emancipation of the untouchables and the*

protection of the cow. When these two desires are fulfilled, there is swaraj, and there lies my soul's deliverance.[36]

Gandhi himself has been introduced as a character towards the end of the novel. Anand draws an excellent, vivid pen-portrait of Mahatma, seated like a child huddled up between two women, Kasturba Gandhi and Miraben. The entire speech made by Gandhi is a collage of his actual statements about untouchability, which makes his picture authentic.

Bakha is intrigued and mystified by Gandhi's speech. "The Mahatma seemed to have touched the most intimate corners of his soul."[37] Momentarily, he even forgets the fact of his own untouchability. The Mahatma had left "a glow of brotherliness and humanitarianism" in his trail.

The author, in this way, with the poignant story of Bakha's experiences in a day, through the stream-of-consciousness technique, shows the injustice of untouchability prevailing in our Hindu society. The author suggests three solutions to this problem. Bakha in his humiliation and disgust hears three appeals for ending this disparity. One appeal is from a Salvationist missionary for his conversion to Christianity where there is no caste-distinction to oppress him. The second one is Gandhi's appeal in the meeting for the emancipation of the outcastes by carrying on propaganda against untouchability, and by doing their own cleaning work by the upper-caste Hindus as Gandhi himself and the inmates of his *ashram* do. The third one is an appeal of a Marxian poet Iqbal Nath Sarashar who wants introduction of machines for doing the jobs of the sweepers which will redeem the untouchable caste from their dirty profession and thus elevate them to a higher rank, putting and end to the injustice of untouchability. Bakha on hearing Gandhi and the poet feels that a solution to the problem is not far away, the redemption is bound to come. To quote E.M. Forster:

His Indian day is over and the next day will be like it, but on the surface of the earth, if not on the depths of the sky, a change is at hand.[38]

In *Untouchable* we thus find the novelist dealing with the social problem of untouchability of 'Hindu Dharma'. Against its political background of the time, depicting at the same time people's faith in Gandhi as their leader in the national movement and his magnetic influence on the masses, it is proper to have a comparative study of the subject. There have been many novelists and story-writers who have introduced Gandhi as a character, but whereas most of them remain merely a documentary, this novel transcends these levels. To quote G.P. Sharma:

> *The introduction of Gandhi serves a very significant purpose here in both aspects of the theme, political and social. Without introducing Gandhi in flesh and blood and with his speech it was difficult to sooth Bakha's oppressed mind; and in this way the novelist would not have been able to show this illiterate, untouchable boy's nationalist feeling in spite of his own problems of life in society. The novelist's success lies in the fact that the portraiture of Gandhi has been quite real and faithful and the speech given to his lips has also been in the exact idiom in which Gandhi spoke in reality.*[39]

Untouchable is thus an eminent work of art. Thematically, the wounded feelings and sufferings of a particular Indian, Hidnu untouchable have attained a universal significance. Stylistically, the use of 'stream-of-consciousness technique' has been quite effective and it also has contributed to the success of this 'great little' novel, to borrow a phrase from the novel where the author has used it to describe Gandhi.

The Road : Gandhi's dream of swaraj yet to be fulfilled

The Road (1961), though not so famous, is an important Gandhian novel of Mulk Raj Anand for our purpose. It deserves to be discussed with *Untouchable*, as the very theme of both is interlinked. Anand, the novelist must have realised that the road leading to the abolition of untouchablity from the Hindu society would be long and arduous, despite the Mahatma's superhuman efforts. He, therefore, in *The Road* shows that although the Government of India, mainly because of Mahatma Gandhi, has officially abolished the social and religious bias against untouchables, Gandhi's dream of *swaraj* still remains unfulfilled because the caste Hindus continue to persist in their attitudes of bigotry and prejudice against the *Harijans*.

Dooli Singh, the village headman, is the central character through which the image of Mahatma Gandhi has been projected. He is the champion of the cause of the untouchables against the cruelty of the caste Hindus like Thakur Singh. Bhiku, the young protagonist, is an untouchable like Bakha, but he is more sensitive and more conscious of his need for freedom and human dignity than Bakha. Bhiku's decision to leave the village for Delhi 'where there would be no caste or outcaste' - despite the local Gandhi's sacrifices and support for the *Harijans* - reminds us that the struggle for the Gandhian values have not yet ended and the mission of the struggle is yet to be realised.

Artistically, however, *The Road* cannot be compared with *Untouchable* or other successful novels of Mulk Raj Anand. To quote G. S. Balaram Gupta:

> *The book is perhaps a typical example wherein the novelist's philosophy and art do at best coexist, but do not coalesce. To this extent, The Road is a failure.*[40]

The conflict between the Marxism and the Gandhism

The Sword and the Sickle is another novel of Mulk Raj Anand which reflects the Indian freedom movement of the twenties and the thirties led by Mahatma Gandhi. This novel is unlike other Indo-Anglian novels which deal with the main trend of Indian national struggle with an approval. The novel mirrors a peasant movement, the leaders of which are devoted to Gandhism as they are to Marxism. Their goal is freedom from the foreign rule as well as from exploitation and oppression of the Indian *Rajas* and *Zamindars.* In their opinion the *Rajas* and the *Zamindars* are the very agents of the foreign rule; and freedom from the oppression of these agents is possible only when the freedom from Birtish rule is attained.

In *The Sword and the Sickle* Anand dramatises the conflict between the Marxist and the Gandhian ideologies in the soul of its protagonist Lal Singh, a *Punjabi* youth who has returned to India after being released from a German prison camp during the First World War. Lalu quits his village again, eloping with the landlord's daughter and led by a political leader of a peasant movement in UP. They arrive at a village, thirty-seven miles away from Allahabad, and become the guest of a Count - the elder brother of the *Raja* of Rajgarh. This Count, Kunwar Rampal Singh, refused to succeed to the landlordship; and thus his younger brother became the *Raja*. Rampal Singh remained a commoner, a benevolent leader of the poor peasants whom he rouses to put an end to the tyranny of the rich over the poor. He imbibed the spirit of Marxism when he was in Germany.

Rampal Singh, with the help of Prof Verma and Lalu, organises the peasants of Rajgarh as well as those of the nearby Nasirabad estate for the revolution to end tyranny, oppression and exploitation by landlords who, in their opinion, are the agents of British government. They, in their thought, belief and method, are inclined to communism though consciously they appear to follow the Congress policy of that time. Their revolutionary plans and activities are, foiled again and again by the reactionary forces of the two estates which are backed by the government until at last their movement dissipates and Rampal Singh, Lalu and other peasant leaders are put in jail.

The author, through this plot has depicted the peasant movement that is undoubtedly not the main trend of National Freedom Movement. Gopal Prasad Sharma comments in this regard:

It highlights one aspect of National Freedom Movement - the Communist movements that gained ground in the villages. This the author does with admirable detachment, bringing to the fore the follies of its leaders, their lack of discernment and understanding of the situation, and want of proper study of the 'ism' they have followed. The author is equally detached from the Congress movement of the time, though he has suggested the great influence of it on the people. Even Gandhi, who has been introduced into the novel as a character, has been an object of mild satire, just as the communist leaders of the movement in the village have been.[41]

A number of examples can be given from the novel to strengthen our logic. 'Count' Rampal Singh, the great communist leader of Rajgarh, who has foregone his landlordship, poses as a communist dedicating his life to the emancipation of the oppressed pesants, quotes Comrade Lenin and Marx frequently, celebrates the anniversary of the Russian Revolution with the peasants. But at the same time, he retains his feudal love for authoritarian power, commanding not only the peasants under his leadership but also trying to command the government police. Though devoted to Lenin and Marx, when he has to choose between Marxist trade union and those of Gandhi, with his wrong-headed attitude he chooses the latter. Naturally he fails to win Gandhi's support for his revolution. Then he tries to win Nehru's support. Nehru seems to him as an ideal revolutionary. The underlying irony here is that none of them knows what type of revolutionary Nehru is.

Here Anand's portrayal of Gandhi is entirely different from that of *Untouchable*. Here Gandhi has been viewed through the eyes of the peasant leaders and workers who do not have real faith in Gandhian ideology; naturally they cannot understand him properly. To quote G.P. Sharma again:

It is for this that the portraiture of Gandhi, too, has not been a very bright one here. The author has not allowed himself to be swept away by the emotional adoration for this great leader.[42]

Nehru, in contrast with Gandhi, appears to the peasants as an idealised character. But here Nehru also has been viewed through the eyes and minds of the peasant revolutionaries, who do not properly understand him either. Nehru is appreciated by them not because of his ideas but because he was "the solemn young son"[43] of Motilal Nehru and he was "known to be a revolutionary."[44]

The novelist here maintains an ambivalent attitude to this aspect of national movement. In fact, the main theme of the novel is more a criticism of the peasant movement of the country of that time than an approbatory picture of it To quote, the criticism of Sharar, a Marxian leader in the novel itself:

You people may have the best intentions, but then they say in English, the road to hell is paved with best intentions! And laziness of the kind, which goes on believing in primitivism and does not lay stress on intelligent organisation and solidarity among the workers, betrays not only a lack of confidence in the revolutionary movement of the people but also a kind of unconscious contempt and hatred of the masses.[45]

This is equally true so far as depiction of Gandhian movement in the novel is concerned. In *The Sword and the Sickle* the novelist depicts one trend of Indian National Movement in its vortex and dissipation though the main movement itself is viewed here from a distance. G.P. Sharma says:

This particular trend has been depicted with a critical attitude so that through the demonstration of the follies of its romantic heroes who merely refurbish their own egos while staging the revolt, people can be made aware of a danger which is likely to befall them as they fight for their freedom.[46]

The novel seems to be an amalgamation of the Count's fantasy comic aspirations and Lalu's absurd undertakings. C.D. Narasimhaiah aptly says:

The reader cannot be sure if the fantastic 'Count', his comic aspirations, and Lalu's absurd undertakings are at all to be taken seriously[47]

To conclude our criticism on Gandhian impact on *The Sword and the Sickle* it can be said that Anand's attitude towords Gandhi is that of an artistic detachment. The Gandhian image projected here is neither romantic nor eulogistic. Gandhi is viewed through the eyes of those who feel the magical pull of the Mahatma's personality but fail to understand the very meaning of his ideas and ideals.

Gandhi's Attitude Towards Industrialism Challenged

The Big Heart (1945) by Mulk Raj Anand is another novel within the purview of our consideration. In this novel the author challenges Gandhi's attitude towards machines and industrialism. Gandhian view is represented by Mahasha Hans Raj, an *Arya Samajist* leader, who through his supporters, particularly Satyapal, a student leader, and with the jobless *thathiars* (coppersmiths) to boycott machines. The *thathiars* are persuaded that the machines are not only the cause of their massive unemployment but they are also against the teachings of Gandhi who thought that the introduction of machinery in India was a symbol of the imposition of British civilisation in India that is also led to the exploitation of poor workers by the rich capitalists. The champion of machines is the protagonist Ananta, who not only wants to usher in the 'Age of Machines' but also trade unionism to better the lot of the working class. He has a strong supporter in Puran Singh Bhagat, a Marxist poet, who repudiates the Gandhian system of values. Their effort to form a Union of unemployed coppersmiths is, however, foiled by Mahasha Hans Raj. Professor Majid, a powerful orator, sways the jobless *thathiars* against Ananta and the factory owners by persuading them "...that the real enemy is hidden here, the factory which is going to convert you all from feudal slaves to wage slaves."[48]

One jobless worker gets out of hand and he forces his way into the factory and starts smashing the machine with a huge hammer. Ananta comes forward to protect the machine and is killed with a smash. The author's attitude towards Ananta and the machine once again, as in *The Sword and the Sickle,* seems ambivalent. It is perhaps best expressed through Iqbal Nath Sarashar in *Untouchable*:

> *I hate the machine. I loathe it. But I shall go against Gandhi there and accept it. And I am sure in time all will learn to love it.*[49]

In *The Big Heart,* the novelist shows his concern for a completely different and quite a new theme — the introduction of machinery and its implications. The author thus shifts here from the story of the problem of exploitation of the poor to the story of the problem of the working class thrown out of their traditional moorings with the advent of the Machine Age — a problem that has also a serious implication for his own age and country.

The *thathiars* or the traditional coppersmiths of Amritsar have lost their traditional job because of the setting up of a new plant for copper works in the locality by two rich coppersmiths. A few have been engaged in the plant as workers; some others have also got piece-works to be done, though these have been quite unrewarding now. The bulk of coppersmiths still remain jobless. This critical situation amidst the jobless coppersmiths has been exploited by the reactionery elements of society like Mahasha Hans Raj, a religio-political *Arya Samajist* who has joined the Congress and has become a protagonist of Mahatama Gandhi's programme of reviving the Golden Age in India. Mahasha Hans Raj has his supporters, a staunch one among them being the student leader, Satyapal. They have spread the idea among the jobless *thathiars* that the machines are the cause of their doom and the teachings of Gandhi are against machines. They plead for scrapping the machines and going back to the age of the spinning wheel as Gandhi has asked them to do.

Ananta, a 'rogue' in popular assessment of the *thathiars*, a flesh eater and a drunkard who has a tubercular young widow as his mistress, is for the introduction of the machine and for a change of the age-old profession, even though he himself is a jobless *thathiars* now, and the piece-work he does earns very little for him. Ananta worked formally at a Naval Dockyard foundry in Bombay where he had experience about the Trade Union Movement coming back to his home town, Amritsar. He welcomes the establishment of the plant and at the same time plans the launching of a movement for the welfare of those workers who are thrown out of their jobs. He intends to launch a movement "... to ensure their right to a proper wage until they are strong enough to displace their exploiters and seize the factory, which by all rights of humanity is theirs."[50]

He being tactless in words and deeds, Ananta cannot carry the people with him. He, however, has a strong supporter, the Marxist poet, Puran Singh Bhagat, who with his learning and the poetic vision of the future world-situation helps him in his task of wooing the jobless coppersmiths to the cause of forming the trade union. But the people find his exhortations also too theoretical and idealised. Gokul Chand, the headman of the utensil-sellers' community, and Murlidhar, the headman of the coppersmith brotherhood, both of whom have together established the plant in the town, hate Ananta and Mahasha Hans Raj equally. A betrothal ceremony at Murli Dhar's house for the marriage of his grandson with Gokul Chand's daughter is marred by the absence of Gokul Chand's own brethren of the old coppersmith brotherhood. The absence is due to the fact that Murli Dhar has not maintained any relation with the men of his own caste, he having risen to a better position now. Murli Dhar and Gokul Chand suspect Ananta for the absence of the few invited workers of the factory and they brood revenge for it.

On the same day about the same time, on the other side, Ananta has given a feast to all the *thathiars* affected by the establishment of the factory with a view to form a union. He has also invited the leaders of his rival faction, Mahasha Hans Raj and few others. When all gather for the feast, Ananta explains to them how these days caste-brotherhood of the old age has gone out of fashion and people should form class-brotherhood for their own welfare. He supports his points by the example of Murli Dhar not inviting his own caste-brothers to the ceremony of his house, they being of a different class now from his. He then appeals for the formation of the union of all the jobless coppersmiths who are of the same class now. Most of the unemployed coppersmiths are convinced about the need of such a union, but Mahasha Hans Raj stands in the way and foils the attempt. Ananta does not abandon hope of forming the Union. Late in the afternoon the same day, with the support of Gokul Chand's son, Kushal Chand who has come over to his side at last, makes another attempt to bring the unemployed coppersmiths to his fold. But coming over of Kushal Chand to Ananta's party has been interpreted by Mahasha Hans Raj as a step by selfish Ananta towards a friendly settlement with the rich factory owners who have created havoc in society. Thus Hans Raj wins the jobless workers to his side when Ananta's last appeal to his brethren for a 'radical change'[51] in the context of their living a 'life of terrible, awful suffering'[52] under the relentless oppression of 'the *Angrezi Sarkar* and the rich of our country'[53] is greeted by them with such terms for him and his followers as 'hypocrites, renegades and traitors'.[54]

Mahasha Hans Raj has another very staunch supporter, Professor Mejid, an intellectual and orator, who, with his superb power of oratory, has roused the jobless coppersmiths, who are already embittered with Ananta, against the factory-owners. He explains to them with his silver tongue that "the real enemy is hidden here, the factory which is going to convert you all from feudal slaves to wage slaves... the greatest danger now facing all nations is the wealth of the rich and the development of the machine."[55]

The jobless coppersmiths thus get impatient with the factory and its owners as well with Ananta, who, to them, is a corroborator with the rich now, until at last a gigantic drunkard, a jobless coppersmith, losing his temper forces his way into the factory and starts smashing the machine with a large hammer. None dares to stop the enraged giant. Ananta along comes forward with the spirit of a true leader and forbids the drunkard giant. At once, Ananta is struck down dead with the same hammer.

Ananta, the protagonist of the machine civilisation, seems to be the author's mouthpiece. Ananta's life is dedicated for bringing in the age of machine and also the formation of the working class, which will master the machine, and not to be a slave of it. This seems to be also the author's vision of the new age. But the question arises as to why the author allows Ananta to perish at last. It is not apt to draw the meaning that Ananta's stand is uncalled for and wrong. Actually the author wishes to draw more sympathy for Ananta. Anand as an artist is never unduly partial to him. Ananta has not been an idealised character. The author has created him a worldly character with all follies and foibles; and these have always been very real before our eyes. Even his death at the hands of the drunkard is quite natural as he himself was tactless and careless. Mahasha Hans Raj in contrast to Ananta is more virtuous. But the author's art has made him an object of hatred in spite of all his devotion to the Gandhian ideals and allegiance to the Congress and *Arya Samaj*. So we have the character of Prof Mejid with all his power of oratory and intellectual flashes. Puran Singh Bhagat, the Marxist poet and the supporter of Ananta, on the other hand, wins our sympathy even when he criticises Gandhi. To quote from the text:

> *Because Gandhi always worshipped the kind of truth which was orthodox, though it was dynamic, because he really accepts the system of property, the vicious circle of the old order can never last in India if it has made a mess of things in the other parts of the world.*[56]

So far as the art of the novelist is concerned the foremost artistic quality in the novel is the author's ambivalence in his portraiture of the character of Ananta who is apparently a rogue, though at the same time an ideal protagonist of the new age. The author's economy in the selection of the episodes and incidents, which are shown as taking place within the framework of a day, is another quality that we have here and this is common to *Untouchable*. The story develops from early morning till night through the actions and conversations in three quarters–in the private life of Ananta and his mistress Janki; in the public places of the Cat Killer's Lane where the coppersmith's community dwells, and in the families of Gokul Chand and Murali Dhar.

As mentioned earlier, Mulk Raj Anand wants the society of his vision to be based on the ideologies of two great foreign political thinkers, Marx and Lenin, and not on the ideology of Gandhi, the father of his own nation, in spite of his deep love and respect for the Mahatma. To quote Puran Singh Bhagat, the Marxist poet, from *The Big Heart*:

> *...we must be on our guard against those in our country who only want to substitute Brown or Yellow rule instead of the White. Certainly, if there is anything which has accrued to me through my pilgrimage of the world, it is the belief that I must help to change the present order built on profit; that I must devote myself entirely to the poor.*[57]

Thus we have viewed the Gandhian novels of Mulk Raj Anand. In these novels and elsewhere, too, we find Anand protesting against the contemporary set-up of society and calling for a new social order where the wretched and the poor would come to the level of the fortunate and the rich, and none would be able to oppress or exploit others. G.P. Sharma observes:

> *Anand is a nationalist writer only in the sense of trying to evolve a better and happier society for his countrymen, not in the sense of upholding whatever is Indian or detesting whatever is foreign.*[58]

Story of oppression of lower class

Coolie (1936) is one of the most popular novels of Mulk Raj Anand. Here we have a similar story of a boy's oppression in the society. The author in this novel has not only shifted from his 'stream-of-consciousness technique' to that of the 'picaresque', but also from the theme of oppression in Hindu society, in particular to that of oppression in Indian society in general; and the oppression of not of lower caste by the higher caste but of the poor lower class by the rich upper class. Anand has, therefore, through this novel, struck a new note as an Indian fiction writer. Here lies the analysis of the plot of the novel.

Munoo, a 14-year old peasant orphan boy, is from the Punjab hills. He is doomed to be a dependent member in the family of his uncle who is a *chaprasi* in Imperial Bank in a distant town. He could not live peacefully in his uncle's family because of the harassment and the nagging tongue of his aunt. His uncle has arranged his job as a house-servant in the house of one of his officers in the bank. Soon he realises in the Sub-Accountant's house that he has fallen from bad to worse. Being tortured, under-fed and under-paid he leaves his job, approaches his uncle hoping to get sympathy from him but finds him as unsympathetic as his master. He realises that they are of the same class, his master suppressing and his uncle exploiting him.

Munoo runs away from the town. In the train he meets Seth Prabh Dayal, a partner in a pickle factory at Daulatpur. He takes him affectionately with him. Munoo finds himself here in a better position, as Prabh Dayal loves him; more so because he has himself risen from a coolie to the position of a factory owner. But Ganpat, a partner in the factory, cannot tolerate Prabh Dayal taking Munoo as a boy of their rank and thus the relation between Ganpat and Prabh Dayal gets strained. Ganpat, who takes all the clients of their joint business to his side, dissolves the partnership of Prabh. As a result, Prabh Dayal runs bankrupt and is relegated to his former hard life as a coolie. Munoo, too, again becomes a porter. He leaves for Bombay where he gets the job of a coolie in a cotton mill. Here Hari and Ratan become his friends. Jemmi Thomas, a white *sahib*, his immediate master, forces him to get a sum of money on high interest for his establishment and offers him straw hut on high rent. Munoo and Ratan ignore the offer leading to the confrontation with foreman *sahib* which ultimately results into dismissal of both from their job.

Here we have a reference to All India Trade Union Congress (AITUC) advocating Ratan's reinstatement. In another development, the management orders the wage-cut of all the coolies. The trade union protests this injustice uttering the slogans:

"Right to work without having to pay bribes"
"Clean houses to live in"[59]
"Freedom from the clutches of the money-lender"
"Good wage"
"Shorter Hours"
"Security against certain dismissal"[60]

The confrontation between the mill-owner and the labourers is turned into the Hindu-Muslim communal riots, and in this emotional issue the original issue between the coolies and mill authority is forgotten. Munoo loses contact with Hari and Ratan and one day is run over by the car of an Anglo-Indian lady in the way to Simla. Wounded Munoo is taken to Simla by her and after his recovery the lady engages him as her rikshaw-puller. To Munoo, his story here is comfortable because of the lady's love for him. But he becomes a victim to tuberculosis and the story ends with the grin prospect of his dying with a feeling of detachment in a lonely isolated hospital of quiet Simla.

On a critical analysis of the novel we find that the author here lays bare a kind of violence in society done to the people of the lower rung by those of the upper class, a universal problem of capitalistic societies shown in the Indian context. To quote a trade union leader in the novel:

"There are only two kinds of people in the world: the rich and the poor, and between the two there is no connection."[61]

In this sense the novel breathes a spirit of proletarian humanism than of a spirit of Indian nationalism or Gandhian idealism. The British do not do the injustice we find here to the Indians but by the rich to the poor, by the bourgeoisie to the proletariat, irrespective of their nationalities. His master oppresses Munoo as a servent, the Sub-Accountant of the bank; and his wife does not understand Munoo's feelings because they belong to a different-class-the middle-class, while Munoo belongs to the working class. Munoo does not have any sympathy from his uncle since he, too, as an employee of the bank has merged middle-class. In the pickle factory, when he is employed, he is loved by Prabh Dayal sincerely and is hated by Ganpat. According to author, it is again due to class difference. Prabh has 'risen from cooliedom to the petit bourgeois.[62] But Ganpat is a thorough bourgeois, the son of a rich man of the town. The rapture between Prabh Dayal and Ganpat is also the result of the class confilict between the *petit bourgeois* and the *big bourgeois*. In the cotton mill difference between Munoo, his friends-his well wishers on one hand and mill owners-Brithishers is more distinct. Here the exploitation and oppression are also more ruthless and cruel. Munoo, in his last employment, under Mrs. Mainwaring, is happier than in his earlier employments because the lady again is a *petit bourgeois*.

To conclude, *Coolie*, as a novel is quite successful in its own way. G.P. Sharma, an eminent Indo-Anglian critic, makes a comparative study of *Coolie* and *Untouchable* :

> *Untouchable showed a more careful craftsmanship, a better economy and a poetic style, being written in the stream-of-consciousness method. Coolie betrays a lesser concern for all these, it being a novel in the picaresque tradition. But while it falls short of the artistic qualities of Untouchable, it gains in its appeal to all classes of readers with its fortuitous story, abundance of action and incidents.*[63]

Variation of the Theme of Oppression

Two Leaves and a Bud (1937) by Mulk Raj Anand is the next novel within our purview. It is variation of same theme of oppression of the poor by the rich. Gangu around whom the story is centered, a peasant from Punjab comes to Assam tea estate to serve as a plantation labourer. But his hope for a better fortune is belied as he finds that the joint income of himself, wife and children as coolies, is insufficient to maintain their livelihood. He is doomed to fall a victim to the moneylender who had already ruined him in Punjab.

He faces a series of tribulations. His wife dies of a cholera epidemic. Unable to perform her funeral due to financial strain, he goes to meet the manager to get loan for the same, pays bribe to the *chaprasi* to meet the manager, but he is cruelly rebuffed. He is forced to get money at high interest. He is very thankful to a white doctor, with the help of whom he gets a plot of cultivable land. He along with his children works hard to pay off his heavy debt.

Gangu is shocked to learn that Reggie Hunt, the assistant manager, who is notorious for his cruelty to the coolies, demands his young daughter Leela to satisfy his sexual lust. He rides his horse upon the coolies in his habitual fits of anger, wounding many in the process. They are badly beaten by the warders at his order. The coolies do not know what to do against this injustice. The sympathetic doctor advises them to go to the manager in a body and seek justice, assuring them that he himself would plead their case there.

The manager, Croft Cooke, is quite unsympathetic when the coolies meet him at his bungalow. What is worse is that the assistant manager with some armed warders comes upon them and the aggrieved coolies are chased away. Gangu with 'the bitterness, the folly and the pain of it all'[69] is together with Narain, his neighbour, whom all the coolies regard as their own brother. He finds all other coolies grumbling over the day's happenings. With his long experience as coolie in tea estate Naraian stoically explains to them:

> *You don't know the ways of the white folk, brother. A coolie of your age, a boy named Sridhar Tilang, was sent to prison because he wanted to go the Cinnamara Tea Gardens in search of work, as he heard that there were many other coolies from his district in that garden.*[64]

Anand through Narain in this novel narrates how the Trade Union Congress Movement spread in the tea gardens of Assam, and how the aggrieved coolies are to suffer so badly at the hands of powerful white men and their government. To quote from the text:

> *The Sahibs can do anything, brother. When they want you, they can force you to remain, when they don't want you, they can compel you to leave...*[65]

In *Two Leaves and a Bud,* we have a glimpse of the bitter relationship that existed between the Britishers and the Indians. The procession of aggrieved coolie to the manager to seek justice is smelt by the Britishers as the bugbear of a mutiny, of the nature of that of 1857. The Army and the Air force are telegraphically informed to be alert to safeguard the Britishers who gather together (except Doctor de la Haver) at Croft Cooke's, the manager's bungalow. The aeroplanes of the Royal Air Force are flying round and round in a bid to save white men in the terror of imagination. The helpless are also terrified beyond measure. Women and children are screaming. The terrified coolies approach the doctor who pleads their case sympathically to the manager. This results in the discharge of the doctor, and the coolies are fined Rs. 50/- each to be deducted from their salary. The novel ends with Reggie Hunt's, assistant manager's attempt of rape at Gangu's daughter, Leela, the failure of which leads him to shoot Gangu. In the trial Hunt is ultimately acquitted, as he is not found guilty by the white judge.

Two Leaves and a Bud is a typical novel of Mulk Raj Anand. Here we have a powerful picture of the exploitation of the poor and the wretched working class by the rich and wealthy bourgeois class. It is different from *Coolie* in the sense that in the latter the exploiting class consisted of both the Indians and Britishers, whereas in this novel the bourgeois class consists mainly of the Britishers. G.P. Sharma observes:

> *...this novel thus can be read as a story of oppression and exploitation of Indians by the British, too. Indeed, in Narain's story of the sufferings of the coolies after the war at the hands of tea planters is backed by the government.*[66]

Nationalism and Gandhism : Co-relative to each other

The novel here assumes a nationalistic colour. Nationalism and Gandhism are co-relative to each other. Here lies the justification of studying this novel under the head of Gandhian novels. To quote G.P Sharma once again:

> *The coolies in Narain's narrative, in their movement to go back home or get better facilities, are backed by the Congress Trade Union leaders while the British tea planters are backed by the British Government.*[67]

Here it deserves to be mentioned that during the British period while all other novels of Anand were banned in India only, *Two Leaves and a Bud* was banned in both India and England.

However, the real theme of the novel is not of the sufferings of the Indians at the hands of British but the oppression and exploitation of the coolies at the hands of the tea-planters — of the working class at the hands of the employers, be they Indians or British or of any other nationality. This idea has been suggested throughout the novel by implications. The European doctor, de la Haver, for this reason, has been shown as a declassed bourgeois and a great sympathiser with the cause of welfare of suffering coolies. Let us see what the author writes about him:

The doctor had resisted Anglo-Indian's belief in British greatness ever since his arrival in this country. At first, perhaps it had been from an instinct to be different from everyone else, an individual. Then he had given up the Imperial Medical Service, because the sentimental romantic in him wanted to make a brave gesture to convince himself that he had really come to regard Indians as human beings and to believe that they had a right not only to rule themselves, but to rule themselves justly by destroying the inequalities of caste, class and creed.[68]

British doctor : Prototype of Gandhi

In the person of the British doctor, de la Haver, the very image of Mahatma Gandhi can be traced who fought for the cause of the sufferers throughout his life. Doctor Haver urges the manager to provide decontaminated water to the coolies in place of the dirty, unhygienic water of the wells. To quote his words from the novel:

I know that thousands of those coolies may be swept off by the parasites in those wells. And I feel conscience-stricken. It would be criminal not to do anything about it since I know the water supply is infected. And considering the company earns millions of pounds every year on their labour, it wouldn't be such a terrible loss for it to spend a lakh to save the coolies from perishing through gnats and pests.[69]

Like Mahatma Gandhi, Doctor Haver has observed the sufferings of the 'swarming under-nourished, bleary, worm-eaten millions of India'.[70] Let us see his concern for the sufferers in one of his many private notes that he has written:

The black coolies clear the forests, plants the fields, toil and garner the harvest, while all the money-grubbing, slave-driving soulless managers and directors draw their salaries and dividends and build up monopolies. Therein lies the necessity of revolution in this country. On the one hand, the vast masses, prisoners of so many chains, bearing the physical signs of grief, of lassitude, even of death, and on the other hand the supercilious rich, wrapped up in their self-assurance and complacency, never once questioning the ideals of glory and power and wealth.[71]

Two Leaves and a Bud, in its artistic aspect, is however, inferior to *Coolie* and *Untouchable.* Gangu could not attained the depth of the agony of Munoo, the coolie or Bakha, the untouchable in his sufferings. Naturally the pathos that lies in the theme of *Untouchable* and *Coolie* is missing here. The personality of Gangu has not been as distinct as that of Bakha or Munoo. Even the sufferings of coolies in general in the tea estates are reported in the novel through the narrative of Narain, though in reality it is the theme of the novel. G.P. Sharma observes:

It is a tragic story of the ruin of a family under the exploitation of the landlords and money- lenders let loose by the British government.[72]

Lalu, the young man, with all his progressive ideas and impatience to do something, has become a helpless spectator as his family is shattered with the hanging of his brother because of the landlord's conspiracy and the death of his father in futile complaints and protests against the agents of British Raj. To quote from the text:

They are heretics, those who side with the angrezi sarkar. They are traitors who sold the Sikh raj. And they will come to bad end if they learn to participate in the machinations of the devil as those ferungis have learnt to precipitate them...[73]

The System responsible for the woes

The author, however, shows that it is not just the British rule which is responsible for the sufferings of the people in India. It is their system of administration that favours the rich in their exploitation of the people which is really responsible for the woes of the people in the country. It is for this that the exploiters here are not just the British. They are rather Indians favoured and corrupted by the British system of administration. Harbans Singh, the landlord, thus is a British creation; Chamanlal the money-lender thrives under the British set-up. Mr. Long, Deputy Commissioner, a Britisher, on the other hand, is the only man in the novel who has realised the situation clearly. The author says about him:

He was said to be strong in justice and friend of the poor. Under the name of Aflatun, he wrote interminable treatises full of wise sayings for edification of the illiterate villagers! And he even flouted the orders of the sarkar in his effort to ameliorate the rot of the peasantry."[4]

The British government, naturally, is not pleased with him and thinks his ideas dangerous. Mr. Long has chalked out a programme to help the farmers of the country. However, his programme cannot be implemented under the prevailing rules and regulations of the government. It merely remains a paper policy. To quote from the text:

He thought it iniquitous that the peasants should be fleeced annually of one-third of their produce but knowing that there was no solution of the difficulty, as the sarkar depended on the landed revenue to maintain a large army, he devised odd schemes to rid the peasantry of their misery, in order to quiet the unrest in his own conscience without conflicting too violently with works of the sarkar.[75]

Embodiment of Gandhian Humanism

Mr. Long has sympathy for the lower class. A parallel line may be drawn between Mr. Long in *The Village* and Dr de la Havre in *Two leaves and a Bud.* Both the characters are akin to each other. Irrespective of caste, colour and creed they embody the Gandhian humanism in best possible way. The character of Mr. Long, together with the characters of landlord and the money- lender, proves that the novel is a protest against the British system of administration only, and not against the British rule. Here lies the justification of studying this novel under the head of Gandhian literature, as Mahatma Gandhi though fought against the Britishers throughout his life, he never hated them.

Thus we have had a study of Mulk Raj Anand's pre-independence novels. To have a comprehensive study on Gandhian impact on Anand's novels it is relevant to have a global view of his post-Independence novels.

Nostalgia in the post-Independence Novels

In the post-Independence novels of Mulk Raj Anand, too, we have a reflection of the period of the freedom struggle with a sense of nostalgia or in a mood of reminiscence. The trilogy, *Seven Summers* (1951), *Morning Face* and *Confession of a Lover* (1976) deserve to be mentioned. As G. P. Sharma observes:

These novels, written in the reminiscent mood of a grown-up man after independence, form the first three volumes of a seven-volume story of man whom the author calls 'Seven Ages of Man'. Here we have the depiction of the development of the mind of an Indian set against the background of India and Europe in the beginning of the century.[76]

In *Seven Summers* we have a child as the central figure who is little aware of all the national or social developments around him. The author mirrors the ideology and activity of *Arya Samaj,* a nationalist organisation. Throughout the novel we have the sketches of national movement lying here and there.

Gandhian Ideas seen through Adolescent Eyes

Morning Face can better be described as the second volume of the series where we see the development of the same hero now in his late childhood and adolescence in the freedom struggle of the country. We see the boy developing his fancy gradually for Gandhi who has just appeared on the national scene to be soon accepted universally as the national leader. The boy-hero is very much impressed with Gandhi when he reads his unique ideals in his book, *Hind Swaraj.* He gets intoxicated with Gandhian ideas. There is a conflict in his mind as to whether he should follow the nationalists to be true to own conscience or to keep away from them and please his father who serves in British Army. The period referred to in the novel is around the First World War. The novel is full of the sketches of freedom movement, Jallianwalla Bagh massacre, when Lala Lajpat Rai became the *doyen* of all freedom loving Indians, and the controversy regarding Montague's Home Rule Act had stormed the country, while C. F. Andrews himself endeared to the Indian nation by his sympathy for the cause of freedom though he himself belonged to the imperialist race. All these reflections of national events in the novel are, however sketchy, seen through the eyes of the adolescent hero. Naturally it is not apt to expect the whole phase of movement here with all its intensity and implication.

In *Confession of a Lover*, the third volume in the series, Anand traces the further development of the national movement of the country with the growth of the same hero who has grown into a young man now. With the story of the young man's emotional life in his relationship with the family and the woman whom he loves passionately the author presents here the roles of Gandhi and Annie Beseant in the freedom movement of this period. Here we have once again the conflict that goes on in the mind of the young man, the hero. Even being impressed with Mahatma Gandhi, the young man cherishes a desire to be like an Englishman. To achieve this aim he prepares for a voyage to Europe. G.P. Sharma writes:

> *This ambivalence in the mind of the hero is significant from the point of view of Indian nationalism. We see the mind of the Indian nation which while accepting Gandhi as its father had also accepted Nehru as his successor and their adored leader–something of wide implication reflected in Bhabani Bhattacharya's Shadow from Laddakh.*[7]

The Sketches of the political crisis

The Private Life of an Indian Prince (1953) is another post-independence novel of Mulk Raj Anand. The author here gives the sketches of political crisis that came with the merger of the Princely states. Here we have the reference of that phase of Indian history when the princes in the native states in free India continued to behave as they did during the British rule in all their absurdities and extravaganza of medieval courts. They failed to understand the new reality and cope with it. The novel reflects an Indian state with its proverbially extravagant, debauched and voluptuous Prince. Anand with his proletarian ideals shows his impatience with such a life and makes the Prince an object of hatred and a butt of ridicule. Indifferent to his own wife and children, he is passionately involved with his concubine, Ganga Dasi. At the end of the novel the Prince, who has become insane, is compelled to sign the instrument of Accession by the Praja Mandal, a nationalist political organisation. In the novel, Anand has looked at the national problem of Gandhian era from the people's point of view, which was identical to the government's stand. The character of the very Prince has been portrayed as an antagonist of Mahatma Gandhi who was an embodiment of austerity and saintliness.

The Old Woman and the Cow (1960) and *The Road* (1961) are two post-independence social novels of Mulk Raj Anand. *The Old Woman and the Cow*, recently published under the title '*Gauri*', is a story which reveals the sorrows and sufferings of many an Indian woman in the villages. It also shows the new consciousness of these women about their own status in the society. Gauri, the main character, quiet and gentle like a traditional Indian woman, tolerates all sufferings not only at the hands of her husband and in-laws but at her own mother's hands also. She, however, meets an enlightened city physician, becomes conscious of her own status in the society. She asserts her identity refusing to be oppressed any more. The novelist, through Gauri's character, shows the significant change in woman's awareness in the Indian society, which was the main spirit of the Gandhian age.

Analytical survey of the short stories

After the critical appreciation of Anand's novels, it would be proper to have a brief analytical survey of his short stories as well. In contrast to his novels we do not find here the same concern for the poor and the wretched. In these stories we have the expressions of man's universal feeling of love irrespective of class or caste or nationality. *The Lost Child and Other Stories* (1934) is the first collection of his short stories. The author here gives an expression to the feelings of human heart and its indomitable spirit to know and to conquer. A *Lament on the Death of a Master of Arts (1939)* is a long story where we see the physical and the mental suffering of an Indian youth in the peculiar Indian situation where physical labour is regarded as indignified. Mahatma Gandhi always stressed on the dignity of manual labour. *The Barber's Trade Union and Other Stories (1944)* is the next volume of short stories. Here the three prose poems of the first volume are reprinted. Here we have three trends of Anand as a short-story writer, revealed, expression of universal feelings of human heart, expression of sympathy for the lowly class, and expression of the sufferings of Indians during the freedom struggle. In *The Tractor and the Corn Goddess (1947),* most of the stories depict universal human feeling. *Birth, The Prodigal Son* and the title-story, *Tractor and the Corn Goddess,* are the three stories which reveal Anand's typical concern with the lower rungs of the society. Mahatma Gandhi was deeply concerned with these lowly people, *the dalits,* whom he lovingly called *the harijans.*

Gandhi's Image with an Artistic Detachment

To sum up, we would do well to quote C.L. Sahani:

Despite Mulk Raj Anand's pronounced Marxist bias, his fictional treatment of Gandhi and Gandhian ideology shows considerable artistic detachment. Though he challenges some of Gandhi's ideas and attitudes, he has never questioned their underlying sincerity and humanism. The images of Gandhi projected in his novels are, therefore, authentic, objective, and free from emotional adoration for the Mahatma.[78]

References

1. Sharma, G.P. *Nationalism in Indo-Anglian Fiction*, p. 102.
2. *Ibid.* p. 103.
3. '*Beyond the Village*', in Critical Writing in English. Ed. M.K. Naik, S.K. Desai, G.S. Amur. Dharwar: Karnataka University, 1968. p. 192.

4. *Nationalism in Indo-Anglian Fiction.* p. 103.
5. Anand, M.R. *Aplogy for Heroism.* New Delhi: Orient Paperbacks Pvt. Ltd. p. 17.
6. *Ibid* p. 129.
7. *Ibid* p. 81.
8. *Young India,* May 25th, 1921.
9. *Ibid* April 1925.
10. *Nationalism in Indo-Anglian Fiction.,* p. 104
11. Anand, Mulk Raj. *Untouchable.* New Delhi: Orient Paperbacks Pvt. Ltd.
12. *The Swan and the Eagle.* Shimla: Indian Institute of Advanced Study, 1969. pp. 39-41.
13. *Ibid.* p. 111.
14. *Untouchable.* p. 63.
15. *Ibid.* p. 100.
16. *Ibid.* p. 1.
17. *Ibid.*
18. *Ibid.* p. 13.
19. *Ibid.* p. 27.
20. *Ibid.* p. 63.
21. *Ibid.* p. 114.
22. *Ibid.* p. 115.
23. *Ibid.*
24. *Ibid.* p. 116.
25. *Ibid.* p. 117.
26. *Ibid.* p. 116.
27. *Ibid.* p. 116
28. *Ibid.* p. 157
29. *Ibid.* p. 152.
30. *Ibid.* p. 122.
31. *Ibid.*
32. *Ibid.* p. 123.
33. *Ibid.* p. 124.
34. *Ibid.* p. 123.
35. *Ibid.* p. 126.
36. *Ibid.* p. 149.
37. *Ibid.* Preface. p. i.
38. Forster, E.M.
39. *Nationalism in Indo-Anglian Fiction.* p. 205.

40. Balarama Gupta, G.S. Prakash Book Depot, 1974. p. 36.

41. *Nationalism in Indo-Anglian Fiction*. pp. 206-07.

42. *Ibid.*

43. Anand, M.R. *The Sword and the Sickle*. New Delhi: Orient Paperbacks Pvt. Ltd. p. 201.

44. *Ibid*. p. 49.

45. *Ibid*. p. 338.

46. *Nationalism in Indo-Anglian Fiction*. p. 208.

47. Narasimhaiah, C.D. Ed. '*National Indentity in Literature and Language*'. K.L. Godwin. London: Heinemann Educational Books, 1970. p. 156.

48. Anand, M.R. *The Big Heart*. New Delhi: Orient Paperbacks Pvt. Ltd. p. 204.

49. *Untouchable*. 167.

50. *The Big Heart*. 148.

51. *Ibid*. p. 195.

52. *Ibid*.

53. *Ibid*.

54. *Ibid*. p. 202.

55. *Ibid*. p. 204.

56. *Ibid*. p. 143.

57. *Ibid*.

58. *Nationalism in Indo-Anglian Fiction*. p. 124.

59. Anand, M.R. *Coolie*. New Delhi: Orient Paperbacks Pvt. Ltd. p. 224.

60. *Ibid*. p. 225.

61. *Ibid*. p. 224.

62. *Ibid*.

63. *Nationalism in Indo-Anglian Fiction*. p. 111.

64. *Ibid*.

65. Anand, M.R. *Two Leaves and a Bud*. Orient Paperbacks Pvt Ltd, New Delhi. p. 192.

66. *Ibid*. p. 210.

67. *Ibid*. p. 211.

68. *Nationalism in Indo-Anglian Fiction*. p. 114.

69. *Ibid*. p. 30.

70. *Ibid*. pp. 30-31.

71. *Ibid*. p. 122.

72. *Ibid*. pp. 123-124.

73. *Ibid*. p. 117.

74. Anand, M.R. *The Village*, New Delhi: Orient Paperbacks Pvt. Ltd. p. 218.

75. *Ibid.*
76. *Nationalism in Indo-Anglian Fiction.* p. 238.
77. *Ibid.* p. 240.
78. Sahani, C.L. Ed. *Advanced Literary Essays.* p. 245.

5

Raja Rao's *Kanthapura* and the Mahatma

The Most Elaborate Treatment of Gandhian Philosophy

Of all Indo-Anglian novels of the pre- independence era it is Raja Rao's *Kanthapura* wherein we have the most elaborate treatment of the Gandhian philosophy. The novel seems to have captured the true spirit of the age. It is saturated with Gandhian references, thought and imagery; and its theme is closely linked with Gandhi's life and philosophy. Gandhi is here eulogised, romanticised and mythologised. In the collective unconscious of the village of Kanthapura, the myth, the legend, the religion, the poetry and the politics – all get mixed up, and the village of Kanthapura becomes the throbbing heart of India, responding to the call of the Mahatma. Although the action of the novel encompasses, directly or indirectly, all the major political and social activitics associated with Gandhi during the thirties such as Gandhi's *Dandi March*, the *Civil Disobedience* Movement, *Satyagraha*, *Harijan* Uplift, *Swadeshi Swaraj*, propaganda against drinking, fasting, spinning wheel and police atrocities on the *Satyagrahis*, Gandhi-Irwin Pact, the Second Round-Table Conference, etc., the major focus of the novel is on the electrifying zeal with which the village of Kanthapura rises to the call of the Indian nationalist movement led by Gandhi.

Kanthapura (1938) is the first novel of the author. Like Anand's *Untouchable,* it stands at a peculiarly advanced position. In contrast to *Untouchable,* which is written in stream-of-consciousness technique,

Kanthpura is written as a dramatic monologue. Its prose in most places verges on poetry. Here we have an old grandmother, who narrates her experiences of the freedom struggle of thirties as it took place in her villages. This is not in the form of a well-knit story. It is rather a string of memories wet with ardour and emotion.

Kanthapura: A Typical Indian Village

Kanthapura, situated in the Mysore state, is a typical Indian village having everything common to all men and women of the country, especially of the villages, during the freedom struggle led by Gandhi. The achievement of the author lies in the fact that he has related the general to the particular. Prior to 1939, no novel has expressed the various aspects of the freedom struggle so distinctly within its compass. Here we have the glimpses of all the major political activities of the Congress during the thirties, i.e., the *Dandi March* of Gandhi and his followers in 1930 to inaugurate the Civil Disobedience Movement (pp. 170-173), the response of the villagers to the Movement by way of launching *Satyagraha* (pp. 182-201), observing non-cooperation by not paying taxes and showing disloyalty to the Government (pp. 206-209), the formation of the Congress Committee in the far-flung villages and their constructive programmes (pp. 100-111), Jawaharlal Nehru's social programmes (pp. 256-257), the decision of Gandhi to attend the second Round Table Conference (pp. 255-257), and above all, Gandhi's all-pervading influence on the nation which runs through the entire story. And then we find here the various social programmes of the Congress during the period, viz. emphasis on the removal of untouchability (pp. 57-66), on spinning as a step towards self-dependence (pp. 8-33), propaganda and demonstrations against liquour consumption (pp. 182-200), and the like. While showing these, the *Satyagraha* of the Congress volunteers (pp. 182-200), fasts by Gandhi's followers (pp. 90-99), police atrocities on the Congress demonstrators (pp. 182-200, 224-253), are also very vividly drawn. To quote G.P. Sharma:

> *What makes this novel a distinctive success is that all these pictures have not remained mere pictures showing the freedom struggle in the surface alone, but they have all combined together to reveal the true spirit of the age of Gandhi–the spirit that strove to win freedom both politically in the common sense and morally in the Gandhian sense.*[1]

Kanthapura: The Very Spirit of the Age

Kanthapura reveals the very spirit of the age. A few aspects of the novel deserves to be analysed here. The very setting of the story in a village is, I think, the first aspect. C.D. Narasimhaiah observes in this context:

> *The setting of the story in the village which has given the author an opportunity to show the traditional Indian religious life which supports an elaborate social structure and preserves its organic character through the ages and serves as a sure foundation for the success of the national movement in Gandhi's hands and, therefore, in the hands of his followers like young Moorthy of the novel.*[2]

Kanthapura is a village situated in the hilly region of Mysore towards the Malabar Coast. It is a village with "narrow, dusty, rut-covered roads" (p. 7). All the inhabitants of this village, whether *Brahmins* or *pariahs*, are steeped in the Hindu religious beliefs. The legendary figures like *Rama*, *Krishna*, *Siva* and other Hindu deities are living realities to them. To quote from the text:

> *There is no village in India, however mean, that has not a rich sthala-purana, or a legendary history, of its own. Some god or godlike hero has passed by the village – Rama might have rested under this pipal- tree, Sita might have dried her clothes, after her bath, on this yellow tree, or the Mahatma himself, on one of his many pilgrimages through the country, might have slept in this hut, the low one by the village gate.*[3]

They celebrate different religious festivals in the temple. At this occasion religious scriptures are read out, explained and heard with reverence. With traditional religious functions there goes *Gandhi-bhajans*, talks on *swaraj*, Hindu-Muslim unity and *khaddar*. The villagers of Kanthapura, who were aware of their religion and rituals, and their paddy-fields, come to know about Gandhi. Gandhi, to them is not merely a political leader standing against the foreign rule, but an incarnation of *Lord Krishna* or *Rama*. To quote the village bard at the *Harikatha* in the temple:

> *You remember how Krishna, when he was but an age of four, had begun to fight against demons and had killed the serpent Kali. So, too, our Mohandas began to fight against the enemies of our country. And as he grew up and after he was duly shaven for the hair ceremony, he began to go out into the villages and assemble people and talk to them, and his voice was so pure, his forehead so brilliant with wisdom, that*

men followed him, more and more men followed him as they did Krishna, the flute-player.[4]

The Grandmother, who is the narrator of the story, sees in him the image of *Lord Rama.* To quote her words:

> *They say the Mahatma will go to the redman's country and he will get us Swaraj. He will bring us swaraj, the Mahatma. And we shall all be happy. And Rama will come back from exile, and Sita will be with him, for Ravana will be slain and Sita freed.*[5]

Gandhi: The Rama, the Krishna

To the people of Kanthapura, Gandhi is the Krishna, the demon- killer, or Rama, the slayer of *Ravana.* What a great race the people of Kanthapura are who see their cultural tradition entangled everywhere in the freedom movement of the country ! The men and women fight the battle with utmost sincerity and dedication facing lathi-charge and gun-fire courting arrest and imprisonment crying the slogans, 'Mahatma Gandhi Ki Jai' and 'Vande–Matarm'.[6]

Moorthy: The Embodiment of Gandhian Virtues

Moorthy, a youngman of noble character embodies Gandhian virtues in the village. He is a saint among men, a varitable Gandhi. About him the people of Kanthapura say:

> *He is our Gandhi. The state of Mysore has a Maharaja, but that Maharaja has another in Heaven, and so everybody has his own Mahatma, and this Moorthy who has been caught in our eyes playing as a child, is now grown up and great, and he has his wisdom in him and he will be our Mahatma.*[7]

Moorthy has won love and affection for his honesty, nobility and sincerity. In the eyes of the villagers, *he is* 'as honest as an elephant'[8] 'who was a nice brahminic boy'[9], who had 'neither smoked nor grew city-hair, nor put on suits and hats and boots'[10] 'a deep voiced god-loving person.'[11] like other villagers he is religious by nature. He has setup a temple in the village with the cooperation of all. *Sankara - Jaynathi* and *Harikatha* are regularly held here. With these cultural functions the *Gandhi-bhajans* and *Gandhi-katha,* the politically biased religious functions are interspersed. He leads Gandhian way of life, visits house to house including *the sudra* and *the pariah* families and advises the people to throw of the caste rules. Being humble he has won the heart of all. A few self-centred people, pretending to be the saviours of Hinduism stand against the Gandhian ideal of society excommunicate Moorthy but in his mission he is firm like Himalaya.

Moorthy is always in touch with the Congress Committee of the nearest town and organises the villagers according to the Congress principles — distributing *Charkha* and cotton freely and exhorting them to wear only home-spun *khaddar*. One of the villagers says:

> *Millions and millions of yards of foreign cloth come to this country, and everything foreign makes us poor and pollutes us. To wear cloth spun and woven with your god-given hands is sacred, says the Mahatma. And it gives work to the workless, and work to the lazy... Our country is being bled to death by foreigners. We have to protect our Mother.*[12]

In the village a Congress Committee is formed and is affiliated to the Provincial Congress Committee. Moorthy works whole-heartedly for the organisation. He is arrested and given three years rigorous imprisonment. When the trial starts the advocates and the barristers come forward to plead his case; the students form Defence Committee and raise fund for their beloved leader and the merchants strive to secure his release. But Moorthy, in all humility, declines their help. To quote his words:

> *" I shall speak that which Truth prompteth , and Truth needeth no defence.*[13]
> *".... If Truth needeth a defence God Himself would need one, for as the Mahatma says, Truth is God."*[14]

Ultimately Moorthy is released. By then Civil Disobedience Movement of Gandhi has started with *Dandi march*. Hearing this the people of Kanthapura get exalted with nationalistic spirit and want Moorthy, their leader to lead them in the movement. To quote one of the villagers:

> *I do not imagine the Mahatma like a man or God, but like the Sahyadri Mountains, blue, high, wide, and the rock of the evening that catches the light of the setting sun. That's what he is. High and yet seeable, firm and yet blue with dust, and as the pilgrims march up the winding path, march through prickles and boulders, thickets and streams, so shall we march up to the top.*[15]

In the village *Satyagraha* is offered by launching a campaign of procession to the toddy-grove. The innocent processionists including Moorthy, the leader become the victim of police atrocity. They are again beatten when in another campaign a procession is led out to the toddy-booth at the coffee-state. The villagers as a part of Civil Disobedience Movement that they call 'don't-touch-the–government' resort to non-payment of revenue to the government. Now the story takes an unexpected turn. Moorthy disappears from the stage. No one knows what has happened to him or where he has gone.

The character of Moorthy can be studied in comparison with Kandan of Venkatramani. Both the authors have created an idealised character in the image of Mahatma Gandhi. G.P. Sharma observes:

> *Moorthy and Kandan play the part of Gandhi in their villages and stand amongst the villagers as pillars of Gandhian ideals, firm and yet humble. But Raja Rao's Moorthy is more distinct, more real and more of an active leader with a definite programme of the movement before him.*[16]

The depiction of the national movement itself of a particular period is the next aspect of the novel that contributes to its success as a great political novel. This depiction is so real, vivid and masterly that it is apt to call the novel a small mirror of our age. Moorthy is inspired with the Gandhian ideal. He propagates the ideas of social reform and in this way becomes a means to spread the Gandhian values and reconstruction of national economy.

Like the peasants of the village the coolies of the nearby Skeffington Coffee Estate have come under the spell of Gandhi. When they came to know that the police will be deployed by the Estate authority, they have the only hope from Gandhi. To quote one of the coolies, "What is a policeman before a Gandhi's man there?"[17] Almost with religious ardour they eagerly wait for Moorthy. Moorthy comes but is not allowed by the police to speak. It leads to disastrous results. Moorthy, being composed, faces the police calmly, but the coolies become uncontrolled and there is police-coolie encounter. Many people get injured. Consequently Moorthy goes on a three-day fast. Obviously this is a replica of Gandhi's self-purificatory fast of 1933 against the violence at Chauri-Chaura. The words that Moorthy spoke are the words spoken by Gandhiji. Moorthy says that this violence is caused because of him. To quote his words:

> *... were he full of radiance of ahimsa such things should never have happened.*[18]

Like a true Gandhian disciple he explains to his people during his fast:

> *If only we could not hate, if only we would be so fearless, calm, affectionate towards our fellow men, we would be stronger, and not only would the enemy yield, but he would be converted.*[19]

Gandhi launches Civil Disobedience Movement and when he marches to *Dandi*, Moorthy is to keep the villagers aware with the latest happenings. The author writes:

... the pilgrim path of Mahatma from day to day; for day after day the Congress Committee sent him information.[20]

The Nationalistic Fervour at its Height

The nationalistic ferver in the whole village is at the highest at this occasion. The people of Kanthapura are sleepless at the night before the day when the Mahatma is to make salt. They do this in the eager wait for his success. All the people of Kanthapura including men, women, boys and girls find themselves in the river to have a dip as the token of their co-operation with the Mahatma crying the slogans: *Mahatma Gandhi Ki Jai* and *Vande- Mataram*. The next morning, the good news of Gandhi's success reaches the village as to how he had taken a hand full of salt after his ablutions and brought it home. To quote the text : "everybody went to the sea to prepare salt, and cart loads and cartloads of it began to be brought back and distributed from house to house with music and clapping of hands."[21]

Now the sad news has reached in the village that the Mahatma has been arrested. The people are stunned. They observe fast. The meetings are held and the *Gandhi-bhajans* organised. The whole village is ready for 'Don't-touch-the-Government' campaign. The campaign is launched and Moorthy exhorts the people. To quote from his speech:

... remember each one of you is responsible for the harm done by another, and the first time violence is done against the police or those that are not with us, we shall stop the movement and wait for six months and more in penance and in prayer that our sins may be purified. Brothers and sisters, remember we are not out to fight the white man or the white man's slaves, the police or the Revenue officials, but against the demonic corruption that has entered their hearts, and the purer we are, the greater will be our victory, for the victory we seek is the victory of the heart.[22]

The Country Charged with the Sprit of Satyagraha

And now not only Kantapura but the whole country is charged with the spirit of *satyagraha* and Civil Disobedience:

It is the same from Kailas to Kanyakumari and from Karachi to Kachar, and shops are closed and bonfires lit, and khadi is the only thing that is sold, while processions and songs and flag salutation go through the streets, picketings and prabhat pherries, and the police will beat and soldiers open fire, and the millions and millions of our brothers and sisters be thrown into prison.[23]

Kanthapura is an epoch-making work in the annals of literature. The impact of Mahatma Gandhi and his ideas on an obscure Indian village as a theme assign it this loftiest place. It is remarkable in many ways. Kanthapura, the village, is a type. It represents the seven lakh villages in India. Indian grandmothers are gifted story-tellers because storytelling is the second nature of their person. This is why the author has chosen a grandmother as a narrator of his story. Our village brothers in India are inveterate myth-makers. The heroes and the heroines of our epics are jostled with the historic personalities, the glorious past and the sordid present are blended together to be projected into a golden future. The political revolution of our freedom is beautifully transcended and assimilated into the racial heritage as myth and legend. Dr K.R.S. Iyenger writes:

> *Gandhi Mahatma is Rama; the red-foreigner or the brown inspector of police who flourishes a lathi is but a soldier in ten-headed Ravana's army of occupation and oppression. Nay more; the Satyagrahi in prison is the divine Krishna himself in Kamsa's prison! Events gather significance after the passage of some years, the humdrum becomes the unique, the trivial becomes the heroic, and the hectic excitement of a day becomes a permanent communal possession.*[24]

The Unexcelled Stylistic Beauty

The stylistic beauty of Raja Rao in *Kanthapura* deserves the appreciation of the critics. This style is unconventional. The author here has attempted to adapt the idiom, the rhythm, the total distinctness of his mothertongue *kannada* into English. Dr K.R.S. Iyengar observes:

> *This is not "babu"-English, this is not English of the sophisticated Indians who meet in an exclusive club in Bombay, Calcutta or New Delhi. This is simply the natural speech of rural folk transmuted into English.*[25]

Reading Raja Rao is to see a familiar landscape through the coloured glasses. To some extent this coloring is unavoidable, but it hardly alters the essential truth of the picture drawn. Raja Rao himself explains this in the very Foreword to *Kanthapura*:

> *One has to convey in a language that is not one's own the spirit that is one's own. One has to convey the various shades and omissions of a certain thought-movement that looks maltreated in an alien language. I use the word 'alien', yet English is not really an alien*

> *language to us. It is language of our intellectual make-up—like Sanskrit or Persian was before - but not of our emotional make-up. We are all instinctively bilingual, many of us writing in our own language and in English. We cannot write like the English. We should not. We cannot write only as Indians. We have grown to look at the large world as part of us ... After language, the next problem is that of style . The tempo of Indian life must be infused into our English expression even as the tempo of America or Irish Life has gone into the making of theirs. We, in India, think quickly, we talk quickly, and when we move we move quickly... we tell one interminable tale ...* [26]

The stylistic beauty of *Kanthapura* has made it a *Gandhi Purana* more than a mere fiction. Dr K.R.S. Iyengar observes:

> *Gandhi is the invisible God, Moorthy is the visible avatar. The reign of the red-men is Asuric rule, and it is resisted by the Devas, the Satyagrahis. The characters sharply divide into two camps: the Rulers (and their supporters) on the one hand and the Satyagrahis (and their sympathisers) on the other. There are various other divisions too: orthodoxy is pitted against reform, exploitation against sufferance, the planter against the coolies, the corrupt official against the self-respecting villager. But these lines grow hazy when the main issue between the Bureaucracy and the the Satyagrahis is joined, for now most people are on one or the other side of the barricades.* [27]

Gandhi launches *Dandi March* with his select band of followers. The whole nation is engaged in the passive resistance of the gorventment. The salt is manufactured in open defiance, the forest laws are broken and toddey shops are picketed. And what happens in the whole nation happens in Kanthapura, too. By no means is it exception. To quote Dr Iyengar:

> *... the telling of the story gives the whole affair of an ithihasic - at least a puranic–dignity. The narrative is hardly very straightforward.* [28]

Here we have involution and digressions, the meaningful backward glances, hypnotic repetitions and refrains. A rhythmic chain of proper names draws our attention: "Rachanna and Chandranna and Madanna; Sampanna and Vaidyanna; Satamma and Rangamma and Puttamma and Seethamma."[29]

Waterfall Venkamma, Nose-scratching Nanjamma, Kanthapura, is a village, a picturesque region, an epoch of social and political change, the region and superstition, idealism and cold, calculation-all spring up before our eyes. Let's see how the people wear tell-tale nick-names:

Front-house Akkamma; Temple Rangappa, Coffee-planter Ramayya, Patwari Nanjundia, Gold-bangle Somanna, Cardamom-field Ramachandra; and there is, of course, Corner-house Moorthy who goes through life as a noble cow, quiet, generous, serene, deferent and brahmanic, a very prince.[30]

The author has put the story on the lips of a 'grandmother.' In the words of Dr Iyengar:

... although the feminine touches and mannerisms, the seemingly effortless rotation of the tongue, the meandering sentences and massive paragraphs are characteristic of the narrator, - there is nevertheless consummate 'art' in all this riot of artlessness, there is careful 'selection' behind the apparent abundance of detail, and there is an adroit polarisation in the plotless grandmother's tale.[31]

Symbolism in the Novel

Symbolism is one of the most beautiful *alankaras,* i.e. ornament in the casket of literature. It adds a grace in the thematic and stylistic pattern of the language. *Kanthapura,* from beginning to end is equipped with symbolism. The village, Kanthapura is a symbol in itself. Moorthy, in the village, is the symbol of Gandhian virtues. Bade Khan, the policeman, is the symbol of oppression and soulless bureaucracy. But the villagers hardly care of him. To quote the text:

What is a policeman before a Gandhi's man? Tell me, does a boar stand before a lion or a jackal before an elephant?[32]

Bhatt symbolises usury, and false orthodoxy and cunningness. Ranage Gowda symbolises sense and stolidity. The river *Himavathy*, the Goddess *Kenchamma,* all are symbols. She is protectress of the people, the guardian of the village. Kanthapura is the symbol of the typical Indian village. The Skeffington Coffee Estate symbolises the impact of industrialisation on the traditional life at Kanthapura. Mahatma Gandhi himself, in the eyes of the villagers is a legendary figure. He has become the subject of *bhajans* and *harikathas.* The splendid mythology and contemporary politics are beautifully blended together.

Siva is the three-eyed, and Swaraj too is three- eyed: Self-purification, Hindu- Muslim unity, Khaddar.[33]

Dr K.R.S. Iyengar on this aspect observes thus:

Gandhi is Siva himself in human shape: he is engaged in slaying the serpent of foreign rule, as the boy Krishna killed the serpent Kaliya.

> *Bhajans and Harikathas mix religion and politics freely and often purposefully, the reading of a newspaper becomes as serious a discipline as the reverent reading of the Gita, and hand- spinning is elevated into a daily ritual like puja. The walls of orthodoxy are suddenly breached: revolution comes as a flood, and carries all before it.*[34]

Character Sketch in Kanthapura

Moorthy is undoubtedly the pivotal character of the novel. In addition to him, we have Rangamma, Range Gowda and Ratana whose characters are moulded on Gandhian ideas. They have spread Gandhian revolution upto the person who stands at the very margin of the society. The movement has become a mass movement due to them. No villager of any caste, creed and profession, either farmer or labourer is untouched with the same. In this movement the *Satyagrahis* are maimed and broken and scattered, and they get settled at *Kashipura,* another village beyond the border. Moorthy, Rangamma, Ratana and some other *Satyagrahis* spend their span in the jail. Gandhi- Irwin Pact hastens their release. Moorthy doubts the wisdom of this truce. However, he is confident that Gandhi can do no wrong. This is why he accepts the truce and patiently awaits the further developments. The position of the old woman is not different. There is neither regrets not recriminations, in her heart. To quote her words:

> *No, sister, no, nothing can ever be the same again. You will say we have lost this, you will say we have lost that. Kenchamma forgive us, but there is something that has entered our hearts, an abundance like the Himavathy on Gauri's night, when lights come floating down from Rampur Corner, lights come floating down from Rampur and Maddur and Tippur, lights lit on the betel leaves, and with flower and kumkum and song we let them go, and they will go down the Ghats to the morning of the sea, the lights on betel leaves, and the Mahatma will gather it all, he will gather it by the sea, and he will bless us.*[35]

Pauranic Significance of Gandhian Movement

To attend the second Round Table Conference Gandhi leaves for England. Let us see how beautifully the author has invested *Puranic* significance of this episode of Gandhian movement:

They say the Mahatma will go to the Red-man's country, and he will get us Swaraj....And we shall all be happy. And Rama will come back from exile. And Sita will be with him, for Ravana will be slain and Sita freed, and he will come back with Sita on his right in a chariot of the air, and brother Bharata will go to meet them with the worshipped sandals of the Master on his head. And as they enter Ayodhya there will be a rain of flowers. Like Bharata we worship the sandals of the Brother saint....[36]

Rhythmic Narrative Technique

These are the most beautiful lines of the author. Here Raja Rao is at the climax of his craftsmanship. Here the poetry and the politics are united together. This unification is between the perennial and the present, between the culture and the nationalism that has made *Kanthapura* a distinctive work of literature. Let us see one more example where the parched plains have been flooded by poetry:

In Vaisakh men plough the fields of Kanthapura. The rains have come, the fine, first-footing rains that skip over the bronze mountains, tiptoe the crags, and leaping into the valleys, go splashing and wind-swung, a winnowed pour, and the coconuts and the betel-nuts and the cardamom plants choke with it and hiss back. And there, there it comes over the Bebbur Hill and the Kanthur Hill and begins to paw upon the tiles, and the cattle come running home... and people leave their querns and rush to the courtyard, and turning towards the Kenchamma Temple, send forth a prayer, saying, 'there, there, the rains have come, Kenchamma; may our houses be white as silver', and the lightning flashes and the thunder stirs the tiles, and children rush to the gutterslabs to sail paper boats down to Kashi....[37]

The novel has such rhythmic narrative prose in abundance. For instance, the brilliant description of the Kartik festival of lights:

Kartik has come to Kanthapura... with the glow of lights and the unpressed footsteps of the wandering gods; white lights from clay-trays and red lights from copper-stands, and diamond lights that glow from the bowers of entrance-leaves; lights that glow from banana-trunks and mango twigs, yellow lights behind white leaves, and green light behind yellow leaves, and white light behind green leaves: and night curls through the shadowed streets, and hissing over bellied boulders and hurrying through dallying drains, night curls through the Brahmin Street and the Pariah Street and the

> *Potters Street and the Weavers' Street and flapping through the mango grove, hangs clawed for one moment to the giant pipal, and then shooting across the broken fields, dies quietly into the river — and gods walk by lighted streets... Kartik is a month of the gods....*[38]

Words here are not mere words, they are more than that. Such impressive prose style has made *Kanthapura* a unique species of fiction. Dr K.R.S. Iyengar comments on the incantatory power of these words:

> *Than blocks of stone they are indeed streams of suggestion, dark rooms with central lights to brighten them, waves of sound making haunting music, and even nuclei charged with tremendous power.*[39]

Moorthy is released from the jail. The people of Kanthapura wait impatiently for him at the roadside. To quote from the text:

> *And hearts began to beat, and yet we saw no Moorthy, and yet no Moorthy, and yet no Moorthy, and yet not a hair of his head was seen, and we were silent asthough in the sanctum at the camphor ceremony. Yet no Moorthy, and no Moorthy, and the bus had surely passed by the river...*[40]

The Discourse on Science

Rangamma is a very eminent character in the novel, just next to Moorthy. The author puts this discourse on science on his lips. To quote:

> *... she knows so many, many things, too, of he plants that weep, of the monkeys that were the men we have become, of the worms, thin-as-bust worms that get into your blood and give you dysentry and plague and cholera. She told us, too, about the blue space long before you were born, long before you were born, or your father was born or your grandfather was born; and just as a day of Brahma is a million years of ours, the day of the stars is a million times our day, and each star has a sun and each sun has a moon, and each moon has an earth, and some there are that have two moons... and you put your eyes to a great tube and see another world with sun and moon and stars, all bright and floating in the diamond dust of god. And that gave us such a shiver, I tell you....*[41]

The soldiers and the coolies are asked to walk over the prostrate *Satyagrahis*. But they decline to do so and join them. To quote:

> *... and the Police, frightened, caned and caned the coolies till they pushed themselves over us; and they put their feet here and they put their hands there, but Rangamma shouted 'Vande Mataram! Lie down, brothers and sisters', and we all lay down so that not a palm-*

width of space lay bare, and the coolies would not move, and we held their hands and we held to their feet and we held to their saris and dhotis and all, while the rain poured on and on. And the police got nervous and they began to kick us in our backs and stomachs, and the crowd shouted 'Mahatma Gandhi Ki Jai!' and someone took a kerosene tin and began to beat it, and someone took a cattle-bell and began to ring it, and they cried, 'With them, brothers, with them!' and they leaped and they ducked and they came down to lie beside us, and we shouted 'Mahatma Gandhi ki jai! Mahatma Gandhi ki jai!.[42]

A Grammar of Gandhian Myth

Dr Iyengar sums up the significance of ***Kanthapura*** in Gandhian literature:

Kanthapura is a veritable Grammar of the Gandhian Myth - the myth that is but a poetic translation of the reality. It will always have a central place in Gandhian literature.[43]

In order to study *Kanthapura* as a Gandhian novel it is our imperative to mark how the author has shown the simple villagers of the country roused to a new national consciousness through the electrifying impact of Mahatma Gandhi.

*The Serpent and the Rope (*1960), *The Cat and* the *Shakespeare* (1965*)* and *Comrade Kirillov (1976*) are the post-independevce novels of Raja Rao. In all these novels we have an exposition of the traditional Indian views, values and attitude to life. These novels are at the climax so far as their artistic excellence is concerned.

The Post-Independence Novels

The Serpent and the Rope was published more than twenty years after *Kanthapura*. This novel is unconventional in its form and theme. This metaphysical novel is written in the stream-of-consciousness technique in a highly poetic style. The reviewers, Diana and Meir Gillon, write in *Sunday Times:*

... it was certainly an epic and could... have been a great novel. Even as it is, it remains a magnificent guide to India, and, for those who are prepared to work for their pleasure, a book to read and re-read.[44]

Another reviewer writes in the *Times*:

It is rather as if the wisdom of Sanskrit had been done into story-book form... The writing is utterly beautiful. No other word will do.[45]

The Ramayana and the Mahabharata

Kanthapura and *The Serpent and the Rope are* epics of our age. Dr K.R.S. Iyengar observes:

To compare the small with the great (in terms of quality, that is, not of quantity), if Kanthapura is Raja Rao's Ramayana, then The Serpent and the Rope is his Mahabharata. If Kanthapura has a recognisable epic–it is almost encyclopaedic in its scope.[46]

Ramaswamy is the central character in the novel. He is a research scholar in Albigensian Heresy in France. He marries a French woman, Madeline, who is a teacher of History. She has keen interest in Indian philosophical tradition. Ramaswamy and Madeline are impressed with each other. This marriage is really a spiritual one. They are blessed with a son whom they name Krishna, later Pierre. Rama visits India and its holy places. He has a profound love for Indian tradition. He loves everything that stands for ancient Indian spiritual tradition. Raja Rao gives a beautiful expression of his love for tradition as well as his poetic sensibility in an adequate poetic style. Ramaswamy pays a visit to Benares. We may see how his poetic sensibility is revitalised. To quote his words from the text:

Benares is eternal. There the dead do not the living live. The dead come to play on the banks of the Ganges, and the living who move about, and even offer rice balls to the manes, live in the illusion of a vast night and a bright city.[47]

To quote another illustration from the text:

Night, a rare and immediate night was covering the vast expanse of the Benares sky. Somewhere on the very banks, the Upanishad sages, perhaps four, five to six thousand years ago, had discussed the roots of human understanding. And Yagyavalka had said to Maitreyi, 'For whose sake verily, does a husband love his wife? Not for the sake of his wife, but verily for the sake of the self in her.[48]

Dr G.P. Sharma remarks:

With such a story, if this scanty device for bringing together the feelings and impressions, thoughts and ideas of a person can be called a story at all, the novel is a nostalgic evocation of all that is best in Indian tradition.[49]

C.D. Narasimhaiah in his illuminating interpretation of the book remarks very clearly:

... the entire novel is an evocation of this Truth, the tradition of India and its vitality especially in its encounters with the West – India seen as an idea, not as an area on the map.[50]

...what is summoned here to our imagination is neither place nor time but something that transcends both—it is what has made the great Indian tradition and sustained it through the vicissitudes of history: the Vedas, the Upanishadas, Brahmasutras, the Gita, the teachers and their lineage.[51]

The Principle of *Vedanta*

The Cat and Shakespeare is the third novel of Raja Rao. It is akin to *The Serpent and the Rope* so far as thematic pattern of the novel is concerned. The author here expresses an ancient Indian philosophical ideas and attitude to life through the thoughts, words, actions, feelings and experience of two men, Govindan Nair and Rama Krishna Pai. Dr C.D. Narsimhaiah observes:

As in the tempest, so here Raja Rao provides an opportunity for his characters to transcend the world while belonging to it. It is done largely through the father figure of Govingdan Nair, the narrator's neighbour... Govingdan Nair is not, as the world's valuation goes, a high ranking personage, but only a second clerk in a ration shop where men and women are buying and selling, cheating and sending others to prison. To this he brings Shakespeare's acceptance of the facts of life and a rare compassion.[52]

The novel is based on an Indian social problem of the time — the canker of corruption. The setting of the time is the Second World War. The novel is full of incidents varying from the sublime to the ridiculous, from political to religious, from mundane to spiritual. Bhoothalinga Iyer, an orthodox Brahmin has *mantras* from the *shastras* always on his lips. Through the dialogues the author reflects the profound principle of *Vedant* philosophy. To quote C. Paul Verghese:

The cat is supposed to refer to marjara Kishora nyaya (i.e., the kitten principle) which is followed by the devotees of the Visistadwaita school of thought. The principle is based on the blissful manner in which the helpless kitten surrenders itself utterly to its mother and is well taken care of, and therefore means that the devotees who adopt an attitude of self-surrender to the Creator need have no fears... In this novel Govindan Nair is the exponent of this principle and spares no pain to express it.[53]

The Cat and Shakespeare thus expounds a special Indian consciousness by placing an Indian social situation against traditional Indian philosophical thought.

In Raja Rao's latest novel titled *Comrade Kirillov* we find a reflection of the Indian identity through the character of an Indian expatriate in the West.

The Cultural Nationalism

Having surveyed the Gandhian impact on the novels of Raja Rao, it would be worthwhile to take a glance at his short stories. In his two volumes of short stories entitled *The Cow of the Barricades* (1947) and *Narsiga*, we have the depiction of the Gandhian impact on the Indian mind, especially on the child-mind during the period of the freedom movement. The very title of the story shows how the religious nature of the people is mingled with national spirit of freedom movement. *Narsiga*, the title story is named after Narsiga, the central character. Dr K.R.S. Iyengar observes that Narsiga symbolises the beauty of an unspoilt shepherd-boy's abiding life-loyalties.[54] Here we have Gandhi's impact on the Indian village with its hallowed traditions and age-long reticence. The personality of Mahatma strikes even a simple shepherd lad like Narsiga. Dr Iyengar says:

> *Raja Rao weaves a pattern of relationships between the revered Master of a local Ashram (it might be Rajaji at his Tiruchengode Ashram!), the Mahatma in the background, and the shepherd boy in the foreground.*[55]

Like *Kanthapura*, here also the author draws an aweful picture of Mahatma. Let us see the dialogue of the shepherd boy, in the text:

> *... there was a big, big man called Gandhiji,and the Master knew him, and had talked to him. And the Master worked for him. Who was this Gandhiji?–Narsa had asked. An old man-a bewitching man, a Saint, you know! ...He looks beautiful as the morning sun, and he wears only a little loincloth like a pariah. And they say he is for us pariahs like the Master is for us pariahs... He is a great man. They say he is an incarnation of God, that is why everybody touches his feet, even Brahmins, my son...* [56]

Here the fact and the fancy are inevitably mixed up. In the eyes of the boy, Narsiga, Gandhi is like *Rama*, the divine hero of *Ramayana,* and the foreigner, the red- rulers, are like *Ravana*. The contemporary history is beautifully mingled with myth and legend. The dream and the reality are blended together. The release of Gandhi from prison is compared with the return of *Rama* from *Lanka*. To quote from the text:

> *... the Rama is going in the air, with his wife Sita, and is seated on a flower-chariot drawn by sixteen steeds, each one more beautiful*

than the other. And they will fly through the air and the heavens will let fall a rain of flowers. The Mahatma will have the Mother on his right, and our Master at his foot, and they will go across the clouds and the stars. And we shall gaze at them... [57]

Hanuman: The Ambassador

Hanuman is one of the noblest character of our national epic *Ramayana*. Being highly indebted *Lord Rama* himself pays his gratitude to him in warm words. To quote Goswami Tulsi Das from *Ram Charit Manas*:

Sunu kapi tohi saman upkari,
Nahi kou sur nar muni tanudhari
Prati upkar karow ka tora,
Sanmukh hoi na sakat man mora.[58]

To quote Tulsi Das again from *Hanuman Chalisa*:

Raghupati kinhi bahut barai,
Tum mam priya Bharat sam bhai.
Sahas badan tumhro yas gawe,
As kahi siriparti kanth lagawe.[59]

To be *Hanuman*, the very dearest of *Lord Rama*, is the grandest achievement for a *bhakta*. Narsiga, a true *Gandhi-bhakta* wishes nothing, except to be a *Hanuman* at the feet of Mahatma.

The Mythical Projection of the Gandhian Struggle

In another title-story, *The Cow of the Barricades*, the Mahatma is again in the background. In the foreground there is the Master, counselling the people. As a central character we have Gauri, the cow that embodies mother-love and infinite compassion, the very Mother herself, *Bharat Matha,* Mother India. The author gives a mythical projection of the freedom struggle. Here we have a reference of a point where it is felt that non-violent battle can no longer be non-violent as there is military on one side and the people armed with crowbars, glistening swords and stolen rifles on the side of the barricades. The Master resigns his leadership because his words have become in vain at the occasion. To save the people of the city from bloodshed he goes into meditation. There is no hope for the common people, who are puzzled. There is ominous hovering of owls in the broad daylight. In this chaotic atmosphere, Gauri, the compassionate cow comes. It is felt that she only can save the situation. People greet her with *Vande Mataram*. She moves to the top of the barricades in a manner as if she knows what she has to do. To quote from the text:

But when they saw the cow and its looks and the tear, clear as a drop of the Ganges, they shouted out, "Victory to the Mahatma! Mahatma Gandhi ki jai!" and joined up with the crowd. But their chief, the red man, saw this and fired a shot. It went through Gauri's head, and she fell as a vehicle of God among lowly men.[60]

Gauri has become a goddes, a legend. To quote the Master from the text: "Gauri is waiting in the Middle Heavens to be … reborn when India sorrows again before she is free."[61]

The people are convinced that the Mahatma may be wrong about politics, but he is right about the fullness of love in all creature – the speechful and the mute.[62]

The Vision of Cow-protection

F.W. Bain, the Anglo-Indian writer, in his Introduction to *A Heifer of the Dawn* observes about the glory of the Cow:

What is the secret of the rooted affection of the Aryan and Iranian, the Veda and the Avesta, for the Cow? Partly, no doubt, its utilitarian value. But they are deceived, who think that this is all. There is religion in it, mysticism, aesthetic affection. The Cow is an Idea... Since then, every heifer, and for the sake of the heifer, even every ox, has possessed for the writer a touch of divinity.[63]

Dr K.R.S. Iyengar observes:

This insistence on the 'divinity' of the cow is much more than a stupid Oriental superstition: it goes back rather to the remotest memories of the race and is purposefully linked up with the symbolism of plenty and bounty and compassion and power.[64]

To quote Sri Aurobindo from *The Secret of the Veda:*

... we see in the Veda that Aditi, the Mother of the Gods, is described both as the Cow and as the general Mother; she is the Supreme Light and all radiances proceed from her... .[65]

Mahatma Gandhi himself has spoken much on the significance of cow protection in Hinduism. He writes in *Young India* dated June 8th 1921:

Cow protection is the dearest possession of the Hindu heart. No one who does not believe in cow protection can possibly be a Hindu. It is a noble belief. Cow worship means to me worship of innocence. For me, the cow is the personification of innocence. Cow protection means the protection of the weak and the helpless, cow protection means brotherhood between man and beast. It is a noble sentiment that must grow by patient toil and tapasya.[66]

Cow protection, according to Mahatma Gandhi, is a great contribution of Hinduism. It meant to him a brotherhood between man and entire sub-human world. To quote him again from Young India dated Oct 6th 1921:

The central fact of Hinduism is cow protection. It takes the human being beyond his species. The cow to me means the entire sup-human world. Man through the cow is enjoined to realise his identity with all that lives. Why the cow was selected for apotheosis is obvious to me. The cow was in India the best companion. She was the giver of plenty. Not only did she give milk, but she also made agriculture possible. The cow is a poem of pity. One reads pity in the gentle animal. She is the mother to millions of Indian mankind. Protection of the cow means protection of the whole dumb creation of God. The ancient seer, whoever he was, began with the cow. The appeal of the lower order of creation is all the more forcible because it is speechless. Cow protection is the *gift of Hinduism to the world. And Hinduism will live so long as there are Hindus to protect the cow.*[67]

In this wider perspective the very vision of Raja Rao in *The Cow of the Barricades* can easily be understood. Dr K.R.S. Iyengar concludes it thus:

It is thus with sure racial insight that Raja Rao has made the Cow's mother-gait and silent tears symbolic of India's, the Mother's travail and the cow's infinite patience and veiled power as symbolic of the Mother's genius for surviving her sorrows and transmuting them into the great joy to come.[68]

The world of Raja Rao is as broad as the Pacific Ocean. It is difficult to fathom the same in a few pages of a chapter. Writing literature was a *sadhana* to him. In one of his interviews published in the *Illustrated Weekly* he says:

For me literature is a sadhana–not a profession but a vocation.... This was so even when I wrote kanthapura... but I was then a confused and a lost person. And that was why I gave up writing for a long time. Then after, I had met my guru Sri Atmananda.[69]

In the light of the above clue received from the author himself, it is apt to say that all the writings of Raja Rao are the part of his *sadhana* or spiritual experience. In this way *Kanthapura, The Serpent and the Rope* and *The Cat and the Shakespeare* should be viewed as steps or paths towards self-realisation. Dr K.R. Srinivasa Iyengar remarks:

If Kanthapura could be described as a Purana, as a Gandhi Purana, and The Serpent and the Rope as an epic, a mini-Mahabharata in the idiom of our age, then The Cat and the Shakespeare is more like one of the longer Upnishads, part narrative, part speculation, and part dialogue or discussion.[70]

The Integration of History, Myth and the Philosophy

To study the novels of Raja Rao is to enjoy a journey. In this journey we move from myths to history and then to philosophy. To quote Dr Iyengar again:

If Raja Rao has moved from the puranic to the ithihasic, and from the ithihasic to the Upnishadic, there has been a parallel movement too: from karma in Kanthapura to jnana in The Serpent and the Rope, and on to bhakti-praptti in The Cat and the Shakespeare.[71]

Moorthy is a man of action, and realisation dawns upon him through the Gandhian *Satyagraha*. Ramaswami is a scholar, an intellectual, metaphysician; realisation comes to him through *jyana.* He realises that he has to do all by himself. This is his '*atma darshan*'. Govindan Nair is no intellectual; he is intelligent but no metaphysician. This is equally true in the case of Ramakrishana Pai. They are common human beings like us. For them the path of devotion, i.e., *bhakti* and path of surrender, i.e., *praptti* mingled together is the best path leading them towards their destination.

Kanthapura, The Serpent and the Rope, and *The Cat and the Shakespeare* form a trilogy presenting a steady progression in Raja Rao's *sadhana.* To conclude, we agree with Dr K.R. Srinivasa Iyengar when he says:

The cat is a 'metaphysical comedy', even as Dante's Paradise is the conclusion of his Divine Comedy. If there are glimpses of Inferno's circles and Purgatory's slopes in Kanthapura and The Serpent and the Rope respectively, in The Cat and the Shakespeare we are whirled by winged words and shown the 'death of death' and the efflorescence of the perfect perfection of Love, truth and harmony.[72]

References

1. *Nationalism in Indo-Anglian Fiction*. p. 210.

2. Godwin, K.L. Ed. *National Identity in Literature and Language: Its Range and Depth in the Novels of Raja Rao* in *National Identity.* London and Melbourne: Heinemann Educational Books, 1970. p. 156.

3. Rao, Raja. *Kanthapura.* New Delhi: Orient Paperbacks Pvt. Ltd.

4. *Ibid.* p. 22.

5. *Ibid.* p. 257.
6. *Ibid.* p. 173.
7. *Ibid.* p. 109.
8. *Ibid.* p. 18.
9. *Ibid.* p. 48.
10. *Ibid.*
11. *Ibid.* p. 51.
12. *Ibid.* p. 29.
13. *Ibid.* p. 125.
14. *Ibid.* p. 126.
15. *Ibid.* p. 176.
16. *Ibid.* p. 214.
17. *Ibid.* p. 84.
18. *Ibid.* p. 90.
19. *Ibid.* p. 96.
20. *Ibid.* p. 172.
21. *Ibid.* p. 174.
22. *Ibid.* p. 180.
23. *Ibid.* p. 228.
24. Iyengar, K.R.S. *Indian Writing in English.* p. 390.
25. *Ibid.* p. 391.
26. *Kanthapura.* pp. i-ii.
27. *Indian Writing in English.* p. 391.
28. *Ibid.* p. 392.
29. *Kanthapura.* p. 9.
30. *Ibid.* p. 11.
31. *Indian Writing in English.* p. 392.
32. *Kanthapura.* p. 84.
33. *Ibid.* p. 24.
34. *Indian Writing in English.* p. 393.
35. *Kanthapura.* p. 51.
36. *Ibid.* p. 55.
37. *Ibid.* p. 59.
38. *Ibid.* p. 61.
39. *Indian Writing in English.* p. 395.
40. *Kanthapura.* p. 65.
41. *Ibid.* p. 70.
42. *Ibid.*, p. 68.
43. *Indian Writing in English* p. 394.

44. *Sunday Times,* Review, Diana and Meir Gillon.
45. *Ibid.*
46. *Ibid.*
47. Rao, Raja. *The Serpent and the Rope*. New Delhi: Orient Paperbacks. p. 22.
48. *Ibid.* p. 24.
49. *Nationalism in Indo-Anglian Fiction*. p. 288.
50. Narasimhaiah, C.D. *The Swan and the Eagle*. Simla: Indian Institute of Advanced Study, 1969. pp. 163-164.
51. *Ibid.* 163-164.
52. Narasimhaiah, C.D. *Raja Rao*. New Delhi: Arnold-Heinemann, n.d. pp. 132-133.
53. Verghese, C. Paul. *Problems of the Indian Creative Writer in English*. Bombay: Somaiya Publications, 1971. p. 152.
54. *Indian Writing in English.* p. 387.
55. *Ibid.* p. 387.
56. Rao, Raja. *Narsiga*. New Delhi: Orient Paperbacks. p. 22.
57. *Ibid.* p. 26.
58. Tulsi Das, Goswami. *Ram Charit Manas, "Sundarkand"*. Gorakhpur: Gita Press. p. 386.
59. Tulsi Das, Goswami. *Hanuman Chalisa*. Gorakhpur: Gita Press. p. 12.
60. Rao, Raja. *The Cow and the Barricades*. New Delhi: Orient Paperbacks. p. 16.
61. *Ibid.* p. 22.
62. *Ibid.* p. 29.
63. Qtd in *Indian Writing in English.* p. 388.
64. *Ibid* p. 389.
65. *The Secret of the Vedas: Shri Aurbindo.* p. 12.
66. *Young India*, June 8, 1921.
67. *Ibid.* October 6, 1921.
68. *Indian Writing in English*. pp. 389-390.
69. *Illustrated Weekly of India*, January 1964.
70. *Indian Writing in English.* p. 409.
71. *Ibid.* p. 410.
72. *Ibid.* p. 411.

6

Into the World of Narayan and Abbas

R.K. Narayan himself has described *Waiting for the Mahatma* (1955) as a novel of Gandhi. Mahatma occupies a pivotal position in this novel, and the love story of Sri Ram and Bharati revolves round him. Here the image of Gandhi is that of warm, loving and good humoured Bapu and the portrayal is authentic. Actually Narayan had written a short story entitled *Gandhi's Appeal* before the Independence. The story deals with the nationalistic theme, i.e., irresistible appeal of Gandhi on the masses. Thematically, *Waiting for the Mahatma* can be described as an extension of this story.

Therefore, it would be worthwhile to make a comparative study of the Gandhian impact on the two cotemporary masterpieces, *Waiting for the Mahatma* and *Inquilab,* by two eminent authors of our time.

Narayan and Anand

Though Narayan and Anand are contemporaries, they are diagonally opposite to each other in the nature of their art and in the objectives of their writing. Gopal Prasad Sharma in his *Nationalism in Indo-Anglian Fiction* writes:

> *Anand writes with a conscious purpose; R. K. Narayan, on the other hand, has taken to art not for any specific purpose but only for observing life in its depth and variety. And as he observes life, he does it always with a detachment and a genial smile. Narayan is*

little concerned with the maladies in the society in which he lives, and shows no desire for reforming it.[1]

Narayan and Abbas

Khwaja Ahmed Abbas's *Inquilab* can be studied with Narayan's *Waiting for the Mahatma*. Both the novels were published in the same year (1955). In *Inquilab* also we find Gandhi portrayed as a prominent national leader, and the novel covers the political events of nearly two decades beginning with Jalianwala Bagh massacre of 1919.

The fictional world of R.K. Narayan is too broad. They are great works of art, but most of them hardly come within the canvas of our study. However, let us have a brief view of the major ones among in order to gather an idea of the lives and deeds portrayed by Narayan. More so because these lives and deeds are typically Indian; and Gandhism is nothing but typical Indian approach and attitude to life.

In Narayan's novels and short stories we have a medium-size South Indian town of his imagination, called 'Malgudi'. The characters he has portrayed are generally middle-class people shown against the backgound of this town.

A Peep into Pre-independence Novels

Swami and Friends (1935) is Narayan's first pre-independence novel. It is the story of a school boy of lower form, Swaminathan, with few of his school friends. Their words, deeds and problems are typically frivolous and characteristic of middle-class children. G.P. Sharma says that this novel is only one of its kinds in Indo-Anglian fiction. The critic observes, *"It is a cross-section of Indian children in towns, Indian children who are free from grim realities of living faced by the poor children of the peasants and the workers in towns and villages."*[2]

In *The Bachelor of Arts* (1937) we have the life of Indian youths in college and out of it portrayed through the life of Chandran in his last year in college and the subsequent years until his marriage. The hero is a youth, a college boy; he goes to England, falls in love with a sparkling girl, but their marriage does not take place as the horoscopes do not match. Frustrated, the boy turns a *sanyasi*, wanders from place to place, returns home ultimately and marries a girl of his parents' choice. In this novel we have lucid depiction of the clamouring for job after completion of education in India; hurdles in marriage based on love caused by various prejudices and superstitions. The true theme of the novel is the realisation of the belief of Indian in traditional pattern of life. The hero, Chandran, who loved a girl in the western way, wanted to marry her against the Indian prejudices, finally realises that the girl chosen by his parents is as fit for him as the one he loved himself. In this novel, Narayan thus takes a long realistic look at life in a typical Indian setting.

The Dark Room (1938) is Narayan's third novel. It is the story of the unhappy conjugal life of a woman who is mother of three children. She being neglected by her husband, when finds him eloped with a flirtatious woman quits the house to commit suicide. Her attempt being foiled, she works and lives in a village temple, feels repentant, longs for her home and children, and finally comes back home to be greeted by her children and husband. Therefore, this novel again is story of the realisation of an Indian woman the values of Indian married life signified by her consequent coming back to the traditional Indian fold. A parallel line may be drawn between *The Bachelor of Arts* and *The Dark Room* so far as the thematic pattern are concerned, i.e. realisation of old traditional values.

The English Teacher (1949) is the fourth novel of the author. Here once again we have the usual mastery of the art of story-telling at its best. It is a continuation of the story of the two phases-childhood and youth - of man's life told in his first two novels. After the story of childhood in *Swami and Friends*, and youth in *The Bachelor of Arts*, we find in *The English Teacher* the story of early manhood. Krishnan, the hero of *The English Teacher* is a lecturer of English in a college, leads a happy conjugal life having a delightful prattle of a little girl. His happiness is cut short when his young wife dies of typhoid. The poor fellow is given to the occult science; establishes a psychic relation with the spirit of his wife; exchanges massages and talks about each other's life and condition. He looses interest in teaching job, resigns his post in the college, sends his daughter away to his village home to be looked after by her grandparents to be free to spend his days with his wife's spirit.

The English Teacher is a gripping story of conjugal love and spiritual re-union. But the question is in which sense it is an Indian novel. Krishnan's later life, when he grows indifferent to the material world, even to his job in the college, and gets absorbed in establishing a spiritual relation with his wife is typically Indian. Despite the fact that the inclusion of occult science diminishes the literary value of the novel, it cannot be denied that it is a perfect work of art. Krishnan's indifference to the material world and his new interest in the spiritual is the outstanding achievement of R.K. Narayan in Indo-Anglian fiction. In fact, it was the result of Narayan's personal experiences at it when, after his wife's premature death, he often used to establish spiritual communication with her.

One of the very important aspects of Narayan's work is the encounter between two civilisations - of the ruling class and of the ruled. To quote G. P. Sharma in this context: "The novelist, however, does not show any leaning to any side here; he remains a dispassionate observer."[3] In *Swami and Friends,* we find this encounter in the picture of the Political Movement of Indian nationalist against the British Government".[4] In *The Bachelor of Arts*, this encounter takes place on the cultural level[5] when Raghavachar, the Professor of History, forms a Historical Association in the college with Chandran as the Secretary of the Association. In *The Dark Room*, however, this aspect is totally absent; while in *The English Teacher* there are scattered lines about it.

R.K. Narayan is also a good story writer; he has had four volumes of short stories to his credit till 1947. These are *Dodu and Other Stories* (1943), *Malgudi Days* (1943), *Cyclone and Other Stories* (1944) and *An Astrologer's Day and Other Stories* (1947). In the short stoires also we observe the same detached view of life and the same felicity of art.

Post-independence Novels of Narayan

Let us now have a review of the post-independence social novels of R.K. Narayan. As stated earlier, the novelist has been an observer, sometimes amused, sometimes detached, of men and manners which may not be necessarily Indian. However, there are occasional reflections of manners or situations which are typically Indian. But it should be remembered that these are only occasional. The slum of Malgudi in *Mr. Sampath* (1949) is typical of an Indian city or town (pp. 5-6). In *The Financial Expert* (1952), the scenes of Margayya sitting under a banyan tree in front of the Bank with his worn out tin box transacting his business with always a semi-circle of peasants sitting around him and in *The Guide* (1958), the scene of Raju undergoing a fast as a holy man for rain, are also typically Indian.

However, there are some internal characteristics, which make Narayan's novels distinctly Indian. Generally he reflects typical Indian attitudes to life in his novels, and very often this is done by him in terms of Indian myths, as Lakshmi Holmstrom has elucidated in *The Novel of R.K. Narayan*. R.K. Narayan shows Indian nationalistic concern in this sense of affirming the Indian attitude to life.

Let us first take up *Mr. Sampath* to illustrate this aspect. Holmstrom points out that the central theme of this novel is the evil consequence of attachment. Srinivas comes to Malgudi with an ideal of his own and starts publishing a periodical. He is dragged away by his rich printer, Sampath, to the production of a film for which Sampath appoints him scriptwriter. Ravi, one of Srinivas's closest friends, is appointed as an artist in the studio when he discovers that the beautiful heroine, Shanti, is his own one-time beloved. His love for her is soon revived; but the producer-director Sampath, too, has fallen in love with her and has found for himself an opportunity to play the role of *Shiva* against her who has played the role of *Parvati*. In the climatic scene of the film, when Sampath as *Shiva* embraces Shanti as *Parvati,* Ravi goes mad, and sabotages Sampath's ambitious venture. Srinivas is thus driven to his old, modest publishing plans again. The excessive involvement with money, fame and love is responsible for the pitiable plight of Sampath. Srinivas is unscathed, free as he is of all attachment. The consequences faced by Sampath conform to all that is preached in the *Gita*. The novelist makes this theme clear by bringing in the myth of *Kamadeva's* distraction when he provoked *Shiva*; the mythological film, which Sampath proposed to produce, was based on this myth.

The Financial Expert also has the same central theme of the pain caused by attachment. Margayya, the moneylender, craves for more and more money to such extenct that he has become a slave to money. He offers *puja* to goddess *Lakshmi* to have a respectable image. To earn more money he publishes a book on sex-life jointly with a firm. The money earned through this venture is again invested in money-lending in a bigger way. His craze for money reaches an improbable height leading to the ruin of his money-lending business. He turns humble in the original way, returns under the banyan tree for money lending. Here again the story is about the perils of attachment; in this case the attachment to money.

In *The Guide* (1958) also, we have the theme of the need for detachment but it is subsidiary to another theme, the progress towards realising one's true nature, again an Indian ideal. There are two cycles of events unfolding this theme: Raju's rise and fall within the worlds of normal experience; and Raju's career outside-beginning as the unknown ex-prisoner, and ending as the unknown Swami. Raju's attachment and its consequence form the first part of the story. He, a petty, self-styled tourist guide of Malgudi, meets Rosie, the lovely wife of an archaeologist,

Marco, who visits Malgudi. Raju falls in love with Rosie and she too reciprocates as her husband neglects her. Rosie, in her relation with Raju, revives her old interest in dancing and with Raju's encouragement she becomes a dancer of repute. Her husband disapproves of this and she is left at his Madras home. Raju then makes an elaborate plan of making much of Rosie, now renamed Nalini. Raju and Nalini are on dance tour in the South Indian cities and her dream of becoming a famous dancer comes true. But everything turns topsy-turvy when a lawsuit is filed against him by Macro and he is put behind the bars consequently.

Now we have the phase of self-realisation and this, too, is equally interesting. Raju, being released from jail, reaches a village and takes shelter in a temple. He is taken as a saint and the simple-minded villagers become his devotees. There is a famine in the village and the people rush to him requesting to dispel his omen for the welfare of the village. Raju is expected to perform miracle for the folk. He undertakes a fast with all the fervor of real holy man but on twelfth day of the fast his condition becomes severe and he 'sags down'. His martyrdom for the masses makes him a great saint. Lakshmi Holmstrom observes:

> *The miracle that happens is not that the rains come, but that Raju becomes the 'swami' dying for his people. The very qualities that he always recognised as his nature—to be involved with people, to anticipate this needs and to provide for them.*[6]

The Man-Eater of Malgudi (1962) is Narayan's next work for consideration. Here we have the Indian tint equally distinct both in surface and depth of the novel. The story of this novel has many episodes though the theme is equally Indian. H. Vasu, M.A., taxidermist, a man of gigantic stature and obnoxious nature, appears in the village and the calm and the quiet life of Malgudi gets stirred. He goes shooting birds and animals in the Mempi forest of Malgudi to the great vexation of the people of Malgudi. The people cannot say anything to him in protest, but they hope like true Indians that a day will come when this demoniac creature would meet his own destruction.

The story has a distinct Indian colour. A poet writes a verse titled *Radha Kalyan;* the story of *Krishan.* A festival at the temple of the *Krishna* is to be celebrated. The people of Malgudi have borrowed a temple elephant for the procession. But Vasu, the cruel taxidermist, intends to shoot that elephant, and the peace-loving people of Malgudi get stirred and dismayed waiting for Vasu with bated breath. The auspicious day passes smoothly but Vasu is not to be seen. The following morning his dead body is found in his room. It is later learnt that he had died from concussion of the brain when he had slapped his own temple to kill a mosquito. The story is a universal theme; of course the ultimate triumph of good over evil, the people of Malgudi embodying good and Vasu representing evil. This universal theme is akin to the Indian mythology where the gods and the demons were constantly at war, the demons being the winners destroying themselves ultimately. Vasu symbolises here the demon, which causes devastation and panic in the world of Malgudi for a while but ultimately destroys himself.

R.K. Narayan's next novel, *The Vendor of Sweets* (1967), deals partly with the theme of renunciation — another Indian ideal, and partly with the problem of crisis of faith of people following Gandhian ideals in contemporary society. Jagan, a prosperous vendor of sweets, a follower of Gandhi and freedom fighter, is simple-minded unlike his only child who gives up his study at college and goes to America by stealing money from his father. He advocates the need of beef eating by Hindus to get rid of food shortage and excessive number of useless cows. The boy lives with a girl; half-American, half-Korean, without marriage. Jagan, the father, completely disillusioned from his son, detaches himself from him and quits his house to retire to a life of peace in the forest. *The Painter of Sings* (1976), too, has a nationalistic theme. Here we have affirmation of Indian attitude to life reflecting contemporary Indian society.

Gandhi appears in Person

Thus we have taken a cursory view of the major works of Narayan, our imperative now is to view *Waiting for the Mahatma*. To put it in the words of K.R. Srinivasa Iyengar:

> *It is exceptional in two respects; the action stays out of Malgudi (going as far as Delhi) and the two central characters (Bharati and Sriram) are existentially 'engaged' in politics.*[7]

Mulk Raj Anand in *Untouchable* gives the Mahatma a part towards the end. Other novelists, whether writing in English or in the regional languages, have likewise exploited the magic of Gandhi's name. Gandhi's role is hardly subsumed in the fiction as a whole. Gandhi is too big to be given a minor role; on the other hand, he is sure to turn the novel into a biography if he is given a major or the central part. To quote Iyengar again with regard to Gandhi's role in *Waiting for the Mahatma*:

> *The best thing for the contemporary novelist would be to keep Gandhi in the background but make his influence felt indirectly.*

In 'Waiting for the Mahatma', the theme is apparently the Bharati-Sriram romance which, however, gains a new dimension in the background of their common allegiance to the Mahatma. Since the stress is not merely on Gandhi's influence but on Gandhi himself - we see him in Malgudi stationed in Nallappa's Grove and we see him, years later, in Delhi on his way to prayer on the fatal day, 30 January, 1948 - the novel develops a duality of interests which is not wholly resolved by the compulsion of art.[8]

Waiting for the Mahatma is an ambitious effort, and an impressive feat; but one also feels that Narayan's art, now denied the security of Maldugi and catapulted into Gandhian or terrorist political action, betrays unsureness and perplexity. Iyengar observes:

Bharati herself is a masterful young heroine, a Malgudi Portia rich only in her natural endowments, whereas Sriram can easily qualify for a Malgudi Bassanio. It is Bharati who makes a patriot and a man of Sriram, and in marriage he is certain to find in her the saviour strength that is 'nari shakti'.[9]

A Regional Novel

Waiting for the Mahatma is known as a regional novel. Just as in England, Arnold Bennett has written his Clayhanger trilogy about the pottery districts of England; Thomas Hardy has immortalised Wessex in his immortal classics; in India, Mr Narayan has also attempted at writing 'regional novels' around Malgudi. H.M. Rosenthal has aptly remarked:

Malgudi exists on no map, but it has a full life, frantic often and full of thought and repose just as often, in the ten novels and 150 short stories of R.K. Narayan. The books of Narayan are written in a style as bland and cool as a plate of curd, but are somehow as zestful and satisfying as a helping of good mutton curry... The Malgudi books are not only entertaining and full of qick revelations about India, but they are unhappily among the very few top-grade novels written in English in India by Indian.[10]

Love, Politics and Idealism

Waiting for the Mahatma is one more Malgudi novel in which Narayan has woven his plot with fine strands of love, politics and idealism-'the pensive comedy' for which R.K. Narayan is famous. The story goes as under:

Sriram turns twenty. As a mark of his coming of age his grandmother allows him the passbook to his savings in the local bank, but Sriram is growing up in other ways also; an enchanting and unpredictable girl leads him into the entourage of Mahatma Gandhi. The novel opens with these events. It is the finest thing the author has yet achieved and his story of the triumphs and tragedies of a raw zealot in the service of Gandhi is distinguished for its warmth, its humours, its lack of sentimentality and the stamp of absolute truth.

Sriram evolves into a man. Bharati, the girl whom he loves, is witty, infuriating, capable, and, wonder of wonders, condescending to the moon-struck Sriram. Her first loyalty, though, is to the Mahatma, a saint, blessed with disconcerting common sense, a man whose tragedy is that he is shown much greater than his followers. Most of them accept his ideas enthusiastically, and without realising it, pervert them to suit their own coarser ones. Gandhi inspires Sriram, but glamorous patriots of the type of Jagdish, a terrorist, too easily influence him. Yet such man, bamboozled by pride and self-sufficiency, are human beings as characteristics of the new India, still swayed by ancient traditions as the practical and far-sighted Bharati.

Depiction of Richness and Diversity of India

In *Waiting for the Mahatma* we find richness and diversity of India and her peoples. R.K. Narayan has rightly been compared to Chekhov and Gogal. In *The Financial Expert* we find the author delighting thousands with his loving pictures of small town society. Here, in *Waiting for the Mahatma,* he has encompassed a wider theme and has handled it with great artistry. It is a love story with a difference.

Sriram was twenty; he was living with his grandmother and she handed over his passbook to him because he was now wise enough to look after his affairs. One day he met Bharati who was collecting funds for the Congress movement. Then Mahatma Gandhi came to Malgudi and he went there to hear the Mahatma. He stuck on there, and when he found that Bharati was there with the Mahatma he decided to follow him. When Bharati heard his intention to be the follower of Mahatmaji she took him to the Mahatma. But as soon as Sriram proposed his love to Bharati on the very first day of their meetng she rebuffed him in no unclear terms:

> *Sriram told Bharati that he loved her but Bharati told him, "This is enough to irritate even the Mahatma. Now what will he think of me if he realises I am encouraging a fellow like you about the place, a fellow whom I have not known even for a full day yet".*[11]

Sriram was fired by the zeal to become a follower of Mahatma. He had to go to his granny to take her permission. She was angry with him but all the same he left his home. The author writes:

Now he was an accredited member of the group, and in many villages he was glad to find himself fussed over and treated with respect by the villagers. They looked on him with wonder. He formed a trio with Bharati and Gorpad; and whenever the villagers wanted to know anything about the Mahatma, they came and spoke to him reverentially, and that gave him an opportunity to work off all the knowledge he had gathered in his contacts with Gorpad and Bharati. It was the way of learning the job while being on it. Till then he had no notion of village life.[12]

When Ghandhiji's tour came to an end Sriram moved to a ruined shrine on a slope of the Mempi Hill. Gandhiji asked Sriram to write regularly to him. As advised by Gandhiji he tried to spin better and better and now he even prepared his own clothes.

Once Bharati came to meet him. It was August of 1942 when Mahatmaji was in prison. She declared that she might be arrested and she advised Sriram to carry on the work of 'Quit India Movement' in the villages.

Sriram also moved in villages writing 'Quit India' everywhere. He had awakward experiences in one or two places in those hill villages. Bharati met him again to tell him that without the sanction of Bapuji she cannot marry him. She was arrested after that and she advised him also to be arrested. Then one day Jagadish, the photographer, came to meet him. The author writes:

Jagadish came because he was in need of an out-of-town lair for his activiies, and he was looking for a place where he could install a small radio set which could also transmit code messages.[13]

Here thus starts Sriram's career as a revolutionary who followed the path of non-violence. Sriram came under the spell of Jagadish and went on transmitting massages and receiving massages verbatim.

Ones he took down the speech of Subhash Chandra Bose from Tokyo and when the speech came to the most important point the transmitter failed. When Jagadish read this he was not disappointed; he gave Sriram cyclostyled copies of the massage and asked him to drop the pamphlets beyond the fence of the camp. Then he was busy with Jagadish in wrecking trains or burning railway stations. All through he believed that he must meet Bharati. But Sriram was now the wanted man; and his photographs were printed everywhere.

Sriram made certain changes in his appearance. On a certain day Jagadish examined Sriram's face and declared, 'the most satisfactory moustache that I ever saw in my life'. With a razor and scissors he helped Sriram to give its end a downward turn. He also produced some old silver-rimmed spectacles, and mounted them on his nose. He also provided him an ill fitting, close-button coat, and a white turban to cover his head. He ordered him to tie up his *dhoti* bifurcated, like all respectable men. When he went to see Bharati in the prison she refused to see him but she gave him a letter. A hurried pencil scribbling was there on it:

> *I cannot bring myself to see you today. It seems degrading to have a meeting under these conditions. Bapu has always said that it is dishonorable to assume subterfuges. In a jail we must observe the rules, or change them by Satyagraha openly, if possible. Forgive me.*[14]

Sriram then went to his house and found that his granny was dead. Her cremation ceremony had to be performed at eight O'clock. Sriram went to the cremation ground beyond the Sarayu River but when they set fire to the funeral pyre the big toe of the lady was seen to move. She was not dead. The body was taken away from the pyre and the doctor was called for. The doctor gives her an injection and his grandmother came to life. But now the problem was that according to superstitions, she became alive after dying and, therefore, if she were taken back to her home some calamity would befall on the city. So she was kept in a place outside the city. She became much better but by then Sriram was arrested by the police. He was in the jail where he did not feel easy in the company he had to live with:

> *Sriram felt uneasy in this rough company, who laughed at the soft-handed, softheaded man. They simply could not make out why he would have courted all this trouble from the police because some one wanted him to do something, and not because such exploits as derailing a train brought him a share of profit. This was a fresh outlook that had not occurred to Sriram in his self-centered political existence. He had a feeling that he was running up against a new species of human being, speaking like monsters, but yet displaying sudden human qualities.*[15]

There were all sorts of people in the prison but Sriram tolerated all this because he was suffering for the sake of Bharati. In the jail he came to know from his friend a bank manager that his grandmother had gone to Benaras. The events in the country were moving fast. Ultimately, he was released from the jail. He went to meet Jagadish, the photographer, and then he wrote a letter to Bharati. He received a letter from Bharati; she was in Noakhali in Bengal along with the Mahatma. He got another letter from her in which she asked him to come to Delhi in the Birla House. He travelled to Delhi and at the station she was there to receive him. There he looked after the children of evacuees along with her. She told him about her experiences during the Noakhali tour:

> *Bapu said his place was where they were suffering and not where they were celebrating. He said that if a country cannot give security to women and children, it's not worth living in. He said it would be worth dying if that would make his philosophy better understood. He walked through villages barefooted on his mission. We followed him. Each day we walked five miles through floods and fields, silently. He walked with bowed head, all through those swamps of East Bengal. We stopped for a day or two in each village, and he spoke to those who had lost their homes, property, wives and children. He spoke kindly to those who had perpetrated crimes-he wept for them, and they swore never to do such things again ... It's no use discussing whether this community committed greater horrors or the other one. Bapuji forbade us to refer to anyone in terms of religion as Muslims, Hindu or Sikh, but just as human beings. He said one day that he sometimes pitied those who committed acts of violence.*[16]

Suffering for Love and Marriage

Sriram then met Mahatmaji who promised to get them married the next day. While departing Mahatmaji said,

> *You don't know. If god wills it I shall come. Otherwise, know my blessing is always on you both. Anyway you are not to put off your marriage for any reason. "Remember," he said, with new command in his voice and Bharati replied, "Yes, Bapu".*[17]

Mahatma was shot dead that day only at the prayer meeting but he had already given permission for the marriage of Sriram and Bharati.

We find that *Waiting for the Mahatma* is one of the best novels of R.K. Narayan and the character of Sriram is wonderfully lifelike. Here we have a lively description of the events from 1941 to 1948. This is a beautiful love story of two followers of the Mahatma. Here the novelist has handled his characters with humour and tolerant irony, smiling all the while at their follies and their conflict between what they want to appear and what they actually are. The depth of human psychology and the springs of actions of our hero Sriram, his love for Bharati, are not less deep simply because Narayan handles them in his aloof, half humours and half whimsical manner. The climax reached with the touch of Mahatma Gandhi has been handled very artistically.

Joseph Conrad once remarked with reference to himself:

I would not like to be left standing as a mere spectator on the bank of the great stream carrying onward so many lives. I would fain claim for myself the faculty of so much insight as can be expressed in a voice of sympathy and compassion.[18]

This, we understand, is equally applicable in the case of R.K. Narayan.

Abbas' Illustrious World

Khawaja Ahmad Abbas is an illustrious novelist of our time. *Tomorrow is Ours*, *Defeat for Death* and *Inquilab* are his very well known works. Of all these *Inquilab* is the prime novel of our discussion and we will have a detailed study of this. It would, however, be relevant to have a brief survey of other works of the author, for they, too, portray the contemporary political scenario, if not the Indian freedom struggle.

Turbulent Period of Freedom Struggle

Tomorrow is Ours (1943) is the first novel of K.A. Abbas. It presents a picture of the turbulent period of our freedom struggle led by Mahatma Gandhi. The picture is only hinted at. The novel is concerned with the personal life of a dancing-girl in conservative Hindu society. The international political scene of the time is disturbed by the Second World War, and the author successfully hints at the way the average Indian mind felt about it.

Parvati is the daughter of a lawyer of Allahabad who joined Non-cooperation Movement launched in 1920, giving up his lucrative practice, and suffered imprisonment and ultimately died as the jail diet was fatel for his health. Parvati, who was a medical student, was doomed to give up her studies at the death of her father and moved city to city as a dancing-girl to earn her livelihood. She was married to a doctor in the course of her travel but her married life was not so happy. Meanwhile, the Indian people feel sympathy for the Communist struggle in China and Russia. Parvati also grows sympathetic towards the people of those two countries. She meets a communist leader of Bengal and becomes his compainion. About this time Indian National Congress decides to send a medical mission of four doctors to China as token of the India's sympathy for the suffering people there; and Parvati is happy to find her husband selected as one. She parts with him with sorrow but feels at the same time in this parting that 'from the east rosy dawn is breaking, holding for the promise of tomorrow.' The novel deserves a place in our discussion especially for depicting the India's relation to the then world situation.

Defeat for Death (1944), the second work of K.A. Abbas, is more satisfactory as a work of art and more serious in the purpose. But it is a peculiar work of fiction. Here we have thirteen small chapters narrating three different stories - one about a child, another about an old man and the third about a city. All stories deal with one theme of oppression by the imperialists. The three stories are narrated in phases and each phase forms a chapter. The book thus may be treated both as a novel with one main plot and two sub-plots and also a collection of short stories. The author himself calls it '*A Story*', though the stories are not told in a formal way through plot and characters. They express the author's feeling and emotions about a few incidents of the war years of the early forties just like a poem. It is better to say this work as a prose-poem expressing the spirit of a man in chains struggling to be free.

The author in this book portrays a little Negro boy who is wounded in a racial riot and is undergoing treatment in a hospital. Having turmoil in his mind, he loses all hopes of life in this world oppressed by the imperialist race. But he gets an inspiration, a hope to live from an old man of seventy who undergoes a fast for him. The old man can easily be identified with Gandhi in his fast in 1942 in jail. The boy hears from the radio about this wonderful and great old man who also has suffered like him at the hands of the imperialists but has conquered most of his enemies through a unique method of his own. The boy grows optimistic when he hears about the successful end of the old man's twenty-one-day fast fulfilling his purpose. The boy asks for medicine, which he had refused to take formally, and says, "I don't want to die."[19] When he heard from the nurse about the city being freed he remarks, "Those who fight for freedom can never suffer defeat."[20] Here lies the significance of the title. To quote G.P. Sharma:

> *Defeat for Death, may, therefore, be called a nationalist story for its theme. But it is nationalist in other aspect, too — Gandhi's historic fast. The author has described the condition of Gandhi, though without even naming him, in every stage of his fast in prison, the influence of this fast on the national scene of the country which was then tense with the freedom struggle, and on the international scene*

> *which was ravaged by the Second World War between Fascism and Democracy.*[21]

A Reverential Image of Gandhi

The author's description of Gandhi is sympathetic and reverential, and his faith in the efficacy of such a fast by such a saintly man is very deep. It is relevant to see a few examples of his narration of the fast to prove the author's sympathy for the great man:

> *For years the old man had been holding back the tide of revolutionary violence. With him in prison, the floodgates were burst open, the dykes were breached, and the whole country was flooded with violent activity. No man was more grieved than the old man. For him it was the undoing of a lifetime's patient work of moral reconstruction.*[22]

And yet this 'life-time devotee of non-violence was represented as a blood-thirsty perperpetrator of violence.'[23] 'His soul was in torment to find such accusations hurled at him.'[24] How to explain himself and vindicate his principles against all accusations, especially when he is in prison? To quote from the text:

> *There was only one way open for him. He must punish his body with self-inflicted starvation. He must, if necessary, face death. It was weapon both of defence and of attack peculiar to himself. He had used it on many occasions before, and every time he had emerged from the ordeal, morally strengthened and spiritually uplifted.*[25]

The author intends to make his story historically authentic. He has reproduced a portion of a letter Gandhi had actually written to the British government explaining reasons for his fast. Let us see the part of that letter giving an insight into Gandhi's mind:

> *You have left me no loopholes for escaping the ordeals I have set before myself... If I do not survive the ordeal, I shall go to the Highest Judgement Seat with fullest faith in my innocence. powerful Government and me as a humble man who has tired Posterity will judge between you as a representative of an all to serve his country and humanity throughout.*[26]

The doctors, after the twelfth day of the fast, declare the old man's condition serious. The author narrates the repercussion in the country and the world:

> *The old man's fast was focal point not only for the country but the entire world. Crack reporters from distant lands had been rushed by*

airplane to 'cover' the fast. Every few hours the doctors issued bulletins about the old man's waning strength. Eight hundred million eyes were anxiously turned in this direction. By telegraph, by telephone, radio, newspapers, the news of the fast was being broadcast every hour of the day and night.[27]

The author remarks: "Life was flowing out of the frail body of the old man. Life was flowing into the anaemic body of the nation."[28]

The old man's condition causes still more anxiety as the days pass. He says to his worried wife sitting beside him, 'Don't worry'. 'I won't die'. People demand from all quarters their leader's release by meetings, resolutions, processions, telegrams, telephones, newspaper letters and statements. On the other side of the globe, the black child on his hospital-bed hears from the radio:

During the last thirty years I have reported over half a dozen titanic conflicts — the last world war, the invasion of Manchuria, the Abyssinia War, the Spanish Civil War, the Sino-Japanese War, and the new Second World War. But today I will tell you about the strangest war waged in the long history of man. This is not a war fought with bombers, tanks and guns. This is the battle between Life and Death. And the battlefield is the frail body of an old man of seventy who had not eaten a grain of food for seventeen days.[29]

There is little hope of the old man's life when more days pass. Let us see how the author describes the scene:

...in mosques and in temples, in chapels and in churches, in the agiaries of Parsis and the synagogues of the Jews, prayers were being offered for his life. After namaz, old Muslim women prayed to Allah, after puja and Gita-path, old Hindu women prayed to Bhagwan: 'You are merciful and beneficent, O God. Have mercy on our land. Spare the life of the old man who is the father of this nation'.[30]

The author further writes:

Festivals and celebrations, marriages and engagements, meetings and conferences had been postponed till the end of the old man's fast. The nation held its collective breath in an agony of suspense.[31]

At last the old man comes out successfully after completing the marathon fast; and the nation is freed from all its anxiety. By depicting the nation's love for their leader and his influence on the whole world, the author's nationalist spirit is revealed. This book is certainly one of the best works of fiction by Abbas in its exposition of the seriousness of purpose and its emotionally charged language.

Inquilab by the author has very comprehensive, all embracing and prolific profile. Although written during 1942-49, the novel actually covers the earlier period commencing from the Rowlatt Bill and the *Jallianwalla Bagh tragedy* to the *Salt Satyagraha* and the Gandhi-Irwin Pact of 1931. Anwar the 'hero' is eight at the beginning, a mere impressionable boy, of 21 when the novel closes, a sad and rather a seasoned young man. The novelist's ambitious intention to project the Gandhian Revolutionary Age, (Inquilab means Revolution) in its entirety, and Gandhi, Motilal Nehru, Jawaharlal Nehru, C.R. Das, Subhash Chandra Bose, Vallabhbhai Patel, Rajagopalachari, Sarojini Naidu, Dr Ansari, Maulana Muhammad Ali, Maulana Azad, Dr Sapru and Mr. M. R. Jayakar (the peace maker), Syed Muhammad, Abdul Gaffar Khan and Pandit Madan Mohan Malaviya are among the many leaders of yesterday whom we momentarily encounter in the pages of the novel.

To quote K.R. Srinavasa Iyengar:

> *Planned like a typical 'character' novel, the aim is comprehension and moving multiplicity rather than dramatic concentration or intensity. Anwar is shifted from place to place, things happen to him, he registers impressions of a various nature and is involved - like a leaf in the storm - in the political cataclysms of his time.*[32]

Chronicle of Gandhian Freedom Struggle

Inquilab is a novel on the lines of Upton Sinclain's *World's End* and other volumes in the same series. The novel vividly chronicles our struggle for freedom in the leadership of Mahatma Gandhi. The hero Anwar is very much impressed with the person of Mahatma Gandhi. It is at Dr Ansari's house that Anwar sees Gandhiji first:

> *... a thin, spindly legged man in coarse 'dhoti' and 'kurta', playing a 'charkha'. He had a white cloth thrown over his head and from a distance Anwar had taken him to be a woman.*[33]

Anwar, now a growing boy, has an emotional interview with Gandhi at Muhammad Ali's house:

> *Now he knew why they called him Mahatma — a Great Soul. On his face was a look of suffering, kindness and pity, as if he personally felt the misery of every single human being. But there was also infinite calm and serenity and the boy's spirits revived as he looked into those gentle eyes.*[34]

The story starts with the year 1933. It portrays a typical, Muslim upper middle-class home in Delhi. Anwar, the hero, is a young boy then.

The description of Anwar's household is very realistic. *Phoophi, Amma*, warring about the boy's health and Gulabo, the servant, telling the stories of fairies to lull the boy to sleep is all wonderfully realistic. In that household. Answer's father and his friends discuss politics of the day. Anwar goes with his father to Lahore.

Jallianwala Bagh Massacre

Then we find a wonderfully realistic and vivid description of the massacre of Jalianwalla Baag.

But somehow the cry made him burn with fierce excitement, the hair on his body seemed to be pulled out of their roots, there was rush of blood to his face and his head reeled as it had once reeled when he had got a sun-stroke.[35]

And then:

It was a nightmarish experience for Anwar as he lay on the ground and watched the bloody drama. The rifles kept barking, the bullets came flying in an uninterrupted stream, men and women and children fell everywhere, there were screams and moans and groans. In their mad rush to the narrow exits people had left behind their shoes and turbans and even their dhoties, those who lay on the ground were trampled on by those who were running, and once Anwar's leg was almost fractured as a heavy boot landed on it. Even for those who were able to reach the exits there was no escape. The Red-face ordered the rifles to be directed at them and they were mown down before they could pass through to safety.[36]

Khilafat Movements and the Hindu-Muslim Riots

The death of the Sikh Jamadar dying with his hands raised in salute puts dramatic finish to that treasury. Years pass by and Anwer becomes more and more nationalistic. Then comes the *Khilafat* Movement and Anwar's father Akbar Ali is arrested. Times pass and we are shown how Anwar sees the split between the Hindus and the Muslims growing wider here. Anwer sees Mahatma Gandhi at the house of Dr Ansari.

Noticing Anwar's Khaddar trousers and sherwani, Mahatma Gandhi was pleased and started talking of the importance of everyone using hand-spun and hand-woven cloth a subject on which he could talk for hours together! But what Anwar, had come to talk about was the riots, only he did not know how to begin. As he listened to the talk on the importance of Khadi, his mind wandered. He was thinking of all the horrible things he had heard about setting fire to each other's houses and defiling each other's places of worship. And above the low monotone of the Mahatma and the reen-reen-reen of the creaking spinning wheel, he heard again those fearful cries- "Maro! Maro!" and "Mar dala! Mar dala!" How could he convey the anguish of his soul to the Mahatma? How could he tell him that he had a Muslim father whom he adored and a Hindu Kaka by whom he had always been taught to love and respect as an uncle - and that the two were no longer friends as they had been all their lives up till now? ... And now all these beautiful friendships were being poisoned by communal hatred. If only he could explain all this to the Mahatma! If only! But words failed, his voice was choked, he felt helpless and miserable. He burst into tears.[37]

Anwar then passed matriculation. At the same time his sister Anjum, who was married young, died in her pregnancy. This is how he took her death:

If god so wills! That was then the ultimate court of appeal. That was why his father spent so much time on the prayer rug imploring the Almighty to spare his daughter's life. That was why Phoopi Amma even then, was tearfully mumbling the one thousand names of Allah or her rosary of beads. Ya Qahar'. Ya Jabbar! Ya Ghaffar! But God was benevolent and beneficent. He would never, never take away an innocent life like Anjum's. At any rate, it was best for Anwar, to augment his father's and aunt's prayers with his own. Was he not told that Gods grant children's prayers promptly because children are so innocent! So, thought he, his prayer will be granted the moment it is made![38]

Anwar joined the Aligarh University and there fell in love with Salmah, the daughter of Prof Saleem. Prof Saleem hoped to make his son-in-law an I.C.S. officer. But Anwar was too nationalist minded to become an officer of the British government. On one occasion he met Jawaharlal Nehru in the train:

Our Jawahar! All over the country - as in Aligarh - young men spoke of him with a peculiarly possessive affection. He belonged to them, he was theirs! ... Anwar had a fleeting impression of great power in that strong handsome face and the lean athletic body.[39]

Bhagat Singh in the Assembly

Ratan, his anarchist friend, took shelter at Aligarh and so the authorities debarred him from the college. Then Anwar got for Ratan a pass for entering the Assembly Chamber at Delhi. With the help of that pass Bhagat Singh and his companions entered the assembly building. The author describes the assembly scene with biting irony:

> *"Trades Disputes Bill Under Fire", but here there was neither fire nor fury, only a never ending, sleep inducing repetition of words, words and words. The only bright interlude was the spirited speech of the Opposition leader Pandit Motilal Nehru who looked an impressive figure in his tight fitting Khadi silk sherwani and Gandhi cap. And then, the sleepy atmosphere, descended once more and Anwar was amazed to see that a member on the Treasury Benches, a fat red-faced Englishman, was actually snoring, while another Englishman sitting next to him was solving a crossword puzzle! And, behind them, in a solid phalanx sat the Nominated Members, those obedient souls who, on bill after bill, voted for the Government with robot regularity.*[40]

Bhagat Singh threw a bomb in the assembly and was arrested. Then came the Lahore Congress where Jawaharlal Nehru unfurled the flag and said:

> *We have now an open conspiracy to free this country from foreign rule, and you comrades, our countrymen and countrywomen are invited to join it. But the rewards that are in store for you are suffering, imprisonment and, may even be, death. But you shall also have the satisfaction that you have done your little bit for India, and have helped a little in the liberation of humanity from its present bondage.*[41]

Netaji and Simant Gandhi

Not only Mahatma Gandhi but Subhas Chandra Bose, Khan Abdul Gaffar Khan and other leaders also feature in the novel and we are also shown the trial of Bhagat Singh. Anwar almost quarreled with Manjoor, a police officer who was Prof Saleem's guest, on the issue of national movement. He broke with Salmah also. In Delhi his father believed in Muslim League as Anwar believed in the Congress.

The Dandi March

Anwar was sick and so when he got slightly better Dr Ansari brought for him the light work of working as an interpreter for an American Journalist, Robert Bills. Both of them covered the memorable *Dandi March:*

> *They arrived just in time as the Mahatma was expected to start on his march that very night and the whole city was in turmoil. The*

programme had been announced in advance and made known to the "enemy". The police knew the number and names of the satyagrahis who would be in the Gandhi Army, the 200-mile route of their March to Dandi on the sea and the villages where they would halt on the way! This was a new kind of army waging a new kind of war and there was no precedent in military history for these tactics and strategy. A new word was required to describe it-Satyagraha! Insistence on Truth! It was in fact the "Battle of Truth".[42]

Anwar saw a lathi charge in Mumbai (Bombay) and saved a Gujarati gril. The girl took him to her home. Her name was Asha Shah. Anwar then met her mother and thereafter others who were all engaged in national work. He also met her father who was a calculated capitalist. In the mean time Anwar heard the news that Salmah was married to Manzoor Ahmad, Deputy Superintendent of Police.

The Hatred of the Muslim League

The political atmosphere was full of despair. His uncle Taya Amjad Ali accompanied by his father addressed a fiery pubic meeting in which he stirred up communalism. Anwar made a speech contradicting his uncle:

Soon he could not hear what Taya Amjad Ali was saying. Nor could he see him. He saw a great many Amjad Alis-Hindu Amjad Alis, Muslim Amjad Alis, Parsee and Sikh and Christian and Harijan Amjad Alis, with beards and top knots and sacred threads and crosses, all shouting, "We are a separate people", brandishing the Sword of Islam, the Sword of Hinduism, the Sword of Sikhism, plunging the blades into the body of India and soon all the swords were dripping with blood.[43]

When they went home his uncle angrily declared that Anwar after all has shown his Kafir blood. He gave out at last that he was the son of Kaka Rameshwar by a prostitute named Chhamia Bai. Anwar rushed out of his house and went to that prostitute's house. But he was shy and she told him.

"Go home son". That is what she had called him. He had been called that by many affectionate people, by Akbar Ali who, till an hour ago, had been his father, by Rameshwar who had known him all along to be his son, and by Ma-ji in Bombay. But the word has never sounded so sweet,, so tender, so full of life's most elemental emotion, as when it was uttered by this degraded woman, this agent of Satan, this daughter of sin and this mother of his![44]

The Political History

He then went back to Akbar Ali and rushed into his waiting arm. Here ends the story of *Inquilab*. The novel closes on the political *plane*, with the Gandhi-Irwin settlement; and on the personnel *plane*, with the explosive revelation that Anwar is really a Hindu merchant's illegitimate son, though brought by a Muslim with more than a father's love.

Evaluating the work critically Dr K.R. Srinivasa Iyengar writes:

> *It cannot be said that politics is properly subsumed in 'Inquilab', that personal and political histories are artistically blended in its narrative. There is too much politics, and much of the writing is journalistic; the canvas is too large, the stage is too crowded; the attempt to comprehend too much has led to a kind of cramming of incidental detail, the multiplicity blurs the main outlines, the historical record scores at the expenses of the human story. It is evident that the large-scale importation of politics and political figures into a novel cannot succeed unless the writer brings into play the sweep of comprehension, the architectonic power and sheer creative energy that have gone into the making of a masterpiece like 'War and Peace'; and the difficulties must be all the greater when the present age (and not the vents of a past age, as in Tolstoy's novel) is the theme of the fictional narrative.*[45]

It is thus a historical novel. The publisher's blurb supports the view:

> *Inquilab is the story of the great revolution that ultimately brought independence to India. It contains several soul-stirring characters young in mind and spirit who poured their bubbling youth to twist and break the heavy chains of imperialism. It represents a magnificent cross-section of the entire Indian-nation during its most critical period....*
>
> *In a lucid and picturesque style and with an unusual warmth and sympathy Khwaja Ahmed Abbas proceeds with the narrative from which emerge more than a dozen of powerful and unforgettable characters.*
>
> *Inquilab finally turns out to be a powerful novel so realistic that several of the elder readers may perhaps find a reflection of their own aspirations of those glorious days portrayed in these pages.*[46]

The story is well told although the author's attempt has been to link up the memorable pages of the struggle of Indian independence round the figure of a nationalist Muslim youth. Even the story element of the love and fortunes of Anwar is powerful enough to keep the reader spellbound. The style is simple and lucid. The English, inter-spersed with Urdu words intentionally used by author for the sake of local colour, is smooth and polished. Truly speaking, it is a powerful and gripping novel of epic dimensions.

Abbas is at his best in this novel. The descriptions are realistic and picturesque. The scene of *Jallianwalla Bagh* is a masterpiece of descriptive art. Thus we find Abbas justifying the words of Goncourts that "...the actual novel is made with documents, related from life, or heightened; just a history is made with written documents. The historians are the narrators of the past, the novelists of the present."[47]

Panorama of the Moving Events

So far as the 'plot' of the novel is concerned, the entire struggle for freedom is the plot; a *kaleidoscopic* panorama of fast moving events, each one episodic in nature and yet properly adjusted and 'composed' in the general pattern of the freedom movement.

In selecting the story of the national struggle Abbas seems to have well kept in mind the very advice of Henry James:

> *Don't let anyone persuade you... That strenuous selection and comparison are not the very essence of art... Form alone takes, and holds and preserves, substance saves it from the welter of helpless Biverage that we swim in as in a sea of tasteless tepid pudding, and that makes one ashamed of an art capable of such degradations .... There is nothing so deplorable as a work of art with a leak in its interest, and there is no such leak of interest as through commonness of form.*[48]

And when we read *Inquilab* we know that there is no 'leak' in its interest.

References

1. Sharma, G.P. *Nationalism is Indo-Anglian Fiction*. p. 125.
2. *Ibid*. p. 126.
3. *Ibid*. p. 128.
4. *Ibid*.
5. *Ibid*. p. 2,
6. Holmstrom, Lakshmi. *The Novels of R.K. Narayan*, Calcutta: Writer's Workshop, 1973.
7. Iyegar, Dr K.R.S. *Indian Writing in English*. p. 372.
8. *Ibid*. pp. 372-73.

9. *Ibid.* 273.
10. Rosenthal, M.H. *New York Time Book Review,* March 23, 1958.
11. Narayan, R.K. *Waiting for the Mahatma.* New Delhi: Orient Paperbacks Pvt. Ltd. p. 37.
12. *Ibid.* p. 87.
13. *Ibid.* p. 143.
14. *Ibid.* p. 172.
15. *Ibid.* p. 193.
16. *Ibid.* pp. 243-244.
17. *Ibid.* p. 253.
18. *A Personal Record : 'A Familiar Preface'.*
19. Abbas, K.A. *Defeat for Death.* New Delhi: Orient Paperbacks Pvt. Ltd. p. 42.
20. *Ibid,* p. 42.
21. Sharma, G.P. *Nationalism is Indo- Anglion Fiction.* p. 222.
22. *Defeat for Death.* pp. 15-18.
23. *Ibid.*
24. *Ibid.*
25. *Ibid.*
26. *Ibid.*
27. *Ibid.* pp. 25-26.
28. *Ibid.*
29. *Ibid.* pp. 31-32.
30. *Ibid.* p. 33.
31. *Ibid.* p. 33.
32. *Indian Writing in English.* p. 284.
33. Abbas, K.A. *Inquilab.* New Delhi: Orient Paperbacks Pvt. Ltd. p. 25.
34. *Ibid.* p. 29.
35. *Ibid.* p. 37.
36. *Ibid.* p. 40.
37. *Ibid.* p. 131.
38. *Ibid.* p. 138.
39. *Ibid.* p. 200.
40. *Ibid.* p. 232.
41. *Ibid.* p. 238.
42. *Ibid.* p. 283.
43. *Ibid.* p. 299.
44. *Ibid.* p. 382.
45. *Indian Writing in English.* p. 285.

46. *Incuilab*. pp. i-ii.
47. Goncourts. Qtd. in *Some Principles of Fiction* by Robert Liddell. p. 99.
48. James, Henry. Qtd. in *Some Principles of Fiction* by Robert Liddell.p. 151.

7

Unfavourable Treatment of Gandhian Ideals

Mahatma Gandhi was a staunch upholder of moral uprightness. Most of his disciples were honest, straightforward and indifferent to power politics. They followed his principles, both in letter and spirit. In the novels of Mulk Raj Anand, Raja Rao, R.K. Narayan and Khwaja Ahmad Abbas, which we have studied in the preceding chapters, we have benign and complimentary images of the Mahatma.

The Unscrupulous Followers

But when independence was achieved and Mahatma Gandhi disappeared from the national scene, things began to change for the worse and people's faith in the disciples of Gandhi began to erode. There was corruption and moral degradation of his unscrupulous followers. As a result, the image of Mahatma Gandhi was badly tarnished. This phase of the diminishing popularity of Mahatma Gandhi has also been presented by some Indo-Anglian novelists. In *Train to Pakistan* by Khushwant Singh, *A Bend in the Ganges* by Manohar Malgonkar, and in *Azadi* by Chaman Nahal we have the expression of this aspect of Gandhian personality.

In this chapter our approach would be to view how these authors have criticised Gandhian ideals. Here our imperative is to examine how these novelists have projected Mahatma Gandhi,–his personality, his ideals, the national freedom movement in his leadership, and such other aspects, in an unfavourable way, contrary to several others who regarded him no less than a deity.

The Portrayal of Communal Violence

Khushwant Singh is one of the most celebrated authors of our time. His *Train to Pakistan* was published in 1956. The novel gave a jolt to the whole reading public with its graphic picture of the nation in its most painful and brutal process of partition. The story is set in a village, Mano Majra, situated in the northwestern region of undivided India. The country has just won that long-sought freedom. It was a great event for the world history, but it meant very little to the illiterate villagers. Their ignorance is a sort of blessing to them, at least temporarily. They do not know that along with freedom "the country is divided into Hindustan and Pakistan."[1]

And that the whole country is bleeding with communal enmity and hatred. The villagers have heard of Mahatma Gandhi, but have not heard of Jinnah. Being unaware with communal riots and bloodshed in the country the Muslims and the Sikhs of the village still cling to the ideals preached by Gandhi, even though Gandhi himself was then walking the bloody paths of the riot-torn India of his dream, lonely and disillusioned. In the eyes of the villagers the image of Gandhi is that of a religious man:

> *Look at Gandhi! I hear he reads the Koran Sharif and the Unjeel along with his Vedas and Shastras. People sing his praise in the four corners of the earth... even the English respect a man of religion.*[2]

All the villagers of Mano Majra, both Muslims and Sikhs, in their happy communal harmony, love and respect equally the Muslim-Mullah, regard him as their common *chacha*, and look forward to him for advice and suggestion. Their unity and fraternity remain intact, even when a trainload of Sikhs and Hindus killed by the Muslims elsewhere is cremated in their village by the government authority with oil and fuel taken from them. And when some Hindu refugees from Pakistan come to them for shelter, not only the Hindus but also the Muslims of Mano Majra come forward with equal earnestness to provide them food and shelter.

However, when they get the news of communal killings and bloodshed elsewhere in the country they get excited. The author writes:

> *Rumours or atrocities committed by Sikhs on Muslims in Patiala, Ambala and Kapurthala which they had heard and dismissed, came back to their minds... Quite suddenly, every Sikh in Mano Majra became a stranger with an evil intent. His long hair and beard appeared barbarous, his Kirpan menacingly anti-Muslim. For the*

first time, the name of Pakistan came to mean something to them – a heaven of refugees where there were no Sikhs.[3]

And its reaction? Once again to quote from the text:

The Sikhs were sullen and angry. 'Never trust a Mussulman'- they said. The last Guru had warned them that the Muslims had no loyalties. He was right... Now a trainload of Sikhs massacred by Muslims had been cremated in Mano Majra. Hindus and Sikhs were fleeing from their homes in Pakistan... These were reasons enough to be angry with some one. So they decided to be angry with Muslims.[4]

But the deep-rooted love and affection of one community for another in the village could not be shaken off so easily. When the life of Muslims in the village is in danger and government wants to evacuate the Muslims for their safety and send them to Pakistan the Sikhs with tears in their eyes assure them for their safety. The village lambardar, a Sikh, says, "This is your village as much as ours."[5] Another Sikh says:

As long as we are here nobody will dare to touch you. We die first and then you look after yourselves.[6]

And the Muslims, too, express the same sentiment and emotion. One of the Muslims says:

What have we to do with Pakistan? We are born here. So were our ancestors. We have lived amongst you as brothers.[7]

But the time and situation has left no option. The communities have to part; the Muslims have to be evacuated from the village and sent to Pakistan for their safety.

But this is not the climax of the story. The situation of the village worsens with the situation of the country. The police, the military, and the administration as well become biased and communal. The innocent peasant Sikhs have been instigated by the educated Sikhs coming from the town for killing two Musalmans "for each Hindu or Sikhs they kill."[8] A section of the Sikhs of Mano Majra is soon won over, and they join the educated Sikhs coming from outside in their plot to massacre the Muslims passing by in a train to Pakistan. Even the news that the Muslim brethren of their village already evacuated will also depart for Pakistan by that train, cannot stop them now from the execution of the plot. However, with the good sense and noble intentions of some of the wise people of the village the planned massacre in the train to Pakistan is averted, at the high cost of martyrdom of a Sikh.

The narrative technique of the novel is not the conventional one. The story develops through some selected episodes, incidents in the village and outside and well-knit plot. The author effectively portrays the communal harmony and the fellow-feelings inherent in the millennium old Indian society, and how same was disrupted by vested interests for their own ends at that crucial point. The story is told in the wake of the nation won freedom showing the lack of fore-sight in the national leadership for not assessing the aftermaths of decision of partition of the nation.

Khushwant Singh holds the miscalculations of *Baniya* politicians at Delhi (an obvious reference to Gandhi) responsible for India's partition resulting in mass massacres during the early autumn of 1947. He also shows the bias and inefficiency of the administration in handling the unfortunate situation. The author thinks that the massacre and the bloodshed at the time of partition is an irony on the entire Gandhian values of freedom movement.

The author attacks the disciples of Gandhi in the government:

> *Ask anyone coming from Delhi and he will tell you that all these Gandhi disciples are minting money. They are as good saints as the crane. They shut their eyes piously and stand on one leg like a yogi doing penance; as soon as a fish comes near - hurrup.*[9]

Khushwant Singh's *I Shall Not Hear the Nightingale* appeared in 1959. It is a popular love story set against the freedom movement and the war years from April 1942 to April 1943 at *Jallianwalla Bagh*. Here we have a good deal of people's involvement in the freedom struggle or their non-cooperation with the British.

Subtle Description of India's Partition

Chaman Nahal's *Azadi* is another novel in our preview. It was published in 1975. Here we have a subtle description of India's partition and the riots and the bloodshed that followed. The people of Sialkot had perfect faith in Gandhi's determination to keep the country united. Lala Kanshi Ram cannot even imagine how the partition could happen. To quote his words from the text:

> *The Congress had a promise to keep with the people. For the last thirty years, since that wizard Gandhi appeared on the scene, it had taken the stand that India was a single nation, not two. And Gandhi was not only a politician, he was a saint. He had his inner voice to satisfy, too. Would that nagging voice of his let him accept the slaughter of so many? That's what it would mean, if Pakistan did come into existence. And Gandhi was shrewd - surely he saw it all. He wouldn't give in to such butchery.*[10]

But when the bombshell of partition falls and the people of Sialkot are doomed to migrate with families and children, their faith in the Mahatma gets shattered.

Exposure of Congress Hypocracy

Manohar Malgonkar's *A Bend in the Ganges* was published in 1964. The political story of the country is told through the personal story of Debidayal, Gian and Sundari. The political aspect comprises the non-violent movement under the leadership of Gandhi around the forties when the extremist movement, too, was at a crucial stage.

In this novel the author uses a two-pronged approach to Gandhism.

He exposes the hypocrisy and hollowness of Mahatma's disciples like Gian. At the same time he probes the Gandhian philosophy of non-violence by posing the question: Could it ever serve as a philosophy of life itself? In the first chapter of the novel Gandhi appears briefly, but his creed of non-violence suffers severe attack throughout the work.

The Extremists: the Nationalists

The author tells the story from the viewpoint of an extremist group of freedom fighters. Actually the extremists were the thoroughbred nationalists who believed in the militant action to get freedom of the nation.

They believed that the freedom was not something that could be achieved through the *tyaga*, the *tapasya*, but it must be snatched from the Britishers. Obviously, the members of this group in the novel had no faith in Gandhi's ideology of *satya* and *ahimsa*. They rather hold Gandhi responsible for the atrocities committed during India's partition.

Non-violence: The Creed of the Coward

The novel begins with the dialogue of a character named Singh who denounces Gandhi's philosophy of non-violence 'as the philosophy of sheep, a creed for cowards, ...the greatest danger to this country.'[11] To quote his words from the text:

> *Gandhi, by weakening the spirit of men, making us all into sheep and cattle, will only multiply the sacrifice. A million shall die, I tell you - a million! For each man who should have died in the cause of freedom, Gandhi will sacrifice ten. That is what non-violence will do to this country.*[12]

Basu is another character in the novel who expresses a similar view:

> *Non-violence is merely a pious thought, a dream of the philosophers.*

I shudder to think what disillusion confronts them; what Gandhi will feel when he sees the holocaust that will engulf this country. He will die a thousand deaths, I tell you, he will suffer for each single man that suffers, Hindu or Moslem, but will he ever recognise that mankind is not prepared for true non- violence–will never be prepared? No! No! He will go on living and preaching his dream.[13]

Non-violence : It cannot be the Philosophy of Nation

Basu is a revolutionary by creed. He capitalises on the fact that Gandhi himself had doubts about the efficacy of non-violence. He quotes Gandhi again and again. Malgonkar, in fact, uses this quotation as an epigraph to the novel:

This non-violence, therefore, seems to be due mainly to our helplessness. It almost appears as if we are nursing in our bosoms the desire to take revenge the first time we get the opportunity. Can true, voluntary non-violence come out of this seeming forced non-violence of the weak? What if, when the fury bursts, not a man, woman or child is safe and every man's hand is raised against his neighbour?[14]

This very epigraph sets the tune of the novel. Even Gian, who puts his faith in the Gandhian creed of non-violence in the beginning of the novel, soon discovers that his 'light–hearted acceptance' of *ahimsa* cannot serve him as a philosophy of life. When his brother is murdered, he forgets his vows to practise the Mahatma's creed. He seeks out Vishnu Dutt, the culprit of his brother's death, and kills him. Tekchand, an industrialist, is a Gandhian in the novel. When he is confronted by the reality of violence unleashed by communal riots, he sees the inefficacy of Gandhian philosophy. The author writes:

Now he could see that as the people of India were concerned, Gandhi's message was merely a political expedient; that for the bulk of them, it had no deeper significance. At best, they had accepted it as an effective weapon against British power. It seemed that the moment the grip of British power was loosened; the population of the sub-continent had discarded non-violence overnight and were now spending themselves on orgies that seemed to fulfill some basic urge.[15]

It seems that the author has used this novel as an instrument to propagate his ideas. He uses his characters as his mouthpiece. After having seen the dialogues of the characters in the novel it is relevant to see the author's ideas. To quote Malgonkar in 'Author's Note':

Only the violence in this story happens to be true; it came in the wake of freedom, to become a part of India's history. What was achieved through non-violence brought with it one of the bloodiest upheavals of history: seventeen million people had to flee, leaving their homes; nearly half a million were killed; over a hundred thousand women, young and old, were abducted, raped, mutilated.[16]

Through *A Bend in the Ganges* the author shows how Gandhi's principle of non-violence was bound to fail perilously as it did with the kind of followers he had. A character in the novel says:

In the midst of Gandhi's non-violence, violence persists. Violence such as no one has ever seen. That is what awaits this country; the violence bottled up in those who pay lip service to non-violence.[17]

Gandhi himself has been introduced in the first chapter of the novel. He is in the vow of silence. One of his followers explains to the assembled crowd the meaning of non-violence in their struggle. To quote his words:

The non-violence of the brave, arising not from cowardice, but from courage, demanding greater sacrifice than ordinary fighting men are called upon to make.[18]

But the author shows how even the devoted followers of Gandhi, like Gian Talwar in the story, were not at heart really brave, not really moral, but were mostly opportunists and cowards for which the movement, in spite of Gandhi, had come to its natural end, soaking the country in a bloodbath.

In the light of these references it is not just to draw the conclusion that the author is recommending violence as a way of life in preference to the Gandhian principle of non-violence. As a creative artist his attitude is very critical and he mirrors the spirit of the age. He is simply exposing the hypocrisy of those followers of Gandhi who pay lip service to non-violence but have really violence bottled up in them. The author's attitude can best be traced in the words of Devi-dayal, an extremist nationalist leader:

Yet what was the alternative? Would terrorism have won freedom at a cheaper price and somehow still kept Hindus and Moslems together? Perhaps not. But at least it would have been an honest sacrifice, honest and manly–not something that had sneaked upon them in the garb of non-violence.[19]

Thus, in the light of above criticism it is apt to say that the author does not uphold extremism as an answer to the question of country's freedom. Dr G.P. Sharma observes:

He does not reject Gandhi's principles, though he is dubious of the people's capability to follow him. He is critical of the effectiveness of

Jinnah's separatist view which is also held responsible in the story for that national holocaust.[20]

Britisher's Prejudice against Indians

Combat of Shadows is a political novel of Manohar Malgonkar. It appeared in 1962. Here the author has been very critical of the Indian nationalism and the Gandhian ideals. With equal detachment, the novelist focuses the doubtful actions, motives and idols of both sides. Thus as the theme of the novel we have the prejudice of the ruling Britishers against Indians, their subject race, and the Indians' consequent hatred for the Britishers.

Henry Winton and Jugal Kishor are the two characters representing the ideas, which are poles apart. Henry Winton is a young Englishman and Jugal Kishor, an Indian Trade Unionist leader. The former, a manager of a British tea estate, in Assam, is generally honest, well intentioned, and guileless while the latter is an unscrupulous Indian political leader. Henry Winton finds himself in a situation that is puzzling, demoralising and dehumanising for him. There was a small theft case in the garden in which Gauri, the niece of Jugal Kishor, the stockman, was caught red-handed. The girl was let to go with a warning, but Jugal Kishor twisted the incident as an attempt of the white manager to molest a tender-aged Indian girl. There is no end to the matter when it had once started.

One trifle matter deserves to be mentioned. In the tea-garden school there is a vacancy for a teacher. When Winton refuses the candidature of Gauri, Jugal Kishor gives it a political colour treating this at a case of racial prejudice.

The life of Henry Winton as a manager in the tea garden becomes a nightmare as his relationship with Jugal Kishor becomes sore. Jugal Kishor fights for the state assembly election, becomes the member of the house and then the Minister of Plantation. Henry Winton now apprehends real danger from him, who can sit on judgment over him for his personal lapses as manager of the estate. He wants to come out of the whole situation and even to leave the country by joining the army to fight in the Second World War. He is selected for a commission but Jugal Kishor stands in the way and using his powers as a minister he does not relieve Winton. Henry Winton thus becomes a victim of the machination of crooked politician.

In *Combat of Shadows*, the author, through the story of racial prejudice of Henry Winton, seems to paint the Indian side in a darker dye.

Though he is not as unscrupulous as Jugal Kishor, his character is drawn in a more or less similar mould. In the tea-garden school he would appoint only Rube Miranda, an Anglo-Indian girl whom he wants as his mistress, though Ruby Miranda does not have adequate qualifications for a teachership. Again, he can love Ruby Miranda or can keep her as his mistress; but he would not marry her because she is not a pure white girl. Later, when he marries a girl of pure British blood and finds that she is friendly with an Anglo-Indian youth, Eddy Trevor, it is inexcusable for him. He explains to his wife why she should not mix up with Anglo-Indian people. To quote his words that clearly reflect arrogance of the ruling class: "It's not a question of liking or disliking them. It's just that they are different from us, the ruling race."[21]

Dark side of Indian Politics

In *Combat of Shadows* we find the author portraying the darker side of Indian politics and that of the politicians of the Gandhian era. Jugal Kishor is the representative of these politicians who, as the followers of Gandhi and Nehru, become the leaders of the people. Jugal Kishor is ugly and repulsive not only in his words and deeds but also in his looks, as he has "blunted, puffy, roundness of feature, the opaque half-closed eyes."[22]

Jugal Kishor is clever enough to twist the matters to serve his own interest. He goes farther to the extent to be mean enough to lay bare the bosom of his young niece, Gauri, before Winton in order to tempt him when the latter had refused her appointment as a teacher.

Jugal Kishor contests the election for the state assembly backed by the labour unions and supported by the Congress. He wins with a massive majority and is made a minister. When Winton comes to know he is going to contest the election, on his face he says to Jugal Kishor:

> *May God help India, if people like you are to be elected to assemblies. You are crooked, without a spark of decency, corrupt, and quite immoral.*[23]

The irony of the situation is to be marked here. Jugal Kishor becomes the Minister of Plantations; labourers' problem in the tea garden miraculously ceases, even though the conditions of the labourers remained unchanged. Winton is unable to understand this mystery until he comes to know from the Resident Director of their group of tea estates that the union leader had been bribed by the planters to keep mum. The Director comments on the motive of the politicians and their politics:

Politics is his business, just as growing tea is yours and mine. We grow tea for no other reason than because it gives us the wherewithal to live according to our standards; he goes into politics for much the same reason.[24]

The commentary of the Resident Director on a politician is a real commentary on the post-independence Indian politicians. To quote his surprising revelation once again:

Did you know that the Brindian Tea Company contributed five thousand rupees to his election expenses, and the other two companies, two thousand each? Do you know that the day he became Minister for Plantations he was given an assurance, on behalf of three companies, that he would be given a monthly remuneration of one thousand rupees if he stayed on our side?[25]

With the depiction of the Britisher's prejudice and hatred against the Indians the author delineates the dark aspects of Indian politics. Here the author shows how the unscrupulous followers of Gandhi and Nehru could sell out the national cause for personal profit and self-interest.

Documentary of the Dirty Politics

Combat of Shadows is a real documentary of Indian politics prevailing in the fourth decade of the 20th century when our freedom movement in the leadership of Mahatma Gandhi was in its highest ebb. It was the time when anything having something to do with the British in India came to be looked upon by the Indians as a political issue, however private or personal it might be. All this made the life of the British in India a nightmare. A triffle incident in the novel deserves to be mentioned. A rogue elephant appears in the villages. The task of killing the elephant falls upon Henry Winton who was supposed to restore the image of white rulers in the minds of the natives. Winton, with the help of a lame Indian *shikari*, confronts the elephant but due to the defective cartridges he has to flee away to save his life. He is saved, but the lame *shikari* is trampled to death. The news spreads in the villages like a wildfire and Winton is charged of having intentionally murdered an Indian. Winton is shocked to see the situation, though the experienced planters had forecast such a reaction well ahead in time. To quote the dialogue:

The Indian ministers will laugh their heads off; and the villagers will whisper behind your back, pointing a finger at you... And there is the press. My God, you don't know the Indian press... If they get a sahib in their mangle, particularly when it concerns something we ourselves profess to do better than the Indians... The political capital the Gandhis and Nehrus will make.[26]

Winton is unable to understand how an accident like this could lead to anything political. Cockburn, the experienced white planter, who had accepted India as his homeland and had a father image among the labourers, says:

In India, everything that concerns a Sahib is political, damn it. His very presence is the basis of all political agitation.[27]

Dr G.P. Sharma observes:

Malgonkar's special success lies in that he has not made any attempt to gloss over the dark aspects either of the Indian side or of the imperialist side. This is typical of Malgonkar as a political novelist and it is this which earns for his novels a distinct place in Indo-Anglian literature.[28]

In *The Princes,* Manohar Malgonkar has attained laudable success. It appeared in 1963. The novel is akin to Mulk Raj Anand's *The Private Life of an Indian Prince* so far as the story and setting in time and history are concerned. Malgonkar as an artist has looked upon the human aspect of the problem while looking at the national problem from his own vantage point which is of course quite opposite to that of Mulk Raj Anand. Dr G.P. Sharma observes:

In these, the novel The Princes becomes a criticism of the Indian National policy after independence regarding the Indian Princely states, which contrasts with the novel The Private Life of an Indian Prince by Anand which supports this policy.[29]

The Romance and the Chivalry

The Princes may be regarded as the best of all the novels of Manohar Malgonkar. Its story is both appealing and objective. In *Combat of Shadows* also we have these elements in fair measure but the melodrama of murder and love intrigues at the end have marred the same. *The Princes* is free of all these evils and the story appeals to both heart and head. Here the popular ingredients of the romance and the adventure, the heroism and the chivalry are beautifully blended together. The author here depicts that phase of our national life when age-old administrative set up was trampled down by us in the zeal of new spirit of democracy with no care for decency.

The story of the novel refers to the period of late thirties to forties when our freedom movement was in its momentum. The *Praja Mandals,* the counterparts of the Congress in the princely states, gave the princes a very difficult time, threatening their existence. The British government did not do anything to keep their promises in spite of their assurance that the British government would scrupulously accept and maintain all treaties and agreements and shall always respect their rights, dignity and honour. To quote Dr G.P. Sharma in this context:

> *This assurance was renewed from time to time by successive British Emperors. It is also suggested how the British were not selflessly interested in them or their welfare; their actual interest was in the Empire. The Princes with their typical naiveté, took it for a genuine interest and placed all their trust in the good will of the British government.*[30]

The author focuses that aspect of post-Independence Indian politics when the princely estates were left to the National Government of India and the *Praja Mandals* of the state to be swallowed up as they liked.

The politics of Begwad, a princely estate, situated in the central India is at the centre of the story. Abhay, the prince's son, the narrator of the story, is completely detached. Contrary to this, his father, Prince Hiroji Maharaj, lacks this detachment, vision and insight, in the changed circumstances. Owing to his medieval idea of his right to rule under all circumstances he is doomed to meet extinction in the new age. At the end of the story his death is inevitable. Abhay, his son, with a clear vision of the past, the present and the future, foresees the inevitability of such an end, but being a human being, with honesty of mind and sincerity of purpose he is not enthusiastic about the way this end has come to his father and his estate. He is a sensitive young man with deep insight, He accepts all the changes that the country is heading for with the great national leaders like Mahatma Gandhi and Pandit Nehru. The followers of these national leaders in the state politics are so unworthy and petty with their mind steeped in jealousy and hatred that he prefers to stick to his father. These despicable politicians are not content with anything less than crushing their personal enemies.

The Follies and the Foibles of Politics

With the criticism of the unscrupulous followers of Gandhi and Nehru, the author criticises the great movement these leaders were associated with. In this way Malgonkar is a novelist with a difference in comparison to his contemporary novelists. But this does not mean that Malgonkar is an advocate of the princely states and is blind to the evil aspects of their lifestyle. In the story he shows the follies and foibles of these rulers as well. The Prince of Begwad seeks sensual pleasure with his concubines to the utter neglect of his own consort who is thrown to the pity and subsequent love of one of his petty officials. When he unexpectedly horsewhips the cobbler's son Kanak Chand in public, his rashness and thoughtless behaviour is reflected. He wastes fifteen thousand to bribe a girl of low origin to keep herself away from his son, who has fallen in love with her. He gets his family history written by an eminent university professor hired for the purpose on extravagant honorarium to prove his lineage and prestige. His blind faith in his divine right to rule is pitiable, at least in a modern age. He is foolishly confident of his position, when the whole nation is crying hoarse for freedom. To quote him:

> *There will always be a Begwad, and there will always be a Bedar ruling it - so long as the sun and the moon go round.*[31]

It was the time when the whole nation had gathered under the banner of national leaders like Gandhi and Nehru, and even the British government had granted self-rule to the British Indian estates. This ruling Prince of Begwad sneers at all these developments and calls the national leaders: "*Goondas* led by traders and lawyers."[32] Elsewhere he asserts: "As far as I am concerned, they do not exist."[33]

However, the author does not neglect to depict the selfish, the narrow-minded, and the dishonest politicians of the country. Kanak Chand, the son of an untouchable, an earnest devotee of Mahatma Gandhi from his school days and advocate of Gandhian ideals is one such politician. He hates the rule of the princes and even spits at the name of the 'state people who are in slavery'.[34] He, despite his being a follower of Mahatma Gandhi and a leader of the *Praja Mandal* of his estate, behaves most shamelessly with the ruling house. He goes to the extent of indulging in all sorts of slander and blatant lies. He, as the President of the *Praja Mandal* of the *Maharaja's* state gives the *Maharaja* all sorts of trouble. To the Government of India, he sends a series of complaints against the *Maharaja*. When the country wins freedom, he becomes more powerful due to his link with the Congress as a *Praja Mandal* leader. He indulges in all sorts of false and highly exaggerated propaganda against *Maharaja's* private life. The irony of the novel is to be marked here.

Kanak Chand though is a disciple of Mahatma Gandhi, he is not fair in his private life. In his childhood he couldn't have even a square meal but now he is in possession of a 'bunglow and a *gaddi*.'[35] He is a typical Indian politician with all the vices of character.

Abhay, the *Maharaja's* son, is progressive-minded. He has seen the imperatives of the age and has accepted the democratic, republic values coped with the Gandhian ideas. He is happy that his father had at last signed the Instrument of Accession. He is unable to understand why Kanak Chand is so inimical to his father or the family. On his accord he talks with Kanak Chand and asks him why he does not want to come to terms but Kanak Chand is not only unyielding but indignant at this very idea. To quote him:

I want revenge. I want to wash away the insult of the poverty... the shame of untouchability.[36]

He gets the state merged with the Indian Union to wash away this shame. Although this was an execution of an Indian national policy without any thought but the very intention of Kanak Chand was soiled.

Malgonkar has sketched the character of Abhay in contrast to the character of the *Maharaja* and Kanak Chand. *Maharaja's* and that of Kanak Chand are the dark pictures while the character of Abhay is all embracing and liberal. Though he is attached to his father, he is not a bit hesitant in grasping the changes in national situation. He does not support the conservative ideas of his father. He looks at the whole process of passing away of the Princely order in the spirit of peculiar detachment. This ambivalence has made his character lovesome and appealing to the readers. To quote him in the text:

We were the princes; no one mourned our death. We were a jest of history, a tribe that had lived long beyond its day because it had been carefully preserved in the strong chemicals of British protection. And when that protection was withdrawn and all of us were exposed to the harsh glare of the sun like frogs under an overturned slab, it was inevitable that we should perish. I realise that it could not have been otherwise, and yet I cannot rid myself of a purely selfish sense of loss."[37]

Dr G.P. Sharma is all praise for the nobility in Abhay's character:

It is this understanding which makes this character noble, and at the same time a significant one making an objective appraisal of the situation when the Princely order dissolved in the white heat of our strong national fervour which brought for the country, freedom and for the people democracy.[38]

Indecency of the Congress Leaders

The Distant Drum is the first novel of Manohar Malgonkar. It was published in 1960. Here we have a political leader of Congress Party who is a living example of indecency. He visits an army regiment office and demands the military *shamiana* to be sent to the City Hall garden where the Congress Committee will receive a leader whose visit is scheduled in the city. No army officer including Colonel Kiran, the Officer-in-charge, would have ever heard such requests in the British period. Naturally, Colonel Kiran expresses his inability to lend military property for political purposes. The Congress leader, whose character is moulded in so called Gandhian values, loses his temper and shouts at the army officer:

> *... the political party of which you talk so lightly is ruling this country to-day. The days of treating us as seditious organisation are gone. Now the party and the government are the same. I would say that in refusing this small favour you are running for a great risk.*[39]

Colonel Kiran soon gets transferred from the Regiment. Kanka Chand in *The Prince* can be viewed in comparison to the Congress leader in *The Distant Drum*. Kanka Chand, the so-called upholder of democracy, becomes the Education Minister after the merger of the state. The picture depicted in the novel shows the new democratic set-up that the author intends to project. A few illustrations deserve to be referred. The national government after the independence of the country invites the *Maharaja* of Begwad to discuss the question of merger of the state. The *Maharaja*, accompanied by his Chief Minister and his son, Abhay, has arrived at exact time in the Secretariat. But the Joint Secretary in the Home Ministry, whom they had to meet, is not ready to meet them because he has not finished his tea. After twenty minutes of wait when they are at last shown into his room, the *Maharaja* has left the place in impatience. The Joint Secretary, whom the author describes as "a dark little man with bulging eyes and a froglike expression to go with them,"[40] is then only 'putting away his cup of coffee. On an empty plate before him, were the crumbs of *samosas* and the remains of a red sauce."[41] "There were neither smiles nor apology for having kept us waiting - only the tray with the dregs of breakfast."[42] Before leaving the place the *Maharaja* comments:

> *The British I feel would have handled it with much more finesse. They would have been civil ... civil as well as punctual.*[43]

Manohar Malgonkar is regarded as an upholder of aristocracy, a novelist of the top dog, a conservative who does not want the liberal ideas to take root. In all his social or socio-political novels in general and *Combat of Shadows*, *Distant Drum* and *The Prince* in particular, Malgonkar has shown a tendency to uphold conservative ideals and values in spite of the fact that he takes meticulous care to paint unpalatable aspects of both the aristocrats and the middle and lowly classes in equal proportions, without an attempt to gloss over the defects of the upper class. His sympathy for the conservative values amounts to repugnance for democratic or proletarian ideals is clear from his portraiture of the politicians and the leaders of our age who were the underdogs of democratic or the Gandhian values. But one should not think that Malgonkar is an advocate of the British regime or the Princelye states. To quote Dr G.P. Sharma:

Like Abhay, he, too, wants the change, but he wants it to come in a proper way and prove itself decent to all. As it is, Malgonkar is not happy with the way the change has come and the way the new set-up has worked. But behind such criticism again, it should be remembered, is the feeling that 'consciousness of the bad is an essential pre-requisite to the promotion of the good.[44]

Criticism of Contemporary Politics

Thus we have viewed how Gandhi and his followers have been made the subject of criticism. These authors have dealt with the political scenario of the Gandhian era as wall as post-independent India with a critical and objective attitude.

Midnight Address to the Nation

It may be a subject of debate and discussion whether the followers of Gandhi were worthy or unworthy. But one thing that is beyond all controversy is that his messages have perennial relevance. Pt. Jawaharlal Nehru in his address to the nation on the midnight of 14th of August, 1947 says:

We have often been unworthy followers of his and have strayed from his message, but not only we but succeeding generations will remember this message and bear the imprint in their hearts of this great son of India, magnificent in his faith and strength and courage and humility.[45]

Tagore's Tribute to Mahatma

We agree with Rabindranath Tagore that Mahatma Gandhi is not only great as a politician, as an organiser, as a moral reformer, he is greater than all these as a man, irrespective of his success or failure in future:

Gandhi ... is the complete man who is absolutely one with his ideas, whose vision perfectly blend with his whole being... Perhaps he may not succeed. Perhaps he may fail as the Buddha failed and as Christ failed to win men from their iniquities, but he will always be remembered as one who made his life a lesson for all ages to come.[46]

References

1. Singh, Khushwant. *Train to Pakistan*. New Delhi: Orient Paperbacks Pvt. Ltd. 20.
2. *Ibid*. p. 47.
3. *Ibid*. pp. 105-06.
4. *Ibid*. p. 106.
5. *Ibid*. p. 109.
6. *Ibid*. p. 110.
7. *Ibid*.
8. *Ibid*. p. 129.
9. Ibid, p. 20
10. Nahal, Chaman. *Azadi*. New Delhi: Orient Paperbacks Pvt. Ltd. pp. 48-49
11. Malgaonkar, Manohar. *A Bend in the Ganges*. New Delhi: Orient Paperbacks Pvt. Ltd. p. 11.
12. *Ibid*. p. 14.
13. *Ibid*. p. 17.
14. *Ibid, Epigraph*. p. i.
15. *Ibid*. p. 51.
16. *Ibid*. p. ii.
17. *Ibid*. p. 98.
18. *Ibid*. p. 12.
19. *Ibid*. p. 366.
20. *Nationalism in Indo-Anglian Fiction*. p. 256.
21. Malgaonkar, Manohar. *Combat of Shadows*. New Delhi: Orient Paperbacks Pvt. Ltd. p. 199.
22. *Ibid*. p. 33.
23. *Ibid*. p. 113.
24. *Ibid*. p. 227.
25. *Ibid*. p. 228.
26. *Ibid*. p. 90.
27. *Ibid*.
28. *Nationalism in Indo-Anglian Fiction*. p. 258.
29. *Ibid*. p. 259.
30. *Ibid*. p. 230.

31. Malgaonkar, Manohar. *The Princes*. New Delhi: Orient Paperbacks Pvt. Ltd. p. 11.

32. *Ibid.* p. 13.

33. *Ibid.* p. 14.

34. *Ibid.* p. 87.

35. *Ibid.* p. 97.

36. *Ibid.* p. 274.

37. *Ibid.* p. 11.

38. *Nationalism in Indo-Anglian Fiction.* p. 263.

39. Malgaonkar, Manohar. *Distant Drum*. New Delhi: Orient Paperbacks Pvt. Ltd. p. 53.

40. *The Princes.* p. 295.

41. *Ibid.*

42. *Ibid.*

43. *Ibid.*

44. *Nationalism in Indo-Anglian Fiction.* p. 265.

45. Nehru's address to Nation. '*The Appointed Day*'. Published in English Reader. New Delhi: NCERT, 1984. p. 26.

46. *The Visva Bharati Quarterly.* Gandhi Memorial Peace Number.

8

Gandhian Philosophy Needs Revalidation in the Changed Context

Mahatma Gandhi was the pivotal figure in our struggle for independence. After the attainment of independence the Indian leaders took a pledge to run the administration of the country in accordance with the ideals and principles enunciated and propagated by him. But when the diplomatic and political problems in the day-to-day running of the administration were encountered, it was felt that the views and principles of the Mahatma were not of much help. This phase of our national consolidation has found expression in the works of some of our contemporary novelists; the noted ones among them being Nayantara Sahgal and Bhabani Bhattacharya. Nayantara Sahgal has four novels to her credit, *A Time to be Happy*, *This Time of Morning*, *Storm in Chandigarh* and *The Day in Shadow*.

Power Politics in the Nehru's Prime Ministership

Nayantara Sahgal's *This Time of Morning* was published in1965. The novelist here has portrayed the power politics in the last days of Nehru's primeministership. The protagonist Kaliash Vrind, a veteran Gandhian in the novel, doubts the creed of non-violence. The author tells about him:

> *He accepted it as the finest way for India at that moment in her history to win her freedom ... but ... he did not accept it as a philosophy of life and it could never apply to a sovereign state which would have to maintain armed strength for defence.*[1]

He also believes that many of Gandhian ideals like prohibition of liquor, cow protection, sexual abstinence, aversion to science and industrialisation are out of tune with the twentieth century. Kalyan Sinha, the antagonist of the novel thinks that Gandhi has emasculated the people.

In *This Time of Morning* the image of Gandhi has pervasively been felt in the reflections of Kailas Vrind. In fact, in his moments of retrospection, he recapitulates the entire history of Gandhian movement and his involvement with the country's progress to self-government beginning with Gandhi's experience in the train from Durban to Pretoria in 1893. One of the chapters has been devoted almost entirely to this purpose. The novel although in the final analysis calls into question the sanctity of the Gandhian tenets in the practical world of politics, it affirms its faith in the Gandhian values by showing the moral degeneration and eventual downfall of a power-mongering politician. Kalyan Sinha sees in Gandhi only a history of India's decay and decline:

> *... decay and decline, culminating fantastically in the person of a man acknowledged saint and leader who had believed that liberating the untouchable from the job of cleaning a latrine was more important than liberating a people from foreign rule.*[2]

Non-violence: Inadequate to Meet the New Challenges of the Nation

This Time of Morning poses a question - Can a sovereign state, which has to maintain armed forces for defense, live up to the ideal of Gandhi's principle of non-violence? This question became crucial during the Chinese invasion on India in 1962. Gandhian philosophy of non-violence was found inadequate to meet the new challenges faced by the nation.

Storm in Chandigarh is the next novel of Nayantara Sahgal. It appeared in 1969. It is akin to *This Time of Morning* so far as the theme of the novel is concerned. Here we have the depiction of the political scenario of the late sixties when Punjab was further divided into Punjab and Haryana turning into an apple of discord between the two states. As per settlement the Punjabi-speaking Sikh part of Punjab remained as Punjab and the Hindi-speaking non-Sikh part of Punjab came of as Haryana.

In the story, Harpal Singh, the Chief Minister of undivided Punjab, himself a Sikh, is a true Gandhian striving for communal harmony and national integration. He is against any further division of Punjab on the basis of religion and language. Gyan Singh represents the modern politicians. The author describes his character not as an individual but as a type. Unfortunately he has become the new rising leader of the Sikhs. To exploit the weak nerve of the people; he has mingled the religion and the language into the politics. In this way he has won the heart of the Punjabi masses. He succeeds to become the chief minister of Punjab; the success does not depend on any sound ideology but on his capability to raise the issues that can appeal the sentiment of people. The socio-economic circumstances also have turned the political situation in his favor. Thousands and thousands of people are poverty-stricken and are unable to get food-grains. It is quite natural that such people can be won over to any side. To quote the author's words:

> *Outbursts of brutal, calculated violence had become a feature of the cities. There were too many in the congestion and chaos who had nothing to lose by violence, too many others who sat inert and indifferent, their sap sucked dry, watching the mount and ebb like some great tidal wave waiting for it to engulf them... violence had become routine and expected. It was given different names, indiscipline unrest and disorder.* [3]

Chaotic period of our National Life

Storm in Chandigarh presents the real picture of the chaotic period of our national life during the sixties and early seventies. The old politicians of Gandhian Age were still alive, but not playing active role in the politics. Although they were dedicated to Gandhian ideals and democratic values, but the young leaders hardly followed them; they only looked for their own interests though always under the garb of some new ideals and values. All these circumstance caused the eclipse of Indian democracy. The internal emergency declared by the then Prime-Minister, Mrs Indira Gandhi, was culmination of this political chaos and disorder. The novelist writes about the then Home Minister of India, a Gandhian and very akin to Harpal Singh in his words and deeds:

> *The Home Minister was known to be strictly a light and shade man himself with a reservoir of patience that explored the farthest reaches of every problem. His admirers found this his finest, and his critics his most infuriating quality. As far as the Minister himself was concerned, there was no other way. He was the last surviving figure of the Gandhian era left in public life.* [4]

The author thinks that the nation suffered a major change, when such dedicated leadership came to an end. To quote from the text:

The map of India, once a uniform piece of territory to administer, was now a welter of separate sensitive identities, resurrected after independence. Psychology seemed to play as important a part in understanding them as did history, geography and economics. Much more than facts and figures were required in coping with political rivalries that had now ceased even to make bargains.[5]

Gyan Singh, the Chief Minister of the new Punjab, typifies the new leader of a new state of this post-independence India. To quote from the text:

In the new states, Punjab and Haryana, just carved out of the former Punjab, the quarrel over boundaries, water, electric power, continued, intensified by the presence of both new state governments in a common capital, Chandigarh, which was claimed exclusively as its own.[6]

Gyan Singh, being a Chief Minister, calls a total stike throughout both the states to demonstrate the strength of his demands. Harpal Singh is worried at this kind of politics. The Home Minister of India is equally worried at this situation and is unable to understand what to do at this new brand of politics. The centre deputes Vishal Dubey, the administrator, a bright and worthy officer to study the case and to report. Being the representative of the union Home Minister he sincerely and faithfully does his job and reports to the centre after a careful study of the situation in Chandigarh, the joint capital. In his report he backs Harpal Singh. In a further development Harpal Singh is assaulted by the supporters of Gyan Singh on the day of the strike and is hospitalised. Vishal Dubey returns Delhi from Chandigarh vexed and frustrated and Home Minister dies unfortunate death to know his mission failed.

Storm in Chandigarh thus shows the end of an epoch of Indian politics by the late sixties. Durga Das observes:

By the end of 1969, the spirit of sacrifice and service which was the hallmark of Congressmen before independence had given place to a naked struggle for power. India's vast problems of stability and progress took a back seat.[7]

Parochial Sentiments Replace the National Values

Nayantara Sahgal thinks that with the passing away of the Gandhian leaders like Harpal Singh, or the Home Minister, a new phase of Indian politics began. In this age the religious, the linguistic, and the parochial sentiments replaced the broader national ideals like communal harmony and the national integration etc. The novelist has expressed the national ideals through the dialogues of Vishal Dubey and Harpal Singh. When Harpal Singh, vexed and perplexed in the face of the new developments, intends to resign from chief ministership, Vishal Dubey convinces him against it. To quote his words:

> *I was thinking that we should all — civil servants, politicians, doctors, lawyers, armed forces, everybody—have resigned in 1947 when India was divided and the very foundation of this country's belief that religion was a private affair, torn up. But I don't suppose that would have been a practical thing to do.*[8]

At this Harpal Singh, like a true leader of the Gandhian order replies:

> *In 1947 there was still an India left to serve. Now there is no such loyalty to bind us. The long vision has disintegrated. At any rate, let someone who believes in the existence of Haryana, and to whom carving out this extra state makes some sense, look after it. I have no heart for this job.*[9]

The story, though ends with this note, is interspersed with the scenes and references to chaos and lawlessness. A few examples deserve to be quoted:

(i) *Labour trouble threatening the industries.*[10]
(ii) *Wanton killing and extraction of money...*[11]
(iii) *The language fever running high among the people.*[12]
(iv) *Ministers indulging in corrupt practices while talking of high ideals, and people and legislators* crying hoarse *against such practices in vain.*[13]
(v) T*he government service running at a snail's pace.*[14]
(vi) *Frequent breaks even in essential services caused by employees.*[15]

Storm in Chandigarh is a significant novel portraying a chaotic period in the era of national consolidation. Nayantara Sahgal's sympathies do not lie with the new who lack the firm Gandhian values and exploit the sentiments of the people.

The Day in Shadow is the last novel of Nayantara Sahgal. It appeared in 1971. It is continuation of the same theme of the new leadership ousting the old. Dr G.P. Sharma observes:

> *But whereas in the earlier novel, she was concerned with the conflict of the two kinds of leadership resulting in the end of one epoch, here she deals with the more serious aspect of the anatomy of the new leadership. For this, she tacitly poses through the story these questions: what is it that drives them to work for a change in the*

national ideals–sheer zeal for people's welfare or something else? Are these leaders really able to bring in a change for the better?[16]

Sumer Singh, the new Minister of Petroleum of the union government, represents the new leadership in the country. He has replaced Sardar Sahib Singh, who was dedicated to Gandhian values resembling Harpal Singh of earlier novel. Sumer Singh has no respect for Gandhi and the values he represents. It can be clearly seen from the statement made by him:

It is time to throw away sentiment, the weak, the worn out liberation of the past, time to bury Gandhi, and write a new page of Indian history.[17]

The novelist thinks that a new India, based on principles other than what Gandhi or Nehru stood for may be built but one cannot really be successful without an inner urge for people's welfare, without a true love for the country, and without a firm ideology to follow. The author discusses these issues through the dialogues of the main characters. She shows that the Oil Minister cannot bring in any welcome change because he is more after power and wealth than for the welfare of the people. As he says:

For him, he was convinced, it meant big things ahead–the prize–the Foreign Ministership which in the coming reshuffle would almost certainly be his. He was sick to die of it and its complications, the never ending controversies about crude, about refinery agreements, and all the homework it meant. He did not want that ministry. The Foreign Minister was a key figure on the world stage.[18]

Through his dialogues with his mistress, Pixie, the author expresses his ambition. To quotes:

If things went as he expected, he would be a force to reckon within his party in a few months' time. Privately he knew he could really count on the support of both the communist parties, too. And one or two of the other leftist groups were solidly behind him... And the independents had not been much of a problem in the vote — thirty thousand rupees per vote was not too much to hand out when the stakes were global.[19]

It is ridiculous that such a leader talks of bringing about a change, of building a New India. That he was a man of lowly ideas about his people whom he professes to serve can be seen from one of his conversations with Pixie:

We had it under Gandhi. He took ahimsa - non-violence -Hinduism's oldest idea and sent a whole nation into battle with nothing but that... You in your generation may have to find a different springboard, but there is no scarcity of ideas among us.[20]

It seems that this new leader wants a clean sweep of the last vestiges of Gandhism from the country. To quote him:

That was why there had to be a clean up, a break away, an end to the Gandhi syndrome, that supposedly long, shining chain of service, begun by the Mahatma that he himself had spun out ad nauseam in speeches.[21]

Raj, the Christian individualist, sees the way out in his own way:

Which is the famous workable idea that will lead us out of our tribulations? No country. Marx abolished frontiers when he united the working class... Not violence either. That would take another Gandhi to promote. So where is it, the touchstone that will work to-day?[22]

The author gives Simrit's view-point:

She could hardly believe it–after all these years to find that Som was a man without pity or concern or even real responsibility. A man, she decided, not quite out of jungle. He is so like Sumer Singh, she concluded in surprise. They are two of a kind though they might be on opposite sides of the fence politically–big business and radical politician. There is no human difference between them.[23]

Diagnosis of National Maladies

The novelist seems to diagnose the disease of the political and the national malaise through the utterances of her characters. Her point of view is well expressed through the dialogue of Ram Krishna:

There has never been any touchstone except any character and example. Any ism under the sun needs that to enthuse and inspire. It takes a Christ, a Lenin, a Mao.[24]

Through Ram Krishna, the novelist ultimately suggests the idea to rescue the nation from the morass. Ram Krishna says: "The nation will think its way out into an answer."[25] He adds, once it has leaders of character and example since humanity needs inspiration to move it even half a step out of the rut.[26] *The Day in Shadow* and all the works of Nayantara Sahgal including *A Time to be Happy, This Time of Morning, Storm in Chandigarh,* are undoubtedly very significant contribution to Indo-Anglian fiction. In all these novels we have the portrayal of that period of national life that led to the declaration of emergency in 1975.

The Conflict between Gandhism and Industrialism

India's military encounter with China on the northern frontier was an unexpected national crisis that our nation faced after its independence. It opened the eyes of our national leaders who were compelled to think in a new perspective. At the occasion of this national calamity it was felt that if India wanted to strengthen its defence power and at the same time become economically self-sufficient, it had to accelerate its pace of industrialisation and technological advancement. Bhabani Bhattacharya gives a powerful expression of this conflict between Gandhism and industrialism in his novel *Shadow from Ladakh.* The author figuratively describes this conflict as "the frail old world wheel of wood set against the giant machines of the modern age."[27]

Gandhi and Nehru: The two different Approaches

Shadow from Laddakh was published in 1966. The war with China forms its backdrop raising a question about India's defence policy after independence. A political novel, it mirrors the socio-political drift of the nation after independence and suggests the direction the author thinks right.

Gandhi and Nehru : The two Approaches

But before discussing the theme of the novel in detail, it is our imperative to see the conflict of ideals in post-independence India arising out of the two ideals of our two national leaders, Mahatma Gandhi and Pt. Jawaharlal Nehru. During our freedom struggle, the nation followed both the leaders unquestioningly. It is also true that Pt. Nehru himself accepted Gandhi as his mentor in the political field and followed him like a true disciple throughout the freedom struggle. In spite of all these, it is a fact widely accepted that Gandhi and Nehru were poles apart representing two different approaches, modes of life, ideals and faith. Durga Das, in this context, observes:

> *One of Gandhi's remarks haunted me. He had said to me, describing his differences with Nehru: 'Jawahar wants Englishmen to go but Angreziat (English ways and culture) to stay. I want Angreziat to go and Englishmen to stay as our friends.' Gandhi wanted to rid India of the western culture which had been imposed on the country and had stifled the order and more natural Indian culture and social traditions. Nehru, although the idol of masses, was aloof from them mentally. He was an Englishmen in Indian skin.*[28]

It is interesting to note that this conflict did not come to the surface on some burning issues such as the aftermath of partition, the merger of the states, the controversy over Kashmir and the like.

The Unexpected Chinese Invasion

But with the passage of time the question whether Gandhi or Nehru should be followed for national policy on industry and agriculture or mode of living and thinking came to be a burning one, and in 1962 when our nation faced unexpected Chinese invasion on its northern border, this question came to the surface–whether India should meet force with force even while following the policy of peaceful existence at the international level, or whether India should meet force with soul force, following the ideals of Gandhi.

These are the questions which form the theme of Bhabani Bhattacharya's *Shadow from Ladakh*. The novel is strongly impregnated in Gandhian thought and symbology. Gandhi's words reverberate throughout the book. The scene is set in *Gandhigram*, a replica of Gandhi's *Sevagram*, an embodiment of the rural India of Gandhi's dreams, representing the Gandhian way of life. Satyajit, a staunch Gandhian, is dedicated to the life of austerity and high principles, through which the image of Gandhi has been projected. Satyajit is a Cambridge-educated young man. As he has served at Shantiniketan, he is selected to lead the village Gandhigram, an ideal village founded by Vinoba Bhave on Gandhian principles as an embodiment of the rural India of Gandhi's dreams. Satyajit has been the choice of Vinoba as he is energetic young man who has acquired western education as wall as Indian ideals at Cambridge and Shantiniketan respectively. This Cambridge-educated young man is a true Gandhian in his austere life and ascetic thought and a true disciple of Tagore in his educational and aesthetic ideals. In this way he is an ideal Indian national in free India whom Vinoba can choose as the worthy leader of his model village Gandhigram.

Suruchi is an ideal match for Satyajit. Hailing from Shantiniketan, the great seat of learning, she has acquired all the good tastes of Tagore. Satyajit and Suruchi have a lovely daughter, Sumita, who has proved to be a worthy child of their tastes. But very soon Satyajit faces a conflict in his domestic life. He demands the same kind of rigid self-discipline from his wife and daughter as he has imposed on himself. It is difficult for Suruchi to live by the austere and ascetic Gandhian code of Satyajit's living. Sumita also in her love for the Tagorean ideal of aesthetician has a tendency to enjoy certain things of life that Satyajit as an austere Gandhian cannot approve. However, both of them, the wife and the daughter, bear a great respect for Satyajit and his ideals and follow him though it is without any enthusiasm.

The Great Dilemma before the Nation

Satyajit is put in great dilemma when the nation is invaded by the Chinese forces on the northern border at NEFA and Laddakh:

India was under invasion, and what could the answer be? Armed resistance. Violence against violence. Had he, Satyajit, a second answer? Had he a clear alternative to conflict?[29]

What would Gandhiji have done under such situations? This question is asked again and again. He remembers:

Gandhi had summoned its [India's] people more than once to meet brute force with soul force in a struggle against the mightiest of empires.[30]

Proposal to Send a Shanti Sena at the Border

Being a true Gandhian, he is confident enough. Yes, he would act like Gandhi. He takes this national cause and puts forward a proposal to the government to send a Peace Mission, Shanti Sena, led by him to Laddakh where China had intruded into Indian territory. "Satyajit follows the footprints left by Gandhi on history, and history will repeat itself."[31]

India being the land of Gandhi whose principle was to meet brute force with soul force, to send *Shanti Sena* will be an ideal response of India to China's armed attack. Satyajit is so much steeped in Gandhian thought that he looks upon himself as another Gandhi. The author remarks: "Today the ground was ready again for Gandhi."[32]

There is anther problem Satyajit is confronted with. He thinks that Lohapur or Steeltown, an industrial city, seriously threatens Gandhigram. A young engineer named Bhaskar Rao who has received his training in the United States of America runs it. Bhaskar is flushed with the ambition of industrialising and modernising the country, sweeping away in the process all that is old and outmoded in his western outlook. The factory needs to be expanded as more and more steel products are needed for defence purposes which will result in annexing Gandhigram–a village of no importance according to him and an anachronism in this modern age. Satyajit is shocked to know that Nehru's government has given him permission to expand the steeltown and annex Gandhigram in the context of the Chinese aggression.

Satyajit, who as a disciple of Gandhi wants decentralised small scale industry, not the large scale industries like that of Bhaskar. Satyajit in this way is racked by two burning problems simultaneously—the threat to the nation by Chinese invasion and the threat to his village by the government's policy of industrialisation.

The conflict between Satyajit and Bhaskar reaches to a point of crisis. It is not a clash of personalities but a clash between two ways of life; a clash that is inevitable in the history of the nation. The Chinese invasion precipitated it.

After viewing the conflicts at three levels that Satyajit faces, it is interesting to see how the author presents the resolution to these conflicts. The Government of India though accepts the proposal to send *Shanti Sena* but in such a modified form that it will take long to do it. By the time Chinese forces are withdrawn unilaterally and in this way the national crisis automatically resolved. But the government's policy on industrialization and annexing the villages like Gandhigram is left unresolved.

Satyajit, being a Gandhian disciple, in order to solve this problem undertakes a fast unto death to protest against Government's decision to set up steeltown by annexing Gandhigram. Meanwhile a club is set up between Steeltown in Gandhigram for a friendly mixing of the people of both the places. This approach to bring the people together bears fruit. Sumita, Satyajit's daughter being a visitor to this club, is deeply impressed with the westernised culture of Steeltown. She is very much attracted to Bhaskar, who is symbol of this culture. Bhaskar is also attracted to her and with reverence appreciates her father Satyajit and the ideals he represents In this way his attitude towards Satyajit and his ideals undergoes changes and he decides not to annex the village Gandhigram in the way he proposed. A procession from Steeltown to Gandhigram is led by Bhaskar to announce Satyajit's victory of Gandhian ideals. G.P. Sharma observes:

> *This victory of Satyajit however, by non-violent means is not an absolute victory — even if we suppose that his victory is not because of his daughter's love but because of his soul force. While Bhaskar has changed in his ideal and attitude to the village, Satyajit has also changed a lot. He has mellowed a good deal following Bhaskar's change of heart, and he now accepts some of the good ideals of Steeltown while abandoning some of his own rigorous principles —*

thus becoming a happy combination of Gandhi, Nehru and Tagore together.[33]

G.P. Sharma sounds quite justified when he says:

The story in this way shows how in the contemporary context none of the ideals of Gandhi and Nehru alone can be a national ideal; only a balanced combination of the two ideals would be an answer to the problems facing the nation today.[34]

Tagorean Ideal of Integration

Thus by dramatising the conflict between Gandhigram and Steeltown, between Gandhism and industrialsm, the author seems to find a synthesis, for the Tagorean ideal of integration. This integration is, in his words, "integration of the simple and the sophisticated; the ancient and the modern; city and village; East and West".[35] Suruchi, Satyajit's wife, suggests the ideal of integration:

There was one way left for Gandhigram. It must make readjustments. That would mean acceptance of life in its totality. But not the Steeltown way; that also was denial of life deep under the surface. Let licence be chastened by restraint. Let restraint find its right level by a leavening of freedom. Let there be a meeting ground of the two extremes; let each shed some of its content and yet remain true to itself.[36]

A Treaty on Gandhism

Of all novels of Bhabani Bhattacharya *Shadow from Laddakh* is the most important novel for our purpose so far as the Gandhian impact on the fiction is concerned though his *Gandhi the Writer: The Image as it Grew* is a comprehensive treaty on Gandhism in which the author has viewed the height and the width of Gandhian ideas. Naturally, other works of Bhabani Bhattacharya may not be exception to this. In the light of this fact it is our imperative to search the references of Gandhian movement in other novels of Bhabani Bhattacharya.

So Many Hungers is the first novel of Bhabani Bhattacharya. It is a unique co-incidence that it appeared in the year of independence, i.e., 1947. Dr G.P. Sharma writes:

Bhabani Bhattacharya's So Many Hungers is not only the last political novel about the freedom struggle of this period but also one of the best of this category. A unique quality of this novel is that it portrays realistically the agony of the age it depicts, a quality which perhaps no other novel of this category published till 1947 possesses.[37]

In *So Many Hungers* the author, with his superb technical skill has shown the injustice of the foreign rulers on the innocent villagers. In this way he has created pathos in the heart of the readers. He has done it by telling the story of two families against the dismal background of the Bengal famine of the war years in the early forties. This novel does not depict the freedom movement of the country as do most of the other novels discussed in this chapter, though there are occasional glimpses. The story of the novel goes to the root–the real cause which was responsible for such a movement, instead of merely depicting the movement itself.

So Many Hungers is the story of the suffering caused by the war and the subsequent famine to the members of a family in particular and to all villagers of Bengal in general, first in the villages and then in the metropolitan city of Calcutta. The Second World War by that time had spread to India and Bengal was apprehending violence on her own soil. Japanese war fleet in the Bay had cordoned off Bengal, and any moment the province could be attacked from the sea. All the boats of the villagers along the coast had been seized and destroyed by the government as a protective measure, though boats were the only kind of transport of this region and means of livelihood of a large section of the population of the area. Like the boatmen and fishermen communities, the cultivators were reduced to paupers when the government requisitioned their paddy without controlling the price of paddy and rice.

In the light of this social plight the novelist portrays the fate of Kajoli, her mother, and her little brother Onu. This little peasant family of the village Baruni is quite helpless. Kajoli's father and elder brother are in jail as a consequence of their participation in the national freedom movement. Kajoli's husband, a young man, who was staying with her, leaves for the city to get a job. Unfortunately he meets an accident and dies. Kajoli and the family members are not aware of this tragedy.

There is not an ounce of foodgrain at home. Kajoli, whose pregnancy is in the advanced stage, with her old mother and little brother is doomed to move for Calcutta city to earn livelihood. But their condition in the city worsens; Kajoli in the city suffers horrible ordeal, e.g., rape, abortion, hospitalisation; then on the footpath, and ultimately, the brothel house. Thus a lady of a noble family turns to ignoble profession of prostitution. The mother commits suicide to see the children starving and dying.

With this surface story of famine the author has told a parallel story. This is the story of the war thrust upon India by the foreign rulers bringing unlimited miseries. This story takes place in the material world of Bengal. The author has elaborately dealt with this aspect of the story. This is why it is so appealing to the readers.

Rahoul, a young scientist, a Cambridge D.Sc., is a Professor of Astrophysics in the University of Calcutta. This intellectual of fine sensibility, busy in study, research and teaching, is upset by the World War spread gradually in the country. It is not because the war has come unexpectedly as a surprise to him. The fact is that he had been expecting such a war against the evil of Fascism right from his Cambridge days.

Political Scenario of Second World War

The story of war is the story of Rahoul. The novelist has moulded his character on the wheel of the Gandhian values. Why should our country join the Allied Powers and fight in the Second World War? This was the question that any Gandhian leader of freedom movement might have faced. And same is the question that Rahoul faces. To quote from the text:

Indian opinion was at one with the progressive forces the world over. But how could a people step out into a war said to be waged for democratic freedom, so long as that very freedom was denied to them?[38]

Indians, who were undecided at first, soon decide to lend support to Britain, for "its fight was with England's diehard rulers, not with her people, who, defeated, would face enslavement, adding to the miseries of human kind."[39]

India, however, wants in return "recognition of the Indian people's right to freedom."[40] Britain, in response to it, sends the leader of the Indian nation to prison because he had "… decried the attempt to drag his people into a war that was none of their seeking, as they were the humblest of slaves."[41]

Rahoul is shocked to learn about the arrest of Mahatma Gandhi:

That leader had often expressed Rahoul's own thought in words and images more beautiful and forceful than he himself could devise. Rahoul was no hero-worshipper. His ideas had been shaped on the anvil of reason, and emotion had no visible place in the process. Yet that one personage who India knew to be her man of destiny stirred his depths.[42]

The British government indulged in many more thoughtless activities like arrests of thousands of Indians and letting loose black-marketeers and hoarders. Rahoul's father, conservative diehard with his influence in government quarters, taking advantage of this situation, has opened a rice supply agency and has become one of its directors. Rahoul is not happy with his father as he knows his father has earned money through immoral means. Yet Rahoul, being a *Suputra*, cannot beat his father, who after all, had sent him to Cambridge and thus helped him become one of the greatest scientists of the nation.

A Reign of Terror in the Country

This was the time when Gandhi had launched 'Quit India Movement' unleashing a reign of terror in the country. And so the British government had arrested him and other prominent leaders. Rahoul, being an ardent nationalist, in this circumstance could not confine himself into the research work in the laboratory. And one day at last from the window of his laboratory he saw thousands of his countrymen marching down the street procession with the national flag in their hand and the army charging them, kicking them and trampling down the national flag underneath their jackboots. The young scientist in the laboratory forgets himself and his research work. He rushes out of the university laboratory into the street and thrusting his way through the jostle of the crowd challenges the military men. Immediately there was lathi-charge and Rahoul is put into the prison-cell for a day with many of his students as co-prisoners. They ask him in the prison-cell, "Is it the hour at last?"[43] With firmness Rahoul replies:

> *The hour is not as yet, but we are apart from it by a hair's breadth. We must stand ready to carry out Gandhi's command, 'Do or die'.*[44]

War Stricken India

The author has drawn the picture of war-stricken India. The city is scarred as though by battle, streets deserted save for men in uniform, armoured cars rolling by, troops standing by street corners with machine guns. The war has caused a famine, and it has wrought havoc in the villages. Hungry masses have rushed to the city with the false hope of finding food and shelter there from the government. The government has become a callous spectator of this situation. He comes out to the streets leaving the laboratory neglected and abandoned, ignoring the comfort of his home and love of his wife and little daughter. Having an instinct to serve the grief-stricken humanity, he forms a Non-Government welfare organisation to serve the poor and the destitute. As the secretary of the welfare society he addresses his students with smouldering rage:

> *This war, he had said, was just a repetition of other wars in history. The Four Freedoms did not include the freedom to be free–not for Asians. This famine, this brutal doom, was the fulfilment of alien rule. The final commentary. Imagine two million Englishmen dying of hunger that was preventable, and the government unaffected, uncensored, unrepented, smug as ever. 'Quit India' cried the two million dead of Bengal. The anger was warm in his voice, and he had paused till his speech was cool again. 'Quit' cried all India. 'You have done us some good along with much evil. For the good you have done you have been paid in full. The accounts have been settled. Now for God's sake, quit.*[45]

The novelist thus draws the situation in the novel parallel to the freedom movement. Rahoul can easily be substituted either by Mahatma Gandhi himself or any of the Gandhian leader of our national movement. Rahoul's address against the government resulted in his arrest and imprisonment. His father is a conservative opportunist. When he gets the news of his son's arrest at the relief camp he remarks: "It was as though they were aliens speaking a language that he did not know. What need had Kunal to join the Army? And Rahoul, could he not serve his country best as a scientist?"[46]

Rahoul's wife is also worried to get the news of his arrest but her sorrow is of different sort. Earlier she had asked him: "Your true place is with your books, your mathematics, your strange instruments in your college room."[47]

Just before the police take Rahoul away from relief center she says to Rahoul on telephone: "I too shall go your way soon… I am not the silly thing I used to be, you know that."[48] Dr G.P. Sharma aptly infers:

> *In this way, this story unfolds the agonies of mind one felt during the war period because of the misrule and wrong policies of the British government that did not care for the good of the country. Instead of merely depicting the famine or the war or the national movement superficially, this novel goes deeper unlike others of its kind and reveals the agony of slavery of the whole nation.*[49]

The author has skillfully linked up the two stories of the peasent family and of the scientist, with the story of Devesh Babu, Rahoul's

70-year old grandfather. He is an ardent nationalist, a devoted freedom-fighter, and the follower of Mahatma Gandhi. When he retired as a teacher he settled at Baruni, a coastal village dedicated to the ideals of national Gandhian movement with a priority to the rural reconstruction programme. He has organised the villagers for this mission and has won their love and respect. He is an active participant of Civil Disobedience Movement and leads the villagers to the seashore to make salt. Rahoul is proud of Devesh Babu whom the villagers regard him as their *Devata*, the god. In this way Rahoul develops a love for the peasants and intimacy with Kajoli's family.

Dr G.P. Sharma remarks on the significance of the character of Devesh Babu:

> *As this old man is the link between the two backgrounds of the story -the city and the village-so is he the link between the story of the famine and the story of the national movement and the war.*[50]

A Typical Gandhian Novel

Thus through the three main characters of the novel–Devesh Babu, Samarendra Basu and Rahoul, all of whom belong to the same family–the author has very skillfully revealed before us all the three social forces that were at work then. And yet all the three are distinctly human in the novel, not mere ideas or types.

The character of Devesh Babu is typically Gandhian. He is a type of man who loves his country sincerely and is ready for any consequence for it. He leads a life of his own ideal. His very presence in *So Many Hungers* has made it a typical Gandhian novel.

The portrait of Rahoul has been very alive. He is a man of fine sensibility embodying all that is best in the western civilisation. He has a great love and respect for his country.

The character of Rahoul is that of a nationalist but there is a fine human touch that has made his person life-like. In his character we have beautiful blending of sentiment and reason, domestic dutifulness and national and universal ideals. He is an ideal son of his mother, a loving husband of his wife, and affectionate father to his little daughter. When the shadow of the war looms before his eyes, he gets the consent from his wife because he cannot keep himself away from joining the same. To quote him from the novel:

> *Six months before I left England, fascist rebels were destroying the Government of Spain elected by the people. Madrid besieged,*

strangles. Then volunteers from many lands rushed to save freedom in Spain. I had an urge in those days to join the army of liberation....And I came back to my homeland. Some sore in me throbs now and then. A greater war of liberation has started, the greatest ever. What am I to do this time?[51]

So Many Hungers is one of those novels which depict the phase of the Indian national struggle under the leadership of Lokmanya Tilak and Mahatma Gandhi, when the nationalist freedom fighters worked for rural reconstruction to remove untouchability and other evils of society for a better and stronger nation.

In addition to *Shadow from Laddakh* and *So Many Hungers* of Bhabani Bhattacharya we have *Music for Mohini, He Who Rides a Tiger* and *A Goddess Named Gold* in his name. These novels are social novels contrary to the former ones which are political novels.

Plague of Hunger in the Wake of War

But national awareness is a common element in all novels of Bhabani Bhattacharya whether political or social, whether published before independence or after. Like most novels of our age, in these novels of Bhabani Bhattacharya we find an awareness of the evils of contemporary society. Hence it is apt to review the social novels of Bhabani Bhattacharya as well.

Music for Mohini appeared in 1952. Here we see a girl of fine sensibility growing up amidst the affluence of a respectable family of Calcutta. The family is orthodox and conservative, but the day the girl is offered in the marriage and she sees hell in the customs and traditions of our age-old society. To quote Dr G.P. Sharma:

With such a theme, the novelist stresses the need for eradicating social evils that are practised in the name of custom and tradition....In showing this kind of realism and detachment in looking at the problems of society the novel rises to the level of a serious work.[52]

He Who Rides a Tiger, Bhattacharya's next novel, was published in 1954. Here we have more intensity of feeling and a greater seriousness of theme. The novel is set in the early forties when there was a historic famine — 'the plague of hunger in the wake of war.'[53] So far as the portrayal of people's miseries in the great famine of Bengal is concerned this novel is akin to *So Many Hungers*. But in *He Who Rides a Tiger* the novelist against this setting, tells here a different story with a different theme. Here it deserves to be mentioned that the protest here is not against the alien rule, responsible for this famine but against certain evils of society which aggravated that critical situation.

A Goddess Named Gold is the last social novel of Bhabani Bhattacharya. It was published in 1960. In this novel the author highlights a post-independence national consciousness, which seeks freedom in the true sense — the real freedom for which our countrymen aspired while fighting against the British. The author shows how the freedom of ours is not the freedom that Mahatma Gandhi sought: it is only a privilege for a handful of wealthy men.

Revalidation of Gandhian Values

Thus *Shadow from Laddakh* offers a revalidation of Gandhian philosophy in the context of the new challenges faced by free India. But it must be kept in mind that Gandhian philosophy is of eternal value. Its relevance is not confined within the frontiers of any nation or the span of any particular age. Romain Rolland says aptly:

> *Gandhi is not only for India a hero of national history whose legendary memory will be enshrined in the millennial epoch. He has renewed, for all the people of the West, the message of their Christ, forgotten or betrayed. He has inscribed his name among the sages and saints of humanity; and the radiance of his figure has penetrated into all the regions of the earth. We, intellectuals, men of science, men of letters, artists, who belong to the panhumanist fraternity, we offer our fervent homage of love and veneration to our master and brother, Gandhi, who is realising, in the heart and in action, our ideal of humanity to come.*[54]

References

1. Sahgal, Nayan Tara. *This Time of Morning*. New Delhi: Orient Paperbacks Pvt. Ltd. p. 46.

2. *Ibid.* p. 218.

3. Sahgal, Nayan Tara. *Storm in Chandigarh*. New Delhi: Orient Paperbacks Pvt. Ltd. p. 6.

4. *Ibid.* p. 7.

5. *Ibid.* p. 9.

6. *Ibid.* p. 13.

7. *Das, Durga, India from Gurzon to Nehru and After Collins, London, 1969,* p. 231.

8. *Ibid.* p. 46.

9. *Ibid.*
10. *Ibid.* p. 50.
11. *Ibid.* p. 65.
12. *Ibid.* p. 141.
13. *Ibid.* p. 144.
14. *Ibid.* p. 165.
15. *Ibid.* p. 204.
16. *Nationalism in Indo-Anglian Fiction*. p. 272.
17. Sahgal, Nayan Tara. *The Day in Shadow*. New Delhi: Orient Paperbacks Pvt. Ltd. p. 186.
18. *Ibid.*
19. *Ibid.* 191.
20. *Ibid.* 234.
21. *Ibid.* 192.
22. *Ibid.* 234.
23. *Ibid.* 222.
24. *Ibid.* 235.
25. *Ibid.*
26. *Ibid.*
27. Bhattacharya, Bhabani. *Shadow from Laddakh*. New Delhi: Orient Paperbacks Pvt. Ltd. p. 95.
28. Das, Durga. *India from Curzon to Nehru and After*. Collins, London, 1969. p. 261.
29. *Shadow from Laddakh*. p. 204.
30. *Ibid.* p. 208.
31. *Ibid.* p. 214.
32. *Ibid.* p. 322.
33. *Nationalism In Indo-Anglian Fiction*. pp. 267-68.
34. *Ibid.* p. 268.
35. *Shadow from Laddakh*. p. 215.
36. *Ibid.* p. 217.
37. *Nationalism in Indo-Anglisn Fiction*. p. 227.
38. *Ibid.* p. 228.
39. Bhattacharya, Bhabani. So Many Hungers. New Delhi: Orient Paperbacks Pvt. Ltd. p. 9.
40. *Ibid.* p. 41.
41. *Ibid.*
42. *Ibid.*
43. *Ibid.* p. 67.

44. *Ibid.*
45. *Ibid.* pp. 212-13.
46. *Ibid.* p. 210.
47. *Ibid.* p. 13.
48. *Ibid.* p. 213.
49. *Nationalism in Indo-Anglian Fiction.* p. 232.
50. *So Many Hungers,* p. 224.
51. *Nationalism in Indo-Anglian Fiction.* p. 233.
52. *Ibid.* 234.
53. Bhattacharya, Bhabani. *He, Who Rides a Tiger.* New Delhi: Orient Paperbacks Pvt. Ltd., New Delhi. p. 15.
54. Radhakrishnan, S. Ed. *Mahatma Gandhi, Essays and Reflections.* pp. 193-94.

9

Conclusion

The Embodiment of Universal Beings

This is the man who has stirred three hundred million people to revolt, who has shaken the foundation of the British Empire, and who has introduced into human politics the strongest religious impetus of the last two thousand years.[1]

Romain Rolland, the renowned French writer, wrote this in his biography of Mahatma Gandhi. His book, *Mahatma Gandhi* sub- titled *The Man Who Became One with the Universal Being*, appeared in translation in several European languages and had a wide circulation. Virtually this was the first time Mahatma Gandhi was presented to the western world. Romain Rolland had learnt a great deal about Gandhi from his conversation with Rabindranath Tagore, C.F. Andrews, Madeleine Slade (Mirabehn) and others.

Romain Rolland had a vivid portrait of Mahatma Gandhi in his mind — the outward visage and the man within. He could see the small frail person with soft dark eyes and a thin face. His body did not count at all. Modest, unassuming, hesistant in making assertions; 'yet you feel his indomitable spirit', Rolland wrote. He makes no compromise and never tries to hide a mistake. Nor is he afraid to admit having been in the wrong, … he is happiest when, in meditative solitude, he can listen to the 'still small voice' within.[2]

Romain Rolland : The Greatest Pacifist of the World

Here it deserves to be mentioned that Romain Rolland (1866-1944) himself was as great a man as Mahatma Gandhi. His novel, *Jean*

Christophe, brought him world acclaim and he received Nobel Prize for Literature in 1915. What is more significant than the prestigious Nobel Prize is that Romain Rolland was the greatest pacifist of the world during the First World War. Being the fearless champion of the oppressed, his humanism was unparalleled at the time. Though his ardent appeal for peace was lost in the fury of nationalist fervour, he declared in his anti-war book titled *Above the Battle*: "For one year, I have been rich in enemies. Let me say this to them: they can hate me, but they will not teach me to hate."[3]

Rolland's internationalism, a compulsive inheritance from Tolstoy, forced him into exile from his homeland, France, and he settled in a quiet village, Villeneuve, near Lake Laman in Switzerland.

A Vision Transformed into Reality

Romain Rolland witnessed the historic significance of Indian National Movement led by Mahatma Gandhi. If Gandhi were merely an idealist Rolland would not have gone out of his own domain of creative writing to bring a personality in the literary horizon. But Gandhi had transformed a vision into reality. He had turned a nebulous idea into an iron-hand technique and appealed it for social and political ends on a massive scale involving millions of men and women in his epochal experiment.

Ramakrishna and Swami Vivekanand

Rolland was drawn towards Ramakrishna Paramhamsa and Swami Vivekanand and wrote the biographies of these two saints. Addressing to the western readers Rolland said:

I desire to reconcile the two antithetical forms of spirit for which the West and the East are wrongly supposed to stand—reason and faith.... The West and the East share them both almost equally although few suspect it... An absurd separation has been made between these two halves of the soul, and it is presumed that they are incompatible. The only incompatibility lies in the narrowness of view, which those who erroneously claim to be their representatives share in common.[4]

On Hinduism

The study of the lives and works of Ramakrishna Paramhamsa, Swami Vivekanand and Mahatma Gandhi made Romain Rolland fascinated to Hinduism. To quote his impression:

I have studied all the religions of Europe and Asia. Hinduism appears to be the best of all. I have conviction that one day the whole world would have to bow before the Hindu Dharma.[5]

Rolland's work on Gandhi is impregnated with profound thoughts. To quote his words from the last chapter of the book:

Gandhi is more than a word; he is an example. He incarnates the spirit of his people. Blessed the man who is a people, his people entombed and then resuscitated in him! But such resurrections are never haphazard. If the spirit of India now surges forth from temples and forests, it is because it holds the message for which the world is sighing...[6]

Let us see how Rolland interprets Gandhi's message of non-violence:

One thing is certain; either Gandhi's spirit will triumph or it will manifest itself again, as were manifested, centuries before, the Messiah and Buddha, till there finally is manifested in a mortal half-god the perfect incarnation of the principle of life which will lead a new humanity on to a new path.[7]

Gandhi and Tolstoy as Rolland views

Rolland compares two great men of East and West. The context was his conversation with Tagore. To quote:

Tagore always looked upon Gandhi as a saint, and I have often heard him speak of him with veneration. When, in referring to the Mahatma, I mentioned Tolstoy, Tagore pointed out to me ... how much more clothed in light and radiance Gandhi's spirit is than Tolstoy's. With Gandhi, everything is nature-modest, simple, pure-while all his struggles are hallowed by religious serenity, whereas with Tolstoy everything is proud revolt against pride, hatred against hatred, passion against passion. Everything in Tolstoy is violence, even his doctrine of non-violence.[8]

It was March 22, 1924, when the direct communication between the two geniuses of the time began. Gandhi wrote his first letter to Rolland, who was projecting Gandhi's ideas in Europe. A collection of *Young India* articles was translated into the French edition, the 'Foreword' of which was written by Romain Rolland:

I saw surging up in the plains of the Indus the citadel of the spirit, which has been raised by the frail and unbreakable Mahatma. And I set myself to rebuild it in Europe.[9]

The true nature of Indian Civil Disobedience Movement was interpreted by him. He pointed out that there was no pacifism in it. It was struggle to achieve her revolutionary progress, one that was "*efficacious enough to wrench the world of man away from the catastrophe into which it is about to plunge.*"[10]

Mira Behn : A Bridge between the East and the West

Rolland's book on Gandhi bore many significant outcomes. It left a tremendous effect on a European reader who inexorably changed her whole course of life. It was Miss Madeleine Slade, the daughter of a British Admiral who had been Commander-in-Chief of the East Indies Squadron. The music of Beethoven brought a spiritual awakening in her and led her to Romain Rolland, an authority on the great German composer. She went to meet him at Villeneuve. Rolland spoke to her about Gandhi and the biographical study that was already in the press. She was deeply impressed to read it. To quote her impressions in her own words:

> *As I read, the dawn in my heart glowed brighter and brighter, and by the time I had finished, the Sun of Truth was pouring his rays into my soul. From that moment I knew my life was dedicated to Bapu. That for which I had been waiting had come, and it was this.*[11]

She decided to offer her services to Gandhi, came to live in *Sabarmati Ashram*. She dedicated herself to the country she adored. In a letter to Romain Rolland on November 13th Gandhi wrote:

> *What a treasure you have sent me! I shall try to be worthy of the great trust. I shall ... assist her to become a bridge between East and West.*[12]

Gandhi gave her the Hindu name 'Mira Behn' and when Gandhi came to Villanueve, she accompanied him. Rolland greeted her with the words: "How lucky you are."[13]

Communion of Gandhi and Romain Rolland

Gandhi had attended world stature in the course of the bygone decade. Being the supreme leader of Indian freedom movement he was revered as the Father of the Nation. He had strong desire to meet Romain Rolland, a humanist compared to Tolstoy. The long cherished desire was fulfilled when the two great souls were together at Villenueve in December 1931. Gandhi's five days stay with Romain Rolland turned Villenueve into a place of pilgrimage. Hundreds of men and women flocked there to see Gandhi. There was language bar as Rolland's sister acted as an interpreter. On the walls of the room there hung eight portraits; four of them were of Ramakrishna, Vivekanand, Gandhi and Tagore.

Rolland drew Gandhi's attention on the crisis growing in Europe, uneasy truce getting worse day by day, and fascist ideology gathering strength. Rolland felt himself weak and said:

How I wish I was twenty years younger, so that I might have carried on a fierce battle against the destructive forces.[14]

Rolland spoke for ninety minutes. But it was Gandhi's day of silence. Next day Gandhi commented on Rolland's remarks of previous day:

My method is empiric. All my conclusions are based on personal experience. I have firm belief in non-violence, which alone could save Europe.[15]

Gandhi and Rolland on the Role of Art in Human Life

Gandhi and Rolland discussed on the role of art in human life. They were on common ground on the topic. Like Tolstoy both of them refuted the concept of "art for art sake". Gandhi said:

For me all art must be based on truth. I reject beautiful things, if instead of expressing truth, they express untruth. I accept the formula 'Art brings joy and is good, but on the condition I mentioned. To achieve Truth in art, I do not expect exact reproductions of external things. Only living things bring living joy to the soul and must elevate the soul[16]

Agreeing Rolland took out one of Goethe's book from his shelf, read out passages from it. Goethe had written forcefully of the storm and stress in man's search for truth, which involved the creative artist in infinite pain.

Rolland put the question: "What do you call God?" Gandhi spoke in the course of his address:

God has many names ... In my early youth ... I used to say that ... God is Truth, above all... Two years ago I went a step further and said that Truth is God. You will see the fine distinction between the two statements, 'God is Truth' and 'Truth is God'. I came to that conclusion after a continuous and relentless search after truth which began fifty years ago.[17]

Rolland pressed the query: "Is it a spiritual personality or a force which rules over the world?" Gandhi's reply flashed:

God is not a person; God is an eternal principle. That is why I say that Truth is God...[18]

Rolland put his reservation: "If it is correct that Truth is God, it lacks one attribute of God, joy." Gandhi clarified: "I recognise no God without joy."[19]

Gandhi and Rolland talked on the prospect of another World War. Looming into the future, Gandhi said:

If one nation possessed the heroism to submit without answering violence with violence, it would be the most effective lesson. But for this an absolute faith is necessary.[20]

Some of Rolland's personal impressions of Gandhi deserve to be quoted:

There was frail, little man, bespectacled and toothless, his head shaven. "His thought was in constant evolution.... Fatigue is a word which does not exist in his vocabulary. He could calmly answer for hours the heckling of a crowd, as he did at Lausanne and Geneva, without a muscle of his face twitching. Motionless, his voice always clear and clam, he replied to his adversaries, open or masked - giving them rude truths which left them silenced and suffocated.[21]

At a public meeting in Lausanne the chairman welcomed Gandhi with these words:

Mahatma Gandhi, how happy we are to have you in our town... We in Europe are afraid of prison and of suffering. But you love these things. You take them gladly. You are not afraid. We know the Sermon on the Mount by heart. You know it and live it... We feel humble before you.[22]

Rolland asked at the time of parting: "What would you like me to do in grateful memory of your visit? Interpret India's non-violent struggle to the world?" Gandhi answered cryptically: "Come and meet India."[23]

Gandhi and Satyagrah : As Rolland Views

Rolland was deeply impressed with his distinguished guest, Gandhi. He writes his impression:

He was too much of a saint, too pure, too free from the animal passions that lie dormant in man.[24]

Gandhi had complete trust in man's goodness; it was a testament of Gandhi's faith. Louis Fischer remarks in this context:

Gandhi did not regard divinity as a monopoly of the great man or the artiste or the elite. Gandhi's uniqueness lay in working with common clay and finding the soul-spark in it.[25]

Rolland had warm regard for Gandhi and his *Satyagraha*. In a letter to an English friend Rolland writes:

If the India of Satyagraha were to go down in the battle, it is Christ himself who would be pierced by it, with a supreme lance thrust, on the Cross. And this time there would be no resurrection.[26]

The warmth between Rolland and Gandhi continued to grow throughout their lives though they never met again. Gandhi wrote to Rolland before he undertook a fast unto death in protest against the Communal Award of British Government.

Dear friend and brother — On the eve of taking the momentous step in my life, I would like to tell you how I prize those days I had with you and your great and devoted sister... I wonder how you have felt over the contemplated step. I can only say that it was decided upon in obedience to the imperative voice of conscience.[27]

Rolland kept himself attached with every step Gandhi had in his *Satyagraha*. When Poona Pact brought Gandhi's fast to an end Rolland cabled to Gandhi: "Rejoice at your great victory of the soul." Gandhi wrote to him in answer to the cable of goodwill: "You were ever present with me during the travail."[28]

Rolland wrote to Gandhi on May 8, 1933, when Gandhi was to undertake a fast once again:

We are with you in these grave days when your life is again at stake. We send forth our fervent prayers... Please permit me to attach to your sacrifice a larger meaning... In these tragic times when the whole world is given over to the most atrocious violence... your immolation before the Goddess of Justice, who is all love and without violence, acquires a universal and sacred value — like the Cross.[29]

W.T. Starr in his book, *Romain Rolland and the World at a War*, writes:

His pacifism is based on direct action, and on the principles of love and faith as motives of our acts, and on sacrifice of self in a noble cause. This is what he found later in Gandhism.[30]

Rolland could not agree with the communists that social revolution could be achieved by violence alone. His friend George Connes in The Tragedy of Romain Rolland observes:

....violence, the only possible means? No, Rolland retorted, there was also the Gandhi method of non-violence, non-cooperation, passive resistance, ahimsa, call it what you like. Look at what Gandhi has done for India... the awakening he has brought to hundreds of millions.[31]

Rolland's Tribute to Gandhi

Romain Rolland's contribution to the values dedicated to Gandhi's seventieth birthday (October 2, 1939) was of great significance. To quote an extract:

He has renewed, for all the peoples of the West, the message of their Christ, forgotten or betrayed. He has inscribed his name among the sages and saints of humanity; and the radiance of his figure has penetrated into all the regions of the earth. In the eyes of Europe he appeared at a moment when such an example seemed almost a miracle. Europe was under the weight of a heavy night, pregnant with misery and despair, without a single ray of light. The appearance of Gandhi, who repudiated all violence... seemed a paradoxical defiance hurled in the face of the politics and the thoughts, traditional, accepted and unquestioned, of the West....

A torrent of recognition and of faith flowed from the West towards him. For many, he was like a return of Christ. For others, for independent thinkers... Gandhi was a new incarnation of Jean-Jacques Rousseau and of Tolstoy, denouncing the illusions and the crimes of civilisation.[32]

Romain Rolland while paying this great homage to Gandhi sadly acknowledged that his message of wisdom and love, even like '*The Sermon on the mount*' could not change the destiny of the world dedicated to destruction. His word expresses the depth of his melancholy:

To be applied to politics, the doctrine of non-violence requires a very different moral climate from that which pervades the Europe of today; it demands a total immense and unanimous sacrifice of self, which has no present chance of success in the fact of the growing ferocity of the new system of totalitarian dictatorships which have been established in the world and which have left their pitiless traces in the blood of millions of men.[33]

Mahatma Gandhi was a humanist. His humanism was one of the profoundest things the history has seen. His pity and love for humanity was designed particularly for the poor and the oppressed. Edward Thompson says:

For the first time since Buddha, India knew a stirring that spread to the remotest places; a breath and voice felt and heard everywhere. Even though the words were not always understood.[34]

Literature Mirrors the Society

Literature is rightly described as the mirror of the society. It reflects the spirit of the age. The heights that Mahatma Gandhi attained in his life and the depth of his ideas gave a new direction to the age. The poets and the novelists could have not got a better subject to depict in their works than the life and works of Mahatma Gandhi. The Indo-Anglian writers of our age like their contemporaries of different Indian languages have given expression of Gandhi's life and his values in their works and in the conclusion of our study we would do well to sum up the same in very brief.

Elaborate Treatment of Gandhian Philosophy

Mulk Raj Anand's *Untouchable* (1935) and Raja Rao's *Kanthapura* (1938) are excellent of all Indo-Anglian novels. In both these novels we have an elaborate treatment of the central concept of Gandhian philosophy.

In *Untouchable,* we find Anand diagnosing the disease of untouchability and recommending the solution as offered by Gandhi. Anand was deeply impressed by Gandhi's ideals; he had himself stayed with Gandhi in his 'Sabarmati Ashram' and this intimacy had not only enriched his creative vision but also filled up his heart with the Buddhist 'Karuna' and compassion. As a result we find *Untouchable* a very sensitive, compassionate and realistic portrayal of the humiliations and indignities suffered by the untouchables. Gandhi has himself been introduced as a character and the novelist has excellently and vividly drawn the pen-portrait of the Mahatma and his electrifying impact on the masses.

In another novel of the Gandhi era titled *The Sword and the Sickle* (1942) Anand has dramatised the conflict between the Marxist and the Gandhian ideologies.

In *The Big Heart* (1945), we find Anand challenging Gandhi's attitude towards machines and industrialism.

In another novel titled *The Road* (1961), Anand regrets that though the government of India has officially abolished untouchability, Gandhi's dream of *Swaraj* still remains unfulfilled as the conventional attitude of bigotry and prejudice against *Harijans* still continues.

The image of Mahatma Gandhi as projected in different novels of Mulk Raj Anand is authentic, objective and free from the emotional adoration of the Mahatma.

Raja Rao's *Kanthapura* (1938) is one of the most celebrated novels, wherein we have the treatment of Gandhi's ideals at its top. Here the author seems to have captured the heart of entire Gandhian movement by depicting the emergence of national consciousness in a village. The novel is full of Gandhian references, thoughts and imagery and the theme is tied with Gandhian life and philosophy. Here we find Gandhi eulogised, romanticised and mythologised. There is a beautiful blending of myths, legend, religion poetry and politics here and *Kanthapura* has become the heart of India responding to the call of Mahatma. Here we have all social and political activities of the thirties associated with Gandhi beautifully depicted, e.g., '*Dandi March*,' Civil Disobedience Movement,' '*Satyagraha*', '*Harijan-Upliftment*,' '*Swadeshi*,' '*Swaraj*,' propaganda against liquor addiction, fasting, and wheel spinning, police-atrocities, 'Gandhi- Irwin Pact,' 'Second Round Table Conference,' etc. Moorthy, the pivotal character in the novel who is rightly described as Gandhiman, is dedicated to all Gandhian ideals, i.e. self-purification, self-sacrifice, non-violence, truth, etc.

In our work our effort has been to see as to how successfully the novelist has treated the Gandhian ideals in his work.

R.K. Narayan has himself described *Waiting for the Mahatma* (1955) as a novel of Gandhi and Gandhi himself occupies a pivotal position in this novel, and the love story of Sri Ram and Bharati revolves around him. Here the image of Gandhi is that of a warm, loving, and good-humoured Bapu and the portrayal is authentic. Actually Narayan had written a story entitled *Gandhi's Appeal* before Independence dealing with the nationalistic theme, i.e. irresistible appeal of Gandhi on the masses. Thematically *Waiting for the Mahatma* can be described as an extension of this story.

Khwaja Ahmad Abbas's *Inquilab* can be studied with Narayan's *Waiting for the Mahatma.* Both the novels were published in the same year (1955). In *Inquilab* also, we find Gandhi portrayed as a prominent national leader and the novel covers the political events of nearly two decades beginning with *Jalianwala Bagh* massacre of 1919 to the Gandhi-Irwain Pact in 1931.

Here our attempt has been to see these novels with an angle as to how far the novelists have succeeded in treating the Gandhian ideals.

Reflection of Moral Degradation

Thus in the preceding chapters we have seen a benign and complimentary image of Mahatma as portrayed by some Indo-Anglian fiction writers. But after the national Independence and subsequent disappearance of Gandhi from the national scene, however, things began to change. Because of the corruption and moral degradation of some of his unscrupulous followers, the image of Mahatma was also tarnished. This phase of diminishing popularity of the Mahatma has also been presented by some novelists.

Khuswant Singh in his *Train to Pakistan* (1956) attacks the disciples of Gandhi in the Government. Mr. Singh holds the miscalculation of '*Baniya*' politician at Delhi (an obvious reference to Gandhi) responsible for India's partition resulting into mass massacres of 1947.

In *A Bend in the Ganges* (1964), Manohar Malgonkar exposes the hypocrisy and emptiness of Mahatma's disciples and probes the Gandhian philosophy of non-violence posing the question, 'could it ever serve as a philosophy of life itself ?' Gandhi himself appears in the book briefly but his creed of non-violence has been attacked severely throughout the book.

Chaman Nahal in *Azadi* (1975) projects a similar view. The people of Sialkot had a perfect faith in Gandhi's determination to keep the nation united but when the partition took place their faith in Mahatma got shattered.

Here our approach has been to see the ideals of Gandhi having been criticised in these novels. We have tried to examine objectively how Gandhi and his ideals have been projected in these novels in an unfavorable way: quite contrary to most other fiction writers.

Need for the Revalidation of Gandhian Philosophy

Nayantara Sahgal's *This Time of Morning* (1965) deals with the power politics in the last days of Nehru's primeministership. The protagonist Kaliash Vrind, a veteran Gandhian, in the novel doubts the creed of non-violence. He accepts non-violence as the finest way for India at that moment in the history of freedom movement, but he never accepts it as a philosophy of life and it could never apply to a sovereign state which has to maintain armed strength for its defence. He also believes that many of Gandhian ideals, e.g. prohibition of liquor, cow protection, sexual abstinence, aversion to science and industrialisation are out of tune with the twentieth century.

Shadow from Laddakh (1966) by Bhabani Bhattacharya powerfully expresses the conflict between Gandhism and industrialism. After Independence it was felt that if India wanted to strengthen its defence power and become economically self-sufficient, it has to accelerate its pace for industrialisation and technological advancement.

By dramatising the conflict between Gandhigram and Steel town, between Gandhism and industrialism, Bhattacharya seems to have brought Tagorian ideals of integration: the integration of the simple and the sophisticated; the ancient and the modern; the city and the village; and the East and the West. So *Shadow from Ladakh* offers a revalidation of Gandhian philosophy in the context of the new challenges facing the free India.

Here our endeavour has been to see the influence of Gandhian ideals on the post-Independence novelists in an entirely changed perspective.

Thus we have viewed the different aspects of our subject. Here our objective has been to have a survey of the impact of Gandhi legend on Indo-Anglian fiction written in different times and perspectives. Mahatma Gandhi was one of the greatest personalities of the millennium, and the way he fought with the most powerful empire of the then world and how he successfully achieved the target with *Satya and ahimsa,* truth and non-violence, gave him a high place in the heart of the masses. Indo-Anglian authors have rightly described him as an *awatar,* an incarnation of *Lord Vishnu.* Albert Einsteen pays homage to Mahatma Gandhi in the most befitting words:

> *Gandhi, ... a man of wisdom and humility, armed with resolve and inflexible consistency, who has devoted all his strength to the uplifting of his people and the betterment of their lot; a man who has confronted the brutality of Europe with the dignity of the simple human being, and thus at all times risen superior. Generations to come, it may be, will scarce believe that such a one as this ever in flesh and blood walked upon this earth.*[35]

References

1. Rolland, Romain. *L'Inde.* , *Mahatma Gandhi: The Man who Became one with the Universa l Being* Romain Rolland, p. 5.

2. *Young India*, March 2, 1922. pp. 1-2.

3. Rolland, Romain. *Above the Battle*. Chicago: The Open Court Publishing Company, 1916.

4. *Preface* to *The Life of Ramakrishna.*

5. *Ibid.* p. 2.

6. Rolland, Romain. *L'Inde.* p. 45.

7. *Ibid.* p. 126.

8. Kripalani, Krishna in the *Visva-Bharati Quarterly*, Gandhi Memorial Peace Number. p. 296.

9. *Young India*, June 25, 1924.
10. Tendulkar, D.G. *Mahatma*. Vol. III. p. 124.
11. Behn, Mira. *The Spirit's Pilgrimage*.
12. *Gandhi Marg*, January 1966. p. 43.
13. *Ibid* March 1966. p. 26.
14. Tendulkar, D.G. *Mahatma*. Vol. III. p. 174.
15. *Ibid* p. 199.
16. Fischer, Louis. *Life of Mahatma Gandhi*. Part II. p. 145.
17. Tendulkar, D.G. *Mahatma*. Vol. III. p. 176.
18. Rolland, Romain. *L'Inde*. p. 346.
19. *Ibid* p. 347.
20. *Ibid* p. 358.
21. *Ibid* p. 25.
22. Jack, Homer A. The Gandhi Reader. *La Figaro Lilleraire*, Paris, February 7, 1948. pp. 387-88.
23. Lester, Muriel. *Entertaining Gandhi*. pp. 164-72.
24. Pyarelal. *Mahatma Gandhi- The Last Phase,* Vol. I. p. 105.
25. Fischer, Louis. *Mahatma Gandhi,* Part II. p. 52.
26. Tendulkar, D.G. *Mahatma*. Vol. III. p. 194.
27. Romain Rolland, *L'Inde,* p. 401.
28. *Ibid*. p. 409.
29. *Ibid*. p. 413.
30. W.T. Starr, *Romian Rolland and a World War.* p. 92.
31. George Connes, *The Tragedy of Romain Rolland*. p. 147.
32. Radhakrishnan, S. Ed. *Mahatma Gandhi, Essays and Reflections*. pp. 197-98.
33. *Ibid*. p. 201.
34. *Ibid*. p. 228.
35. Einstein, Albert. Qtd. in Tendulkar, D.G. *Mahatma*. Vol. VI. p. 286.

Bibliography

PRIMARY SOURCES

Anand Mulk Raj, *Untouchable,* Orient Paperbacks, New Delhi, 1935.

Anand Mulk Raj, *The Sword and the Sickle,* Orient Paperbacks, New Delhi, 1942.

Anand Mulk Raj The Big Heart, Orient Paperbacks, New Delhi, 1945.

Anand Mulk Raj, *The Road,* Orient Paperbacks, New Delhi, 1961.

Anand Mulk Raj, *Apology for Heroism*, Orient Paperbacks, New Delhi.

Anand Mulk Raj, *Coolie,* Orient Paperbacks, New Delhi, 1936.

Anand Mulk Raj, *Two Leaves and a Bud*, Orient Paperbacks, New Delhi, 1937.

Anand Mulk Raj, *The Village,* Orient Paperbacks, New Delhi, 1939.

Anand Mulk Raj, *Across the Black Water,* Orient Paperbacks, New Delhi, 1940.

Anand Mulk Raj, *Seven Summers,* Orient Paperbacks, New Delhi, 1951.

Anand Mulk Raj, *Morning Face,* Orient Paperbacks, New Delhi, 1968.

Anand Mulk Raj, *Confession of a Lover,* Orient Paperbacks, New Delhi, 1976.

Anand Mulk Raj, *The Private Life of an India Prince,* Orient Paperbacks, New Delhi, 1953.

Anand Mulk Raj, *Death of a Hero,* Orient Paperbacks, New Delhi, 1963.

Anand Mulk Raj, *The Old Woman and the Cow,* Orient Paperbacks, New Delhi, 1960.

Anand Mulk Raj, *The Lost Child and Other Stories,* Orient Paperbacks, New Delhi, 1934.

Anand Mulk Raj, *A Lament on the Death of a Master of Arts*, Orient Paperbacks, New Delhi, 1939.

Anand Mulk Raj, *The Barber's Trade Union and Other Stories,* Orient Paperbacks, New Delhi, 1944.

Anand Mulk Raj, *The Tractor and the Corn Goddess,* Orient Paperbacks, New Delhi, 1947.

Abbas Khwaja Ahmad, *Inquilab,* Orient Paperbacks, New Delhi, 1955.

Abbas Khwaja Ahmad, *Defeat for Death,* Orient Paperbacks, New Delhi, 1944.

Abbas Khwaja Ahmad, *Tomorrow is Ours*, Orient Paperbacks, New Delhi, 1943.

Bhattacharya Bhabani, *Shadow from Laddakh*, Orient Paperbacks, New Delhi, 1966.

Bhattacharya Bhabani, *He, Who Rides a Tiger,* Orient Paperbacks, New Delhi, 1954.

Bhattacharya Bhabani, *So Many Hungers,* Orient Paperbacks, New Delhi, 1947.

Bhattacharya Bhabani, *A Goddess Named Gold*, Orient Paperbacks, New Delhi, 1960.

Bhattacharya Bhabani, *Music for Mohini*, Orient Paperbacks, New Delhi, 1952.

Malgaonkar Manohar *A Bend in the Ganges,* Orient Paperbacks, New Delhi, 1964.

Malgaonkar Manohar, *Combat of Shadows*, Orient Paperbacks, New Delhi, 1962.

Malgaonkar Manohar, *The Princes*, Orient Paperbacks, New Delhi, 1963.

Malgaonkar Manohar, *Distant Drum*, Orient Paperbacks, New Delhi, 1960.

Nahal Chaman, *Azadi*, Orient Paperbacks, New Delhi, 1975.

Narayan R.K., *Waiting for The Mahatma,* Orient Paperbacks, New Delhi.

Narayan R.K., *Swami and Friends,* Orient Paperbacks, New Delhi, 1935.

Narayan R.K., *The Bachelor of Arts,* Orient Paperbacks, New Delhi, 1937.

Narayan R.K., *The Dark Room,* Orient Paperbacks, New Delhi, 1938.

Narayan R.K., *The English Teacher*, Orient Paperbacks, New Delhi, 1949.

Narayan R.K., *The Financial Expert,* Orient Paperbacks, New Delhi, 1952.

Narayan R.K., *Malgudi Days,* Orient Paperbacks, New Delhi, 1943.

Narayan R.K., *The Guide,* Orient Paperbacks, New Delhi, 1958.

Narayan R.K., *The Man-Eater of Malgudi,* Orient Paperbacks, New Delhi, 1962.

Narayan R.K., *The Vendor of Sweets,* Orient Paperbacks, New Delhi, 1967.

Narayan R.K., *The Painter of Sings*, Orient Paperbacks, New Delhi, 1976.

Narayan R.K., *Dodu and Other Stories,* Orient Paperbacks, New Delhi, 1943.

Narayan R.K., *Cyclone and Other Stories,* Orient Paperbacks, New Delhi, 1944.

Narayan R.K., *An Astrologer's Day and Other Stories,* Orient Paperbacks. New Delhi, 1947.

Narayan R.K., *A Horse and Two Goats,* Orient Paperbacks, New Delhi, 1970.

Narayan R.K., *An Astrologer's Day and Other Stories,* Orient Paperbacks, New Delhi, 1947.

Narayan R.K., *A Horse and Two Goats,* Orient Paperbacks, New Delhi, 1970.

Nagrajan K. *The Chronicles of Kedarm,* Orient Paperbacks, New Delhi, 1961.

Rao Raja, *Kanthapura,* Orient Paperbacks, New Delhi, 1938.

Rao Raja, *The Serpent and the Rope,* Orient Paperbacks, New Delhi, 1960.

Rao Raja, *Narsiga,* Orient Paperbacks, New Delhi.

Rao Raja, *The Cow and the Barricades,* Orient Paperbacks, New Delhi, 1947.

Rao Raja, *The Cat and Shakespeare*, Orient Paperbacks, New Delhi, 1965.

Rao Raja, *Comrade Kirillov*, Orient Paperbacks, New Delhi, 1976.

Sahgal Nayan Tara, *Storm in Chandigarh,* Orient Paperbacks, New Delhi, 1969.

Sahgal Nayan Tara, *This Time of Morning*, Orient Paperbacks, New Delhi, 1965.

Sahgal Nayan Tara, *The Day in Shadow,* Orient Paperbacks, New Delhi, 1971.

Sahgal Nayan Tara, *A Time to be Happy*, Orient Paperbacks, New Delhi, 1957.

Sahgal Nayan Tara, *A Time to be Happy*, Orient Paperbacks, New Delhi, 1957.

Singh Khuswant, *Train to Pakistan*, Orient Paperbacks, New Delhi, 1956.

Singh Khuswant, *I Shall not Hear the Nightingale*, Orient Paperbacks, New Delhi, 1959.

Venkatramani K.S, *Kandan, the Patriot,* Orient Paperbacks, New Delhi, 1932.

Venkatramani K.S, *Murugan, the tiller* Orient Paperbacks, New Delhi, 1927.

SECONDARY SOURCES

Anand Mulk Raj, *Apology for Heroism*, Orient Paperbacks, New Delhi.

Advani. Lalkrishna, My Country, My Life, Rupa and Company, New Delhi, 2007.

Bajpeyee, Atal Bihari, *Jagriti Ke Swar*, Lokhit Prakashan, Lucknow, 1969, Rpt, *Meri Ekyavan Kavitayen*, Kitab Ghar, New Delhi, 1998.

Bondurant, Joan V., *Conquest of Violence: The Gandhian Philosophy of Conflict*, Princeton University Press, 1958.

Bhattacharya, Bhabani, *Gandhi the Writer, The Image As It Grew,* National Book Trust, New Delhi, 1969.

Behn Mira, *The Spirit's Pilgrimage*.

Contemporary Indian Literature, Sahitya Akademi, New Delhi, 1959.

Connes George, *The Tragedy of Romain Rolland*.

Chattopadhayaya Bankim Chandra, *Anand Math*.

Cunnigham Dr *History of Sikh*.

Dinkar. Ramdhri Singh, *Kurukshetra*, Rajpal and Sons, New Delhi.

Das, Goswami Tulsi, *Ram Charit Manas, Sundarkand,* Gita Press, Gorakhpur.

Das, Goswami Tulsi, *Hanuman Chalisa,* Gita Press, Gorakhpur.

Dinkar. Ramdhari Singh, *Bapu,* Lok Bharati Prakashan, Allahabad.

Das Durga, *India from Curzon to Nehru and After,* Collins, London, 1969.

Dash Gopalbandhu, *Bandire Atmakatha*, Loksevak Mandal 1941 Cuttuck, Reprint Satyabadi Press, 1957. Puri, India.

Dash Gopabandhu, *Abakash Chinta*, Odisha Sahitya Akademi 1951, Bhubaneshwar.

Dixit Rajiva: *Bharat Swabhiman: Complete works.*

Dwivedi, Sohan Lal, *Gandhi Marg.*

Dwivedi Hazari Prasad: *Sambhiman Lecture Series*, Website.

Einstein Albert qtd by D.G Tendulkar in *Mahatma*, Vol. VI.

Fischer, Louis, *Gandhi—His Life and Message for the World.*

Gowda H.H. Anniah, '*East West Encounter*'.

Gandhi, M.K., The Preface, *The Story of my Experiments with Truth*, Navajivan Publication, 1925.

Gandhi, M.K., Ruskin's *Unto This Last*, A Paraphrase, Ahmedabad, Navajivan Publishing House, 1951.

Gandhi, M.K., *Discourses on the Gita*, Ahmedabad, Navajivan Publishing House, 1960.

Geeta Bhagwad, Gita Press, Gorakhpur.

Gupta, G.S.Balram, *Mulk Raj Anand*, Prakash Book Depot, Bareilly, 1974.

Guru Granth Sahib Hymns.

Gupta, Maithili Sharan, *Gandhi Marg.*

Ishwaran, Manjeri S, *Venkatramani: Writer and Thinker*, An Appreciation, The People's Printing and Publishing House, Madras, 1932.

Iyengar, Dr K.R. Srinivasa, *Indian Writing in English*, Sterling Publishers Pvt Ltd, New Delhi, 1962. Rpt. Asia Publishing House, Bombay, 1962.

Jagriti, Hindi film, Song by Kavi Pradeep i.e. Pt. Ram Chandra Dwivedi.

James Henry qtd by Robert Liddell in "*Some Principles of Fiction*".

Jack Homer A, *The Gandhi Reader, La Figaro Lilleraire,* Paris, 1948.

Kamlesh, Padma Singh Sharma, *Gujrati Aur Uska Sahitya*, Rajkamal Prakashan, New Delhi, 1960.

Kingsford Anna and Maitland Edward, *The Perfect Way or The Finding of Christ*, Kumar Jainendra, *Contemporary Indian Literature*, New Delhi, Preface. London, John H. Watking, 1923.

Kumar Satish: Schumacher Lecture Series, London.

K.S. Venkatramani' in *Fiction and the Reading Public in India*, ed. C.D. Narasimahiah, University of Mysore, 1967.

Lippincott, B.E., *Victorian Critics of Democracy*, Oxford University Press, London 1938.

Lester Muriel, *Entertaining Gandhi.*

Longfellow, Henrry Wordsworth, *A Psalm of Life*, Colleted in Anthology of Poems, *Wingeed Bird* by David Green.

Mukherjee Meenakshi, *Beyond the Village*, in Critical Writing in English ed. M.K. Naik, S.K. Desai, G.S. Amur, Karnataka University, Dharwar, 1968.

Narasimhaiah, Dr C.D., *National Identity in Literature and Language: Its Range and Depth in the novels of Raja Rao*' in *National Identity*, ed. K.L Godwin, Heinemann Educational Books, London and Melbourne, 1970.

Narasimhaiah, Dr C.D., *The Swan and the Eagle,* Indian Institute of *Advanced* Study, Simla, 1969.

Narasimhaiah, Dr C.D., *Raja Rao*, Arnold- Heinemann, New Delhi.

Nehru Jawaharlal, *Address to the Nation*, titled *The Appointed Day*, published in English Reader, Class XI, NCERT. New Delhi. 1984.

Narayan R.K. *The Novels of Lakshmi Holmstrom*, Writers' Workshop, Calcutta, 1973.

Pyarelal, *Mahatma Gandhi-The Early Phase,* part-1. Ahmedabad, Navjivan Publishing House.

Polak Henry's *Mahatma Gandhi,* Brailsford and Lord Pethic-Lawrence, London, 1949.

Radhakrishnan Dr S. (Ed.) *Mahatma Gandhi: 100 Years,* Gandhi Peace Foundation, New Delhi.

Radhakrishnan Dr S. (Ed.), *Mahatma Gandhi, Essays and Reflections*, Gandhi Peace Foundation, New Delhi.

Rolland Romain, *L'Inde,* The Open Court Publishing Company, Chicago.

Rolland Romain *Above the Battle*, The Open Court Publishing Company, Chicago, 1916.

Rolland Romain, *The Life of Ramakrishna,* Preface.

Sharma, Giridhari Prashad, *Gujrati Sahitya Ka Itihasa*, Gaya Prashad and sons, Agra, 1962.

Sharma, G.P, *Nationalism in Indo-Anglian Fiction,* 1978.

Sheean, Vincent, *Lead, Kindly Light*, Random House, New York, 1949.

Starr W.T., Romian Rolland and a World War.

Swami Ramdevji Maharaj. Bharat Patanjili Yogapeeth Songs.

The Mahatma Gandhi and shrimad Rajchandra quoted in Pyarelal, Ahmedabad, Navjivan Publishing House.

Tendulkar, D.G., *Mahatma*, Vol. VI, Foreword by Jawaharlal Nehru, New Delhi, The Publication Division, 1963.

Thant U, in S.Radhakrishnan (Ed.) *Mahatma Gandhi: 100 Years,* Gandhi Peace Foundation, New Delhi.

Verghese, C. Paul, *Problems of the Indian Creative Writer in English,* Somaiya Publications, Bombay. 1971.

Yamunacharya M, in *Gandhi Marg*, July 1959.

JOURNALS AND NEW PAPERS

A Personal Record : 'A Familiar Preface'.

Evening with Gandhi–editorial in *The Spectator* (London), October 24, 1931.

Emerson and Gandhi by the same writer in the *Emerson Society Quarterly,* No. 2, 1956.

Gandhiji and Indian writing in English, The Banasthali Patrika, July, 1970.

Gandhi Marg.

George Hedrick in *Gandhi Marg*, July 1959.

Harijan, (Mahatma Gandhi).

Indian Litreture Today. (Mahatma Gandhi).

Indian Opinion, (Mahatma Gandhi).

Illustrated Weekly of India, January 1964.

Indian Opinion, 1903.

Journal des Goncourts, Oct. 24, 1864, Quoted by Robert Liddell in "*Some Principles of Fiction*".

Krishna Kripalani in the *Visva-Bharati Quarterly*, Gandhi Memorial Peace Number.

Navajivan, September 7, 1919.

New York Time Book Review, M.H. Rosenthal, March 23, 1958.

Omeo Kr. Das in *Gandhi Marg*, January 1959.

Sunday Times.

The Natal Mercury, December 12, 1894.

The Natal Advertiser, February 1, 1895.

The Influence of Thoreau's Civil Disobedience on Gandhi's Satyagraha in New England Quarterly, December 1956.

The Times, London, January 27, 1896.

U.K. Oza. published in Gandhi Memorial Peace number.

Young India (Mahatma Gandhi).

Yamunacharya M, in *Gandhi Marg*, July 1959.

Index